Photograph by Eva Lindblad

Kajsa Ekis Ekman was born in Stockholm in 1980. She is an author and a critic at the Swedish daily *Dagens Nyheter* and a member of the editoral collective of the anarchist magazine *Brand*. She has a Master's Degree in Literature from Södertörn University. Her first book *Varat och varan* [Being and Being Bought] was published in Sweden in 2010 by Leopard Förlag. Her second book, *Skulden – eurokrisen sedd från Aten* [Debt as a Weapon: The euro crisis seen from Athens] was published in September 2013 (Leopard Förlag). She has founded the network, Feminists Against Surrogacy and the climate action group, Klimax.

Being and Being Bought

Prostitution, Surrogacy and the Split Self

Kajsa Ekis Ekman

Translated by
Suzanne Martin Cheadle

First published by Spinifex Press, 2013

Spinifex Press Pty Ltd
504 Queensberry St
North Melbourne, Victoria 3051
Australia
women@spinifexpress.com.au
<http://www.spinifexpress.com.au>

First published in Swedish by Leopard Förlag, 2010
Translated from Swedish by Suzanne Martin Cheadle
Supported by a grant from the Swedish Arts Council

SWEDISH
ARTSCOUNCIL

Editor: Renate Klein
Copy editor: Maree Hawken
Cover design: Deb Snibson
Typesetting: Palmer Higgs
Typeset in Adobe Caslon
Index: Jane Purton
Printed by McPhersons Printing Group

National Library of Australia
Cataloguing-in-Publication data:
Ekman, Kajsa Ekis, 1980– author.
Being and being bought: prostitution, surrogacy and the split self / Kajsa Ekis Ekman; translated by Suzanne Martin Cheadle.
    9781742198767 (paperback)
    9781742198712 (ebook: pdf)
    9781742198736 (ebook: epub)
    9781742198729 (ebook: kindle)
Includes bibliographical references and index.
Prostitution–Psychological aspects.
Surrogate motherhood–Psychological aspects.
Sex oriented businesses.
Surrogate mothers–Developing countries.
Martin Cheadle, Suzanne, translator.
176.5

Contents

Acknowledgments

This book is dedicated to all the women and girls out there struggling to move on through the tangled jungle that is life.

While working on this book I have sought assistance from many people. I am indebted to the following people for reading the manuscript, sharing important insights and recommendations and much more:

Ander Basabe Wittek, Malin Björk of the European Women's Lobby, Nina Björk, Eric Blyth, Angela Bravo, Ainhoa Carlin, Carolina, Hubert Dubois, Louise Eek, Gunilla Ekberg, Donette Ferrer Pleguezuelos, Lisa Fors, Emma Helgesson, Tanya Holm, Lea Honorine, Tobias Hübinette, Sheila Jeffreys, Sabrina Joitteau, Amely-James Koh Bela, Ann Mari Langemar, Hugo Letiche, Claudia Lindén, Lisen Lindström and Karin Sidenvall at the Stockholm Prostitution Unit, Marie-Victoire Louis, Andreas Malm, Maria, Nicole Montén, Florence Montreynaud, Sven-Axel Månsson, Nuria and Amadeu, Kurt Nurmi at Pockettidningen R, Nätverket PRIS, Olga, Hanna Olsson, Origins USA , Gabi Rolandi, Sharon Smith, Fredrika Spindler, Eva-Britt Svensson, Ragni Svensson, Colette de Troy, Cecilia Tzaou, Emma Wallin, Jenny Westerstrand, Zam, and Lisa Åkesson from the Malmö women's shelter. Last but not least, my thanks go to Jessica Brogren at Leopard Press for giving me the opportunity to write this book.

For the English language publication I thank Melissa Farley for initiating the project and Susan Hawthorne and Spinifex Press for taking on the translation. Suzanne Martin Cheadle has worked tirelessly and produced a fantastic translation and I also thank Linda Schenck for supervising the translation and even going to the library and finding missing references. Renate Klein has put in long hours of editing, Deb Snibson has produced a beautiful cover design, and Maree Hawken expertly copy edited the book. Translations bring special challenges with them and I cannot express in words how impressed I am by the work you have all put into my book.

In spite of all this assistance, there may be things I have misunderstood, and in that case, of course, the blame is entirely on me.

Preface

Prostitution is, in reality, very simple. It is sex between two people—between one who wants it and one who doesn't. Since desire is absent, payment takes its place.

This inequality of lust is the basis of all prostitution, be it 'VIP escort services' or the modern slavery of trafficking. The same condition is always present: one person wants to have sex, one doesn't. Money may get the buyer 'consent' and even fake appreciation during the act, but it only highlights the fact that the other party has sex even though s/he *does not really want to*. No matter how much is said or done to cover this up, if there were mutual desire, there wouldn't be any payment—and we all know it.

Prostitution is therefore an enemy of sexual liberation, of lust, and of free will.

This, of course, is only one of the problems associated with prostitution. There is also the violence, the poverty, the high mortality rates, the pimps—be it the mafia or the state—and the whole industry that feeds off the inequality of lust.

The writing of this book came about at a time when theory and practice converged in my own life. It was 2005 and I was living in Barcelona, sharing a flat with several other women. One of them was Oksana, a thirty-year-old Russian immigrant who prostituted herself on the highway. She would leave home in the evening with her boyfriend, come back at night and say "It went to hell!" and wake everyone else up to drink with her, cry and listen to sentimental music.

The flat was a hangout for pimps who would often try to get the rest of us to do the same thing. I remember one of them always using the line: "Your guy doesn't seem to take care of you very well. Does he give you things? You could have a much better life ..." With some of the other women he wasn't as gentle: he would enter their room, pull out his dick and throw a ten-euro bill on the bed.

It was not the first time I had been approached by pimps: one time in Amsterdam I was almost kidnapped by one whose pick-up line was "I am an honest guy."

Oksana dreamt of going back to Russia with enough money to build a big house and have her son back living with her. Her boyfriend first told me he made his living by robbing banks, but it soon became clear that he spent all his time at the local café or in front of the computer. When would he have time to rob banks? In reality, he lived off Oksana's money, with which she also had to pay the lawyer for his brother, who was in jail.

I eventually moved back to Sweden in 2006, only to find that a debate had started about whether prostitution was, in fact, a free 'choice' and 'liberating' for strong women. As readers may know, Sweden had passed a law in 1998 prohibiting the purchase of sexual services. It was the first time in the world that prostitution legislation had targeted the buyers. At the time, there was not much criticism—the law was passed as part of a package of measures for equality and the reduction of violence against women. It was, and is, supported by 80% of the population.

But suddenly, books, articles and TV shows appeared denouncing the law as puritan and moralistic, claiming it was anyone's right to sell her body if she wanted to. However shallow and neo-liberal these arguments might have been by themselves, they may have made some sense in countries where the selling of sex is still criminalized. In this case, though, the imported nature of the argument was very clear. One *does* have the right to *sell* sex in Sweden—it is the *buying* that is prohibited. Yet the buying was seldom discussed in the debate. It was all about the right to be a 'sex worker' and, to my shock, feminists and part of the left-wing movement fell prey to this sex work discourse.

However, I did not involve myself in the debate until I learned of Oksana's death a year later. At that time I decided that enough was enough and immersed myself in all the prostitution literature I could find. This would turn into four years of deep frustration.

I learned of the overwhelming evidence about the damage prostitution does to people and to society. The mortality rate and the abuse alone should suffice as reasons why prostitution cannot be accepted as work. At the same time, some anthropologists were claiming that not even children in prostitution are victims, but in fact 'free agents' who know what they are doing.

Over the last decade, quite a number of feminists have forcefully contested this neo-liberal current and presented facts on the harms of prostitution. So why another book? While many activists opposing prostitution know about the Swedish law focusing on the sex buyers, not much is known in English-speaking countries about Swedish particularities. It also seemed to me that there was something besides the physical harm and the male dominance, something psychological that constituted the core of prostitution but was often overlooked.

This is the paradox of the prostitution contract: on the one hand, we have the replacement of desire with money. From the point of view of the sex work proponents, this is totally acceptable: few people love their jobs, why should selling sex be different? On the other hand, the buyers refuse to see this reality. He—it is as good as always a man—does not want her to act as if she is doing an 'ordinary' job. He wants the prostitute to show desire for him. Which, of course, means that she has to fake it. This dilemma, this lie, pervades the whole world of prostitution. For the people who sell sex, this has dire consequences: it essentially forces them to create a Split Self: the being, and the one who is being bought.

When I was halfway through writing this book, another debate gained prominence in Sweden. It was the question of surrogacy, and it mirrored the prostitution debate. Surrogacy was booming in places like India and Ukraine, where poor women became pregnant for money, never to see their children again after they gave birth to them. Suddenly, well-off people started pushing for the legalization of surrogacy contracts. The term 'baby trade' was seldom brought up. Rather, it was claimed that being pregnant for money was a free choice, a job like any other, even a celebration of women's love of being pregnant.

The parallels between prostitution and surrogacy were immediately evident to me. Two industries profit from women's bodies: one from her sex, the other from her uterus. Two industries commercialize basic human phenomena: sexuality and reproduction. And these, as it happens, are also the basis of the historical oppression of women and the ongoing division of women into 'whores and madonnas'.

This issue, however, is not only about gender. It is about *power* and how it manifests itself in relation to class, ethnicity, age, social standing, etc. Both industries are based on the concept that the body of a poor person (in prostitution it is not only women) is to be used for the benefit of the rich—without limitations. The powerful people say: "I want sex, I want it this way, I want you to do this, say this," and pay someone to do it. The powerful people say: "We want children, newborn babies, we want them to look like us," and pay someone to bear the child and give it up, never to see it again. The powerful even go as far as to call their wishes 'human rights'.

Some developments have occurred since the original publication of this book in Swedish in 2010. Apart from Sweden and Norway, Iceland has also adopted a ban on the purchase of sexual services and has criminalized the buyers. Norway went even further and also criminalized the purchase of sex abroad, thereby taking on the responsibility for stopping sex tourism. There are now positive signs that France and Ireland might be next. More and more countries are realizing that targeting—and reducing—demand is the best way to deal with prostitution: Great Britain and Finland have both adopted laws criminalizing the buying of sex from a trafficked person. However, these laws do not go far enough and have often proved hard to implement.

Sweden assessed the effects of the new prostitution law in 2010. The evaluation showed that prostitution had diminished significantly since the ban in 1998; fewer men bought sex and there did not seem to be any evidence of an increase in so-called underground prostitution. Whereas 1 in 8 men had bought sex prior to the legislation in 1998, the number today is 1 in 13.

As for surrogacy, in 2011 the European Parliament adopted a resolution stating that surrogacy is a violation of human rights. The Indian Government, which had previously tried to adopt 'surrogate-friendly' laws in order to attract fertility tourists, now circumscribes and regulates the buyers' rights. Unfortunately, the Swedish Parliament went the other way in 2012 and voted to investigate the possible legalization of surrogacy.

Since the first publication of this book I have given more than 100 talks all over Sweden, as well as in Denmark, The Netherlands, Serbia, France, Germany, Cuba and the European Parliament. What I remember most clearly are the words of a teenage girl who came up to me after a speech and said: "I always had the feeling prostitution was wrong, but I didn't dare to say it, I thought you had to agree with it."

Her reaction sums up a climate in which proponents of prostitution and surrogacy have effectively managed to revile anyone who stands up against these businesses. Paradoxically, a person may be simultaneously rebuked as being both a Christian and a radical feminist, patriarchal and man-hating, sex negative and moralist, a supporter of biological determinism and unable to understand the biological male sex drive, and so forth.

Personally, I simply define myself as a feminist. I don't think there is any reason to be scared by such name-calling. To fight against prostitution and surrogacy is to fight for free sexuality and women's reproductive autonomy or, to put it differently, the idea that we should be able to have sex and have children when we want to, when we desire it and feel ready for it—not because somebody pays us, forces us, manipulates us, or makes us feel guilty if we don't.

The fight against prostitution and surrogacy may seem peripheral or trivial to some. But I believe it is through this fight that we define what it is to be human.

Kajsa Ekis Ekman
Stockholm, July 2013

PART I

PROSTITUTION

The Story of the Sex Worker or How Prostitution Became the World's Most Modern Profession

Prostitution has become big business. Since 1998, when the International Labor Organization (ILO) recommended that governments legalize prostitution so they could collect some of the revenue, Holland, Germany and New Zealand have taken this route. Some states in Australia had already legalized prostitution (Sullivan, 2007). While Sweden and Norway are now combating prostitution by imposing fines on the purchase of sexual services, other countries are doing exactly the opposite and institutionalizing it. In Germany alone, the prostitution industry involves—on a daily basis—400,000 prostituted women and 1.2 million male buyers at a calculated annual value of 6 billion euros. Governments profit from prostitution; multinational companies organize it; it is even listed on the Australian stock exchange. The mafia delivers women to it—trafficking in human beings is also on the rise as a consequence of the global sex industry. The ILO estimates profits from trafficking alone to be 28.7 billion USD per year.[1] It is difficult to know how many people are involved in the sex trade. The victims of human trafficking are estimated by the UN and

---

1   Cited in 'Human Trafficking for Sexual Exploitation' [European Conference] (2009) Swedish National Committee for UNIFEM.

the ILO to be between 2 and 4 million people (Marcovich, 2007, p. 331).

In spite of frequent claims to the contrary, the sex trade is a highly gendered phenomenon. It primarily involves women and girls being sold to men: 98% of the people whose lives are sold through trafficking are women and girls.[2] A minority are men and boys whose lives are sold to other men.

Simultaneously, a new way of talking about prostitution has arisen.

It is called 'sex work'.

Its promoters say that prostitution is a job, just like any other. That selling sex should not be seen as a *violation* of our rights, but more as a right in itself. That we ought to focus on the condom use and proper payment. They say that if prostitution is legalized, its negative features will disappear, the authorities will be able to control it and prostitutes will be able to establish unions and be better paid. They claim that prostitution is not harmful in itself, that what happens between two consenting adults is their own business (Kempadoo, 1998, p. 5). Not infrequently, feminist and socialist organizations are mouthpieces for this line of argument: work, unions, rights and self-determination. In the world of prostitution, 'working' has long been used as a euphemism to avoid naming what is happening, a kind of perversely ironic usage. Someone asked "Are you working?" with a certain look, and the other person got the drift. But today the term 'work' is used in all seriousness by social commentators, politicians and international organizations: prostitution has become a job.

This opinion is put forward by Swedish scholars such as Susanne Dodillet and Don Kulick and social commentators such as Petra Östergren and Maria Abrahamsson. We hear it from the Swedish right-wing industrial think tank Timbro, as well as from the postmodern left-wingers writing in the Swedish magazine *Arena*. It echoes from the youth leagues of political parties: both

---

2   'A global alliance against forced labor: Global report under the follow-up to the ILO Declaration on Fundamental Principles and Rights at Work' (2005) International Labor Organization, pp. 10 and 14–15.

the Swedish Centre and the Liberal Party youth leagues have adopted the idea that prostitution can be a job.

According to this way of thinking, prostitution has nothing to do with the relationship between women and men but instead is quite simply a business transaction. We are to speak, then, in business-related terms. Although the absolute majority of people in prostitution in the world are women and girls and the absolute majority of buyers are men, we are not supposed to speak about women and men, but about 'sellers' and 'customers'. Instead of prostitution we are to say 'commercial sex' and instead of prostitutes, 'sex workers'—terms that provide a semblance of neutrality. In Holland, where all aspects of prostitution are legal, brothel owners are called 'independent entrepreneurs'; in Australia, 'service providers'. Petra Östergren defines prostitution as "an income-earning activity or job for people of all sexes" (2006a p. 48). Political scientist Carole Pateman has called this 'the universal argument', as if the reality—in which prostitution is about women being sold to men—was subordinated to theoretical, 'virtual' prostitution, where any person can sell him or herself to any other person (1988, p. 192).

In spite of this genderless surface, the story of the sex worker is above all a story of the woman. At the center stands not the man who does the buying, but the woman who does the selling. This story strives to modernize the picture of this woman, elevating her from prostitute to 'sex worker'. A 'sex worker', they say, is a strong and independent person. She is attractive, smart, a businesswoman or an employee, she knows what she is doing and doesn't take shit from anyone. The 'sex worker' is, as scholar Jenny Westerstrand has written, a postmodern version of "the happy hooker" (2009; see also Rachel Moran's autobiography *Paid For*, 2013). She is popularized in novels with names like *Belle de Jour: The intimate adventures of a London call girl* and *Anett's World: A hooker's diary*, where she is always an escort with a high income and often another job on the side. *Vecko-Revyn*, a Swedish magazine for girls in their early teens, does its part to glamorize the life of a prostitute. In an article from 2007, one woman says: "I sell sex—and actually like it!" The article describes the alluring aspects of the life of a prostitute, like how much money and great sex she gets. The illustration is a model's slender legs covered in glittery stockings and wearing high-heeled shoes (*Vecko-Revyn*, 2007).

When the ILO recommended legalization of the sex industry in 1998, their main argument was that governments should be able to garner a share of a lucrative industry. But in order to assert this, it was, of course, necessary for prostitution also to be legitimated as *morally acceptable*. The narcotics trade and murder-for-hire are other lucrative industries from which governments can also profit, but few international organizations would recommend totally legalizing them. By renaming prostitution 'sex work', explaining that it can be the result of free choice, that society has to "admit the individual's right to work as a prostitute," and then fight for better working conditions, the ILO gave governments the moral legitimacy to profit from prostitution (Lim, 1998, p. 15). The story of the sex worker has replaced earlier biological and eugenic myths. Today it is the primary story used when the porn industry wants to advance its interests. It is used by men who defend buying sex. It is used by governments and lobbyists to legalize the trade in women. But how does this story work? What does it suggest? How did it come about and who is behind it?

The 'Sex Worker' and the Feminist

An article in the Swedish daily paper *Svenska Dagbladet* by doctor of theology Susanne Wigorts Yngvesson featured the following headline: 'Att sälja sin kropp är en moralisk rättighet' ['It is a moral right to sell your body'] (19 December 2006).

The article is about prostitution, but there is nothing in it about what prostitution is. If we didn't know better, we might think prostitution was a strictly female affair. There is hardly a single word about men; instead, the main roles are occupied by two women: the female 'sex worker' and the feminist. The 'sex workers' are "a stigmatized group that feels oppressed"; however, "not by men, but by other women, radical feminists and politicians."

Wigorts Yngvesson's article is a commentary on Petra Östergren's book *Porr, Horor och Feminister* [Porn, Whores and Feminists], published in 2006. The article is constructed so that these two groups—'sex workers' and feminists—are set against each other and assigned opposing characteristics. We aren't told what actually *happens* in prostitution, but rather what the women in these two groups *are like*. It is a typical example of how the story of the sex worker functions.

The 'sex worker' is described as both stigmatized and oppressed and at the same time thoroughly admirable. Wigorts Yngvesson describes her as an active individual who makes free choices, who exercises her "right to decide over her body" and who "actively protests" against claims that she doesn't know what's best for her.

Feminists and politicians are, by contrast, not exactly depicted as likeable characters that you would want as dinner guests. According to Wigorts Yngvesson, feminists *violate* and *stigmatize* 'sex workers' and consider them to be worth less than other people: "Women who say that they sell sex voluntarily are considered stupid." Feminists, Wigorts Yngvesson clarifies in her article, restrict women's rights to their own bodies, and in addition, imply that their attitude is due to 'sexual hostility': when "it is about women's sexuality, radical feminists seem to think that a woman's right to her own body ceases." Feminists "paint all of the sex workers with the same brush and claim that they are victims" and even think "that sex workers themselves are not conscious of their roles as victims." They are real know-it-alls, she suggests:

> The rhetoric from left-wing [female Swedish] politicians like Inger Segelström and Gudrun Schyman is based on the idea that the sex workers themselves are not conscious of their roles as victims and the constant assaults to which they are subjected. In order to be regarded as reliable, they first have to understand how wrong they are and get some distance from their earlier lives. Then they can be saved from the depths of hell and be helped out of their misery. All sex workers with whom Petra Östergren spoke described this rhetoric as insulting.

This kind of rhetoric: "roles as victims," "get some distance from their earlier lives" and "be saved from the depths of hell," is hardly reminiscent of something feminist politicians Schyman or Segelström would have said. Rather it more accurately resembles the Christian rhetoric of sin and penance. The author herself is a doctor of theology, and in the next sentence she defends the Christian anti-prostitution stance: "For a theologian, there is every reason to argue against even voluntary sex trade, because we conceive of the body as a gift from God." Wigorts Yngvesson goes on, however, to state her opinion that others have no legitimate reason to be against prostitution: "So what reasons can secular feminists present for women wanting to sell their bodies voluntarily?" She does not actually present these reasons, but merely hints—with some suspicion—that they might have something to do with a belief in the nuclear family. She then quickly states that there really are *no* valid reasons: secular feminists must, quite simply, surrender their opposition to prostitution.

Historian of ideas Susanne Dodillet similarly asserts in her dissertation 'Är sex arbete?' ['Is sex work?'] (2009) that prostitution can be "an active choice on the part of a strong-willed woman" and that prostitutes are "business-minded individuals" and "feminists who can show other women the way" (pp. 309, 258). She positions the prostitute as a role model for all women today.

When Dennis Magnusson's play *Jenny från Hörby* [Jenny from Hörby], about a young woman who decides to become a porn actress, opened on the *Intiman* stage of the Malmö City Theater, many critics stressed what a heroic character Jenny is. She is "a free-thinking *femme fatale*" who "single-mindedly goes out into the world by riding on the commercial sexualizing of our consciousness instead of being a victim of it," the daily newspaper *Svenska Dagbladet* wrote (Benér, 25 February 2008). It was frequently pointed out what power Jenny exercised when she became a porn actress:

> Jenny is no victim of the porn industry; she takes it over. 'In many ways, she is the ultimate feminist who goes in and creates her own

rules in a patriarchal world', says Alexander Karim who plays the boyfriend, porn actor Simson (Peterson, 18 February 2008).

The 'sex worker' is said to be the ultimate feminist, but she is always set *against* feminists because the feminist who does not sell sex is given only negative characteristics. A critic from the Malmö-based newspaper *Sydsvenskan* wrote:

> In *Jenny from Hörby* at *Intiman* in Malmö, the religious father's role has been taken over by a feminist author-aunt. Her reactions to her adopted daughter's career choice reflect politically correct Swedish feminism à la the turn of the millennium rather than beliefs of the Christian right (Larsson, 1 March 2008).

In Petra Östergren's *Porn, Whores and Feminists*, this juxtaposition is taken to an extreme. 'Whores' and 'feminists' have the leading roles and are positioned against each other: whores are active subjects and feminists the unsympathetic oppressors. Östergren interviewed twelve women whom she chose, she says, because they had positive experiences with prostitution.[3] They "love being whores," are active subjects for whom prostitution was a "conscious choice" so they would not "be dependent on a man," they rail "against outdated female models," take "the command over men," are "not afraid to stand up and be themselves," and "have thought through the analysis of power" (Östergren, 2006a, pp. 212, 282 and 205). Feminists, on the other hand, want to protect and punish, and their suggestion for measures to combat the sex industry only have to do "with censorship and control" (p. 238). Östergren wants the reader to believe that *feminists are actually Christian patriarchs*.

The leading roles, then, are occupied by the 'sex worker' and the feminist. But while the feminist is painted in the blackest of terms, the 'sex worker' takes on what once was the role of the feminist: it is she who, like Jenny from Hörby, is the "ultimate feminist who

---

3   "Most sex workers I've met do not have primarily negative experiences of prostitution. Nor have they found themselves in forced situations. That I have not attempted to make contact with this group of sex workers depends on a number of factors ... Nor would this type of interview help my work" (Östergren, 2006a, p. 168).

goes in and dictates her own rules in a patriarchal world," while the feminist becomes the patriarch (Peterson, 18 February 2008).

The story of the sex worker makes no claim of telling what prostitution is or how it works in practice. Neither Östergren nor Dodillet nor Wigorts Yngvesson uses research on the causes or consequences of prostitution to back up their claims. Instead, they construct a narrative drama of a struggle between good and evil. On the one side there are "the women who have sexual relations with many men and those who sell their bodies for money" and on the other the "radical feminists and politicians" (Wigorts Yngvesson, 19 December 2006). Having sex with many men (emancipated sexuality) is associated with selling one's body for money. Feminists, on the other hand, are associated with power. Feminists stand out as a thoroughly privileged group; they are not ordinary women who are active in a women's group or young activists, but women in positions of power—notoriously known as 'elite feminists'! Wigorts Yngvesson is also consistent about putting the word *radical* in front of feminists, giving the term a tone of extremism—lo and behold, feminists are not just women in positions of power, but *crazy* women in positions of power!

Sexual Orientation

Prostitution, these social commentators clarify, is about women's right to work, to receive payment for formerly unpaid women's work—not unlike the stay-at-home mother, as Susanne Dodillet writes. At the same time, they see prostitution as being about sexuality. They define it as a sexual orientation comparable to homosexuality. British historian Jeffrey Weeks writes:

> Transvestites, transsexuals, pedophiles, sado-masochists, fetishists, bisexuals, prostitutes and others—each group marked by specific sexual tastes, or aptitudes ... have all appeared on the world's stage to claim their space and 'rights' (in Jeffreys, 1997, p. 95).

Two ideas are at play here: sexuality and work. When prostitution is described as a job, it should be subjected to the terms and conditions of the labor market. When it is described as a form of sexuality, it suddenly becomes private, something with which society should not interfere. So it becomes a sexual orientation, precisely the opposite of an everyday profession. In this scenario, the people who are presumed to have a "specific sexual taste" for prostitution are clearly the prostituted women rather than the men who buy sex. In her article 'It is a moral right to sell your body' (19 December 2006), Susanne Wigorts Yngvesson groups prostitutes with all "women who have sexual relations with many men," giving the impression that prostitution is simply some women's sexual orientation. The reader gets a picture of a group of people who simply practice an alternative sexuality, who are different and enjoy their difference, but who are treated unsympathetically and even persecuted by society: a group that will eventually overcome prejudices and be accepted by society. It is not difficult to see through her efforts to liken prostitution to homosexual liberation.

One hundred years ago, many researchers saw prostitution as a necessary evil for the preservation of the institution of marriage and social order. Today, researchers and queer theorists see it instead as a norm-violating practice that breaks down boundaries and calls gender roles into question. Prostitution, it is said, is not only sex but also revolution. Australian scholars Chris Ryan and Michael C. Hall claim in *Sex Tourism: Marginal people and liminalities* (2001) that the meeting between a Western man and a Thai woman in a Bangkok brothel is an encounter between two marginalized people, two outsiders, "two liminal peoples, peoples separated from the mainstream of society" (p. 22). This encounter possesses revolutionary potential, since the two "may be thought to challenge the very legitimacy and structure of order, becoming agents or instances of chaos" (p. 22). According to Ryan and Hall, the reason the sex tourist is also a marginalized character is that he, just like the woman, is scantily clad. They clarify, not without gloating over their impressive powers of observation, that these men go bare-chested, dressed only in shorts, on the beach! Consequently, they *must* have something in common with the prostitute, who wears underwear and stiletto heels on the bar scene.

Anthropologist Don Kulick follows in the same track, taking the side of the sex-buying men. The title of his 2005 essay, '400 000 perversa svenskar' ['400,000 perverted Swedes'], refers to Swedish men who have bought sex, whom Kulick asserts are "the queerest people around today" (p. 98). They deserve the 'queer award' because they "threaten heteronormativity" and commit "crimes against the dictates of the ideology of equality" (pp. 97, 75). Susanne Dodillet also describes how prostitution can be seen as "an enterprise with revolutionizing potential" because she read somewhere that one woman raised herself up out of poverty through prostitution, and another dared "to quit her job as a secretary" (2009, pp. 260, 252).

It doesn't take much for some writers to call prostitution 'revolutionary'. For Maggie O'Neill, author of *Prostitution and Feminism: Towards a politics of feeling* (2001), it suffices to swear at your pimp. O'Neill interviewed a group of street prostitutes who spoke clearly and plainly about how they were abused both before and in prostitution. But rather than devoting herself to studying this abuse, she searches for traces of opposition to a hegemonic masculinity in the jargon of prostitutes:

> The gendered relations operating between prostitutes, clients and pimps/partners are complex, and women do engage in resistances to hegemonic heterosexual masculinities through language, discursive practices and actions/behaviours (p. 77).

While these thinkers try to create associations between prostituted individuals, sexual orientation and revolutionary norm-violating behavior, they describe the opponents of prostitution as authoritarian oppressors. When Petra Östergren discusses the censorship of porn, she is able to connect the dots from "the anti-porn radical feminists," to "a totalitarian society," to "ecclesiasticism and right-wing fundamentalists, often with Nazis at the helm," and the "true, pure and righteous person with his or her true and singular normal sexuality" all the way to "consequences when the feminists want to be in control." In the midst of this cascade of horrors, she hammers down the exact dividing line:

For in all cultures and political movements, there is a struggle between Dionysian ecstasy, pleasures and festivities on the one side and Puritanical order, conscientiousness, sobriety and attention to public health issues on the other (2006a, p. 153).

Östergren's point, however, is not to criticize the church, sobriety or right-wing extremism. These are only included as repulsive elements, to set feminism and opposition to porn in poor company. It is also important to note that Östergren does not create these associations using the tools of critical analysis—we aren't given the opportunity to stop and consider what Dionysian ecstasy and prostitution have in common, or why sobriety would have anything to do with feminism. Enumeration is an associative genre, not an analytical one. By associating prostitution with things we perceive as enjoyable, like festivals and pleasure, we are instilled with positive feelings about it. And by associating the opponents with disagreeable or boring things like Puritanism, Nazism and the Vatican, we are instilled with negative feelings about them. *Openness* is set against *censorship*, *subject* against *victim*, *authoritative* against *helpless*, *active* against *passive*, *liberating* against *moralistic*. This is not an analysis of porn and prostitution, but a way of blocking analytical thinking and manipulating us into abandoning our opposition to prostitution.

Such patterns of associations, which have become innumerable in the story of the sex worker, were first seen in the work of American anthropologist Gayle Rubin. In her 1984 essay 'Thinking sex: Notes for a radical theory of the politics of sexuality', she declared all unconventional types of sex to be revolutionary. According to 'Thinking sex', there is a single conventionally accepted type of sexuality: heterosexual, monogamous, reproductive, non-commercial and private sex, in which the participants are of the same generation. Then there is forbidden sexuality: homosexual, unmarried, commercial, public, pornographic and sadomasochistic, inter-generational sex. To practice the latter, explains Rubin, is to be dissident. Consequently, even the struggle for legitimacy of pedophiles and johns is a valid one—society's opposition to them is nothing but moral panic. Political scientist and feminist Sheila Jeffreys has pointed out in *Anticlimax* (1990/2011) that if the sexual liberalism of the 1960s was about seeing *all* sex as positive and natural, this developed in the 1980s into a sexual libertarianism where it was the sexual minorities who came to be seen as the radical avant-garde. Rubin places prostitution firmly in the latter category (Jeffreys, 1990/2011, p. 269). Rubin doesn't seem compelled to try and explain what pedophilia, homosexuality, prostitution and extramarital sex actually have in common; that all of them have been condemned by society is enough to group them together. Prostitution is thus confirmed as a type of oppressed sexuality.

But the main target of Rubin's criticism in 'Thinking sex' wasn't the government of the United States of America or Christian fundamentalists. It was feminists. The final section of her essay is called 'The limits of feminism' and is a sweeping condemnation of everything feminism stands for. Apart from the liberal current, feminism, according to Rubin, is conservative and anti-sex, prejudiced against all sexual variation except monogamous lesbianism—all other sex is censored (p. 301). It is a "demonology" and a "demon sexology" that "presents most sexual behavior in the worst possible light." Opponents of pornography are the absolute worst. They make constant use, Rubin claims, of the most disgusting pornography to show how horrible it is. This is not their only tactic: they also attack the sex industry as the genesis of sexism (p. 304). This, thunders Rubin, makes feminists responsible for "some of the most retrogressive sexual thinking this side of the Vatican." To be sure, says Rubin, the sex industry is not a feminist utopia, but to single it out as the root problem is a logical fallacy, as sexism exists elsewhere in society. According to Rubin, feminists are overly preoccupied with the sex industry and all but ignore other societal problems such as the family, religion, education, media, and workplace and income inequality (p. 302).

Rubin, oddly, doesn't seem much interested in discussing these subjects herself. Her work on trafficking in women as a cornerstone for patriarchy, 'The traffic in women' (1975), established her as an influential feminist writer. Ten years later, in 'Thinking sex', she distanced herself from it. Maybe the traffic in women plays a role for tribes in 'backward' parts of the world, but "it is surely not an adequate formulation for sexuality in Western industrial societies" (p. 307).

It is ironic that Rubin dismissed her own theory precisely at the time when the traffic in women began to dramatically increase in the Western world. Instead, she says, the time had come to talk about sex. But she didn't really talk about sex in 'Thinking sex'. According to Rubin, how we feel about sex, what we do and why, what prostitution is, why men want to buy sex and what sexual freedom is are the wrong questions to ask. In fact, we should not ask any questions—that brings us too close to making a clinical diagnosis—but instead simply accept all forms of sex. Thus 'sex' is freed from taboo, while talk of relationships between people becomes taboo. Discussions of what gives us pleasure and what makes us feel good are gone, as are power relationships, age, and economic inequality, while 'sex' stands enthroned in solitary majesty. As long as something is 'sex', it is untouchable. And as long as this 'sex' can be said to have lower status than mainstream sex, it is revolutionary.

The Victim and the Subject

At the heart of the story of the sex worker stands a telling phrase. It reads: 'The sex worker is not a victim, but a strong person who knows what she wants'. When someone tries to show how prostitution hurts people, the response is: 'Sex workers are strong and active—not victims!' Susanne Dodillet claims: "the Sex Purchase Act [introduced in Sweden in 1998] assigns to the sex worker the role of passive victim, incapable of arriving at independent decisions" (16 March 2009). She goes on to write that society should instead see them as "active and acting subjects who make rational decisions," citing Norwegian researcher Kirsten Frigard, who says:

> Most prostitutes are strong women who have taken responsibility for
> their situation, and they do not want to be described in that way [i.e.,
> as passive victims], because they are not victims in the traditional sense
> (in Dodillet, 2009, p. 333).

In her dissertation (2009), Dodillet always uses the word 'victim' as
if it were a character description: "victims who don't know what's
best for them," "passive victims," "helpless and innocent victims,"
and "powerless victims" are just a few examples (pp. 104, 331, and
333). This, she says later, is the view social workers and feminists
have of prostitutes, based on their claim that prostitution harms
women.

Honoring the strong, active subject and setting it against the
passive, weak victim is becoming legion. In an interview with
administrator Suzann Larsdotter of the Swedish Federation for
Lesbian, Gay, Bisexual and Transgender Rights (RFSL), which
launched a project to interview men who sold themselves to
other men, she said: "We are not starting [this project] with the
traditional attitude that only sees sex workers as victims. We will
meet the individuals without prejudice and listen to what they have
to say" (in Jonsson, 5 October 2009).

By creating an opposition between victim and subject,
proponents of 'sex work' attempt to rewrite its history. This
rewriting stems from the idea that society had previously viewed
prostitutes as helpless victims, but now that we have begun to
listen to the 'sex workers' themselves, we realize that they are
strong individuals who 'choose' to sell sex. This view is repeated
so often nowadays that it has become something of a truism in
certain circles, and is accepted without any proof of exactly *who*
saw prostitutes as victims, what a victim is, and what separates a
strong woman from a weak one. The argument that society hasn't
listened to prostitutes may be valid in certain countries, not least
in the Anglo-Saxon countries since the argument "she is an agent,
not a victim" is primarily imported from the USA. But in order to
assert this in Sweden, one would have to ignore all of the Swedish
research on prostitution.

Swedish research has been exceptional precisely because it was built on the voices of people in prostitution. Since the late 1970s, the basis of Swedish prostitution research has been just that: meeting people without prejudice, and listening to what they have to say. When the Prostitution Inquiry was launched in 1977, the experts did something quite unusual for government investigations both then and now: they spent three years in places where prostitution was taking place. They left their desks and went to sex clubs all over Sweden, interviewed prostitutes, buyers, and others who traveled in these circles. They not only wanted to map out the prevalence of prostitution, but also to understand what prostitution was. The result was an 800-page report of which 140 pages were people's own testimonies (Borg *et al.*, 1981). On page after page, prostituted women told about their upbringings, about their paths to prostitution, about the buyers (family men, managers, criminals), about the role of alcohol and narcotics, about different types of relationships with pimps, about how prostitution affected them, about violence, shame, strength, and survival strategies. This perspective was unique. Previous researchers had labeled prostitutes as deviants, and prostitution had been positioned at the margins of society. With the Prostitution Inquiry, however, stories from the world of prostitution laid the foundation for a whole new analysis in which prostitution was understood to be an extreme, concentrated version of the general relationship between the sexes. The word 'victim' is not prominent in the report—on the contrary, the report tells a great deal about violence, exploitation and the societal inequality of the people involved.

Even during the investigative work, conflicts arose among the ten experts and the lead investigator Inger Lindqvist, a political conservative. Lindqvist had not taken part in the research work itself, but had been invited by the owner of the strip club Chat Noir to visit the club and had taken his side on the question of whether strip clubs should exist at all (Ribbing, 13 July 1980). When the investigation was finished, Lindqvist dismissed all experts, edited out all personal testimony and, instead of the planned 800-page publication, published only a thin report with statistics about the prevalence of prostitution in Sweden. There was not a single voice left from the world of prostitution. Her intention was that the original material would never be published (pers. comm. Lindqvist to investigators/Minister Karin Söder, 14 July 1980). But after a storm of protests from the women's movement, the original report of the Inquiry was published in its entirety (Borg *et al.*, 1981).

The report dropped like a bombshell, instantly becoming a landmark study that transformed society's view of prostitution. It paved the way for prostitution research all over Scandinavia. Prostitution, like rape, had suddenly become political: part of gender politics as much as of social politics. And the Inquiry gave prostitution research a whole new point of departure. Much of the research from the early 1900s—where the causes of prostitution were sought in a woman's personality and alleged illnesses—was thrown out. The creation of a new set of knowledge began, in which the causes were sought in the relationship between women and men and in society at large. And where did researchers find the sources of this new knowledge? They found it in the stories of prostituted people.

The 1980s and 1990s brought many new observations to the field of research on prostitution. The 'Prostitution Group' in Gothenburg, Sweden, interviewed sex-buying men and investigated their motives in the book *Könsköparna* [The Sex-buyers] (1996). In the 'Malmö Project' (1977–1981), a new way of working was tested that helped many prostituted women by means of debt forgiveness and therapy. Based on that project, in which 111 women were able to leave prostitution, Stig Larsson wrote *Könshandeln: Om prostituerades villkor* [The Sex Trade: On the conditions for prostitutes] (1983). This book, based on the stories of the 224 prostitutes they worked with, described the sex trade "above all, from the prostitutes' own perspective" (back cover). Norwegian criminologists Cecilie Høigård and Liv Finstad added to the knowledge of defense mechanisms used by prostitutes by listening to women involved in Norwegian street prostitution (1992). Sven-Axel Månsson investigated the relationship between prostitutes and pimps in his doctoral dissertation 'Könshandelns främjare och profitörer' ['Promoters and profiteers of the sex trade'] (1981). And Sven-Axel Månsson and Ulla-Carin Hedin collected information about what causes women to enter and leave prostitution in *Vägen Ut: Om kvinnors uppbrott ur prostitutionen* [The Way Out: On women's departure from prostitution] (1998), in which they interviewed women who had left the sex industry. All of this research laid the groundwork for the Act Prohibiting the Purchase of Sexual Services, which came into force in Sweden in 1999.

To claim—as Östergren, Dodillet and others do—that we in Sweden have not listened to people in prostitution, therefore, is rather absurd once one learns about all the prostitution research that has been carried out. But what if one doesn't learn about it? What if more and more articles and books are written that pretend it never happened, that count on us not having done our research?

This is exactly Susanne Dodillet's supposition in her 2009 dissertation in the field of the History of Ideas, 'Är sex arbete?' ['Is sex work?']. Dodillet's hypothesis is that in Sweden, unlike Germany, it "has not been the prostitutes themselves who described their roles," but rather politicians and social workers who regarded prostitutes as "more or less helpless." Dodillet delves into the Inquiry from 1977, and what she does with it is intriguing to say the least. She recasts the whole course of events and claims that it was the lead investigator Inger Lindqvist who thought that prostitutes "must be taken at their word" and the experts who "looked at them as helpless victims." Not only that, Dodillet refers to the 140-plus pages in which prostituted people tell their stories as "a few short quotes." These 'few short quotes' total 219, which cannot in any sense be called 'a few'. They aren't short, either; many are more than half a page.[4] When I sit with the report in my hands and envisage what courage must have been required of these women to lay bare their innermost experiences and feelings, I am dumbfounded by Dodillet's audacity.

---

4 Borg *et al.* (1981) pp. 20–41, 203–205, 288–303, 306–336, 338, 340, 343, 345–358, 363–365, 370–376, 378–389, 399–413, 415–422, 425–427, 430, 437–441 and 446–448.

Dodillet's dissertation was reported for fraud by scholars Sven-Axel Månsson and Jenny Westerstrand, but the university refused to investigate the facts, instead referring the debate to 'the public arena'.[5] And thus, with the university's refusal to acknowledge the severity of Dodillet's deception, we have a key example of how the story of the 'empowered sex worker' has wrongly been given historic legitimacy by silencing precisely those voices it said it wanted to represent.

In sum, 'abolishing the victim' is the battle cry of pro-prostitution advocates. Depicting prostitutes as strong women is a beloved practice in the international 'sex worker' debate. Indeed, Jo Doezema, from the lobby group Network of Sex Work Projects believes that we should abolish the idea of the vulnerable subject completely. In its place she prefers

> to change the focus of our concern from the vulnerable subject (capable of being hurt) needing protection, to the desiring subject whose primary requirement is not passively confirmed 'rights' but a political arena conductive to the practice of freedom (in Westerstrand, 2008, p. 362).

A Slippery Slope: From the Independent Escort ...

At first glance, the story of the sex worker seems fairly restrained. Petra Östergren emphasizes that she is talking about consensual adults, not children or victims of human trafficking. Maria Abrahamsson writes similarly in *Svenska Dagbladet*:

> I simply do not understand how one can equate people who sell sex voluntarily with those poor wretches who, for reasons of misery or feeble minds, end up in the claws of cynical human traffickers (1 March 2009).

In this framework some people get to be victims—but only if they are passive and stupid. Those who make conscious 'choices' clearly cannot find themselves in trouble. Trafficking and child prostitution

5 'Angående anmälan om oredlighet i forskning' ['Regarding the report of fraudulent research'] (19 June 2009).

become a garbage bin for all that is wrong with prostitution, and there is a lot that can easily be thrown in: violence, misery and, to use Abrahamsson's term, 'poor wretches'. Once we are rid of those things, we can get to work constructing the idea of an ecological, fair-trade domestic prostitution industry with ethical independent entrepreneurs—an industry that is clearly outside the garbage bin.

… to Human Trafficking

In countries where prostitution has been legalized, these boundaries have begun to blur. Once the ideal of a well-managed prostitution industry has been established, even the contents of the garbage bin can be sanitized, and even trafficking can be made to look like a myth. Sociologist Laura Agustín, who has been employed by various lobby groups such as the Network of Sex Work Projects and the European Network for HIV/STI Prevention and Health Promotion among Migrant Sex Workers (TAMPEP), has written many books about trafficking as a media myth. She also contributes texts on this topic to the British daily *The Guardian* which she alternates with texts about strong women in burkas who have 'freely chosen' to wear this garment. Agustín's primary aim is to stop us from talking about 'trafficking'—she claims that the term itself turns people into victims. Accordingly, she has renamed trafficking victims 'migrant sex workers' and depicts the woman who is forced into prostitution as fortunate,

> she works in multicultural, multilingual clubs, brothels, apartments and bars … *Milieux* are 'workplaces' for those selling sexual services in them, who spend many hours in the bar, socialising, talking and drinking with each other and the clientele as well as other workers like cooks, waiters, cashiers and bouncers. In the case of flats, some people live in them while others arrive to work shifts. The experience of spending most of their time in such ambiances, if people adapt to them at all, produces cosmopolitan subjects, who, by definition, have a special relationship vis-a-vis 'place'. The cosmopolite considers the world his oyster, not his home … (2002, pp. 110–117).

The reader gets the idea that a trafficking victim is someone who parties around town with the upper crust, hangs out at metropolitan nightclubs and maybe lends a hand now and then behind the bar. Words such as 'cosmopolitan' and 'oyster' serve as symbolic ornaments, reinforcing the impression that we are talking about a life of luxury (see Rachel Moran's autobiography, 2013, for a contrasting view). It should be noted that the activities that comprise the 'work' are not described anywhere else in the text.

In another text, in which Agustín addresses the human rights violations when trafficked women are confined to apartments for several months without being allowed to leave, she diminishes their imprisonment:

> The relationship involving women who live inside sex establishments and rarely leave until they are moved to another place without being consulted receives the media's usual attention, it being taken for granted that this represents a total loss of freedom. In many cases, however, migrant workers *prefer* this situation, for any of a number of reasons: if they don't leave the premises they don't spend money; if they don't have working papers, they feel safer inside in a controlled situation; if someone else does the work of finding new venues and making arrangements, they don't have to do it; or having come on a three-month tourist visa they want to spend as much time as possible making money (2006, pp. 29–47).

… and Children

Some people are even beginning to refuse to see children as victims. In her contribution to the anthology *Global Sex Workers* (1998), social anthropologist Heather Montgomery strives to cast doubt on the idea of children as mere victims of prostitution. Montgomery studied a Thai village and noticed traits that, in her opinion, disprove the image of children as exploited. She begins by establishing that it is a poor community "without running water and only intermittent access to electricity" located in close proximity to a tourist resort (1998, p. 142). In the village there are 65 children under 15 years of age, and at least 40 of them have "worked as prostitutes at some point" (p. 143). But while the media often reports child prostitution as "an evil which must be eradicated by all means possible," Montgomery wants to provide another image of children as active, rational subjects:

> The children that I knew did have 'a sense of decision and control' and to deny them this is to deny the skillful way that they use the very small amount of control that they do have. The search for victims of child abuse sometimes obscures the acknowledgement of children's agency (p. 146).

Montgomery criticizes people who think that all prostituted children are "sexually exploited." She believes that although children may not enjoy prostitution, they find a way of dealing with it:

> None of the children liked prostitution but they did have strategies for rationalizing it and coming to terms with it. They had found an ethical system whereby the public selling of their bodies did not affect their private sense of humanity and virtues (p. 143).

Prostitution, therefore, does not affect the Thai children as much as we might think, she claims. The key, according to Montgomery, is not to compare them with Western children:

> The effects were often very obvious in the forms of bruises, STDs or drug use. However, I do not believe that Western models of psychology can be applied directly to children in other countries and still be useful (p. 147).

In Thailand the connection between sexuality and identity is not as strong, Montgomery claims; therefore, we cannot be certain that Thai children are harmed as much as Western children by prostitution. That the children in many ways tried to avoid seeing themselves as prostitutes by referring to the buyers as 'friends' and by saying they are 'having guests' or 'going out and having fun with foreigners', rather than saying it is prostitution, proves to Montgomery that we cannot say with certainty that prostitution negatively impacts their character. Another positive aspect, she notes, is that the older children acted as pimps for younger children:

The older children formed entourages of younger children that they could control and grant favors to in the knowledge that these younger children were indebted to them. In this way, prestige, status and power were built up as certain children could command the time and attention of others. It may not seem a very great power to outsiders but it indicated the skillful way in which the children sought to optimize their status and make use of their limited options (p. 148).

As a matter of fact, Montgomery seems impressed by any and all initiatives or actions on the children's part; clearly she thinks that those who are outraged over child prostitution believe the children are some sort of apathetic beings. Older children controlling younger ones in an advanced imitation of indentured servitude is, to her, a show of the children's strength. And with her next sentence, she hammers it home: "Such discussions show up the difficulty of speaking about choice and force in relation to child prostitutes."

There seem to be very few ways a prostituted Thai child could act that Montgomery would *not* see as representative of an active subject, as one with power and control over their situation. Even when children are obviously passive, she finds that this should not be seen as passivity: "What is seen as passivity by outsiders may in fact be a form of protest" (p. 148). To yield and not protest when the strange men insert their penises into their bodies "is not a sign that they have given up" because "they do not have to believe in what they have to do" (p. 148).

Montgomery knows she is running through a minefield, and repeatedly makes excuses throughout the text: "It is hard not to sound like a moral relativist and argue that if the children do not see abuses, then no abuse has occurred." She assures us that she is, of course, aware that the children are exploited and forced into "lifestyles that exposed them to many forms of abuse and oppression" (p. 149). Note, however, that the text is clinically freed from all corporeal words that would turn our thoughts toward what the men actually *do* with the children. Even so, she tries to plant the seeds of doubt in the one-sided condemnation of child prostitution. She does this with the customary tentativeness, acting as if nothing is black or white, telling us that we must see things from different angles and that we must listen to the children themselves. Moreover, she adds, if these children weren't being 'fucked' by 'dirty old men' from Western countries, they "still would have been impoverished" or "scavenging or collecting garbage, neither of which pay nearly as well as prostitution" (p. 149).

This way of thinking has taken root in those parts of the world where prostitution is already accepted and legalized. In Australia, where prostitution is legal and prevalent in many states, child prostitution is growing. In Australia's National Plan of Action Against the Commercial Sexual Exploitation of Children (2000), the section on child prostitution is introduced by the story of Peter, a homeless nine-year-old boy, who was approached by a group of men on the street. The men took Peter home with them, spent the whole night raping him repeatedly and then left 50 dollars on the bed. The report describes the events in the following manner:

> Some men took him home to bed, gave him a good dinner and breakfast and a warm bed for the night. Sex was involved but in the morning they gave him $50. Peter thought this was terrific—a warm bed, lots of 'affection', food and more spending money than he had ever had in his life. The money also gave him enormous kudos among his peer group shivering under bridges and in doorways. They were so impressed they asked to be introduced to such men and Peter obliged ('Tomorrow's children', p. 7).

Mirroring the writings of Agustín and Montgomery, the focus in this description of Peter's rape is on everything that is not sexual. An eternal paradox in the story of the sex worker is that although it seems to be a pro-sex narrative, it actually euphemizes all sex acts as if to purify the discourse itself. This story, for example, emphasizes that what Peter got out of the arrangement was some food to eat and a warm bed to sleep in. The authors of the report seem to have conveniently forgotten that this should be a human right and not a luxury for a nine-year-old. They also tell us that Peter "thought this was terrific" but without revealing how they happen to know how he felt. The assault is described in passive terms: "sex was involved." There are no perpetrators, victims or even actors. We aren't told how many men violated the child, what they did and how long it went on, all of these facts are brushed aside in favor of the news that Peter received 50 dollars.

The Invulnerable Person

Why this fear of calling someone a victim? Why is it so important to prove that prostituted individuals cannot, ever, be victims?

Like all systems that accept inequalities, the neoliberal order hates victims. To speak of a 'vulnerable person' points to the lack of, and need for, a just society and a social safety net. Making it a taboo to talk about victims is a step towards legitimizing class divisions and gender inequality. This takes place in two stages. First we are told that the victim is *by definition* weak, passive and helpless. But because in reality vulnerable people develop a variety of strategies to cope with their situation, it is 'revealed' that the idea of the victim is false. The vulnerable person was not passive and helpless, but exactly the opposite: she was strong and brave with a devil-may-care attitude. As a consequence, victimhood must be abolished. It follows, therefore, that we must accept the existing social order—including prostitution, a class society, global inequalities—if we want to resist labeling people as passive and helpless.

But there is something strange about this definition of victimhood. A victim, according to the Oxford English Dictionary, is "a person who is put to death or subjected to torture by another; one who suffers severely in body or property through cruel or oppressive treatment" or "one who is reduced or destined to suffer under some oppressive or destructive agency." That is, someone who is subjected to something by someone else. Nothing is said about the characteristics of the subjected person in this definition— it is all about what *someone else does* to him or her. Someone hits, robs, cheats, is cruel towards or takes advantage of someone else in some way.

What characterizes the neoliberal definition of the victim, however, is that *victimhood has become a characteristic*. It means that a person is weak, that we can be *either* passive victims *or* active subjects. We cannot be both. In this way, the victim is depicted so negatively that the concept must eventually be abolished completely.

Instead of the vulnerable person (who has now disappeared), the illusion of the invulnerable person is created—the person who, by definition, cannot become a victim. No one—not women, drug abusers, people subjected to human trafficking, people living in poverty, illegal immigrants, or even children with no other option but to dig in the trash for food—can be called 'subjugated'. The ideal of the superman/superwoman becomes the natural condition of the human. For whatever this invulnerable person's fate—to be screwed by multiple men per day, take drugs and contract HIV/AIDS at ten years of age, have her body covered in bruises, lie passively and let herself be used, or turn other children into slaves—she is, by definition, an active subject who exercises opposition and control. The only possible violence that can be exerted against her is by calling her a victim. It is worse than any other physical or psychological violation to speak of her as subjugated—only *then* does she become a victim.

A consequence of this belief system is the conviction that if there are no victims, there can be no perpetrators. The unmentionables, the men, are completely exonerated in a highly convenient, imperceptible way. In the writings of Agustín, Dodillet and Montgomery, men appear as mere shadows on the wall, movie extras who sneak into the story now and then and in some magical way see all of their desires justified by the happy ending. While Montgomery's focus was on Thai women and children—she studied them, she interviewed them, she counted and described them—she asked no questions at all of the men. Not even the most basic one: Why do you do this?

The phrase 'she is an agent, not a victim' is not only tossed around in the prostitution debate. We hear it repeated in a multitude of contexts; it flies through the air like a dandelion seed and sows itself everywhere. It becomes a refrain in the stories of people who are in vulnerable or powerless situations: *they are agents, not victims …*

Two young Muslim women who choose to wear headscarves are described in exactly this way in a *Metro* article entitled: 'De vägrar se sig som offer' ['They refuse to see themselves as victims'] (Zaitzewsky, 18 January 2008). "They want to be understood as active and capable individuals, not as passive victims," one ethnologist is quoted as saying. In other words, a person is *either* capable *or* a victim. Per Wirtén writes in a similar vein in the Swedish evening newspaper *Expressen* about refugees who come to Sweden via people smugglers: "The stereotype of smuggled people as victims is fading. Instead, a more self-aware subject steps forward" (16 June 2007). This binary system is exactly the same: one cannot be both victim and agent simultaneously. Under the surface lies the same victim-blaming ideology: victimhood is for the feeble; those who are capable and self-aware don't become victims.

It is interesting to study *how* these authors claim justification for not seeing people as victims. In Per Wirtén's text about refugees, it is because they *do* things: they negotiate actively between intermediaries, they bribe officials, they pay for hotel rooms. If they had been victims, they obviously would not have been able to do anything at all; we see an image of a pathetic, emaciated type, standing silent with a downcast gaze as she is yanked away by a greedy people smuggler. Doing business and making decisions excludes us from being a victim. The interesting thing is that this is regardless of what is done *to* us, even if someone robs us, rapes us or restricts our movement; it is how *we* behave that determines whether or not we are victims. In the article about the women wearing headscarves, it is telling that they are described as actively *choosing* their subordination. The ethnologist claims: "These women believe that being submissive in certain situations is a woman's independent decision." Here the writer attempts to make the very power relationship irrelevant, as if it were the person's *attitude* that determined victimhood. If we choose our status voluntarily, then we are clearly not victims—regardless of how submissive we might be.

This type of rhetoric consistently presents the position of the victim as related to the behavior of the vulnerable person. There is a value judgment here as well as an imperative: don't be a victim! Being a victim is for losers! Victimhood becomes an *identity* associated with a variety of negative qualities nobody wants to have. The doctrine of the invulnerable person quickly develops into an imperative to be the responsible, liberal individual. Regardless of what we do, we should always see ourselves as strong, active beings and act accordingly. No matter if you are unemployed, disabled, or a refugee—oh dear, you wouldn't want to be seen as a victim!

This is the neoliberal version of the old myth of the strong slave, the hardened working-class woman, the black 'superwoman', the thick-skinned colonized woman who doesn't feel the whippings and beatings: history is teeming with examples of how living conditions are reinterpreted as character traits, not least in relation to American slavery. Michele Wallace described the myth of the black superwoman in her book *Black Macho and the Myth of the Superwoman* (1990) as

> a woman of inordinate strength, with an ability for tolerating an unusual amount of misery and heavy, distasteful work. This woman does not have the same fears, weaknesses and insecurities as other women, but believes herself to be and is, in fact, stronger emotionally than most men (Wallace, 1990, p. 107).

While the white woman was seen as fragile, frail and in need of protection, the black woman was seen as ready to handle anything. But the most vulnerable individual is always the one who is depicted as strong. Her alleged strength becomes a way for society as a whole to escape having to feel any solidarity with her.

This opposition between subject and victim, however, is asymmetrical and false. Australian women's studies scholar Belinda J. Carpenter writes in *Re-thinking Prostitution: Feminism, sex and the self* (2000) that this is a nonsensical dichotomy—subject and victim are not each other's opposites, but are intimately interwoven (p. 132). It is like saying 'she's not angry, she's running'. The opposite of subject is not victim, but *object*. The opposite of victim is not subject, but *perpetrator*. What the alleged subject-victim dichotomy actually claims, of course, is that *the victim is an object*, that a person who becomes a victim is no longer a person who thinks, feels and acts. This fictitious opposition exposes an unfathomable contempt for any kind of weakness.

Returning to the topic of prostitution, Belinda Carpenter writes that it is the prostituted woman's ambiguous state as both subject and object in the agreement that makes her alienation possible (p. 118). When she enters into an agreement between herself and a buyer, she is both the subject—a partner in the business arrangement—and the object—the commodity being sold. It is this very ambiguity that forces a distancing from the body, from what is sold. Prostitution must be understood in relation to this duality, says Carpenter. Similarly, Sven-Axel Månsson writes in response to Susanne Dodillet about the Malmö Project:

> It is completely clear that many of those women we had contact with were victims of poverty, drug-addicted and violent parents, emotionally impoverished childhood environments, prolonged periods in foster-homes and institutions, and in some cases, sexual assault. Life had been hard for them, which had affected their choices in life. Understanding these mechanisms is, meanwhile, not synonymous with depriving women of their potential for action, as Dodillet seems to believe. We never considered the women to be helpless or incapable (12 March 2009).

The Narrator

What we have so far is a story about prostitution that begins by simultaneously depicting prostitution as a job, as sexual liberation, as a human right and a sort of feminist revolt. Who, then, is portrayed as the narrator of this story? Yes—the prostituted woman. Though only a minority of those who talk about 'sex work' are prostitutes themselves, these women are unfailingly described as the 'real' narrators of the story. Often the story is introduced with explicit reference to prostituted women. Kamala Kempadoo introduces the anthology *Global Sex Workers* with talk of how "prostitutes and other sex workers were fighting to keep brothels open" and how these stories excited and puzzled her (Kempadoo, 1998, p. 2). The author is a professor at the University of Colorado, but she writes as if prostitutes were the authors of her anthology. Kempadoo continues by asserting: "This collection testifies to the courage and determination of sex workers to tell their own stories" (p. 2). Of the book's 15 authors, only 2 are said to have been prostitutes, but the reader is given the impression that, in some mysterious way, they are the book's 'true' authors.

Petra Östergren takes the same approach and succeeds in making her book appear as if it were written by women in prostitution. She interviews 12 women, all of whom she chose because of their positive experiences with prostitution. Their stories are not published in their entirety but instead serve as short illustrations of Östergren's theories. This is not a problem in itself, however; the real issue is that the book was marketed as if these women, not Östergren, were the writers. The reviews of the book repeated this misrepresentation with titles such as 'När sexsäljare själva får tala' ['When sex workers speak for themselves'] and 'Hör horan' ['Hear the whore'].⁶ Maria Abrahamsson (2006) even went so far as to claim that "for what might be the first time ever, we can now hear some of the women themselves"—thereby revealing that she is less than familiar with the history of Swedish prostitution research.

In Petra Östergren's 2006 article 'De oberörbara' ['The untouchables'] in the Swedish politics and arts journal *Arena*, she begins with a supposed quote from a prostituted woman: "'Hey Petra, isn't that book coming out soon?' Ingegärd wonders." Thus the prostitute grants the academic legitimacy: she gives Östergren the floor and we, the readers, are therefore supposed to understand that the opinions presented later are those of prostitutes. Östergren claims that she herself is impartial: "I do not take a position on

---

6   Josefsson (2006); Demirbag-Sten (2006).

whether prostitution is good or bad per se. Instead, I listen to what these women want" (in Mallik, 2004, p. 348). We are supposed to see Östergren as a neutral medium who doesn't analyze what she presents, who doesn't have her own opinions but only presents someone else's—which, aside from being false, is a strange stance for an intellectual to take.

The point here is not whether the chain of events is accurate: how Kempadoo and Östergren first heard about the 'fighting sex workers', became curious and/or irate, and then appointed themselves to be their mouthpieces. The point is not to suspect whether or not any prostitute ever really asked eagerly if Östergren's book was coming out soon, or to deny that there are prostitutes who are pro-prostitution. What it *is* about is how advocates of the story of the sex worker—academics, journalists and critics—create a narrative structure in which they present themselves as spokespersons for prostitutes. This structure exempts the intellectuals from taking responsibility for their own positions. They can present themselves as impartial, even *against* prostitution—all they want, they say, is to let 'the prostitutes' speak for themselves. Susanne Dodillet, for example, argues for decriminalizing the purchase of sex and simultaneously states: "I would never say that I advocate prostitution" (in Sandblad, 27 February 2009). In Francophone and Anglophone countries, opponents of prostitution call themselves 'abolitionists', hearkening back to the nineteenth century movement to abolish slavery. However, those who want to keep prostitution don't call themselves pro-prostitution, but *'anti-abolitionists.'* They don't have the courage to say that they are *for* prostitution—they are simply against the opponents. Interestingly, advocates of slavery used exactly the same word: anti-abolitionism.

Through this smokescreen, academics avoid taking responsibility and avoid being labeled advocates of prostitution. They let 'the prostitutes' do the work and can even, in a cowardly move, present themselves as counterweights. Author Lotta Lundberg, who has written in favor of German prostitution legislation numerous times, introduced her 2006 article 'Lotta Lundberg om prostitution: Att välja att sälja sig' ['Lotta Lundberg on prostitution: Choosing to sell yourself'] with the words: "Lolette is a whore. I ask her if I should say whore or prostitute. And she says whore." The article is constructed so that all positive opinions of prostitution end up coming from Lolette's mouth, while the objections are from Lundberg's. Lolette says of Swedish women: "[Y]ou seem to be scared of your sexuality and to despise men"; that the Swedish government believes that "men are animals"; that when she's working, she makes her own decisions; and that she made the conscious choice at 45 to become a whore. Lundberg's response is that "in Sweden, we believe that no one wants to become a whore" and "whores are either junkies trying desperately to support their habit, or [women] who have been sexually abused" (Lundberg, 2006). The message is clear—prostitution is a free choice by an independent woman, yet Lundberg, author of the article, is not to be held responsible for this viewpoint.

Dagens Nyheter journalist Nathan Shachar used the same strategy in a 2008 interview with an Argentinian woman, prostituted since she was 15, who organized a protest against police violence. In Argentina, the woman told Shachar, police terrorize street prostitutes, fine them and imprison them on arbitrary grounds. Shachar then described to her the Swedish Sex Purchase Act in a striking manner, using her words to then rail against the Swedish law:

> Like many honest Latin Americans, Elena takes it for granted that Sweden manages these sorts of things more reasonably and more humanely. When I first told her that ten years ago, we began allocating a great deal of funding to imposing the same criminalizing laws she had dedicated her life to fighting against, she nearly fell off her chair (Shachar, 9 September 2008).

In the remainder of the article, he abandons her comments about police violence and the difficulties of raising children as a single mother in Argentina and instead embarks on a full-scale critique of Sweden for fining sex buyers. Although fining buyers is not at all the same thing as fining prostitutes—just the opposite, really— Shachar ignores this difference. Nor does he address that in

Argentina, prostitution is legal. Police repression, harassment and fining of prostitutes go hand in hand with complete tolerance for prostitution *as a system* (see Sullivan, 2007 on further problems with legalized prostitution). This essential difference, compared with the Swedish law that focuses on buyers, is revealed neither to the reader nor to Elena.

Instead Elena believes—from what Shachar has told her—that Sweden is "imposing the *same* criminalizing laws she had dedicated her life to fighting." He gets what he wants from her: a statement against the Sex Purchase Act that he can use at home in support of his own position. She states very clearly: "The only people who are affected by prohibition politics are the streetwalkers, while the brothel owners rake in the profits." This is all too true in countries where brothel prostitution is legal and illegal street prostitutes are punished, but it doesn't apply to the Swedish context, where brothel owners are hardly "rak[ing] in the profits."

The Cult of the Whore

The cultural equivalent of sex workers' rights is the 'cult of the whore'. In intellectual circles, praising the whore is fashionable. The whore is quintessentially hip. The word 'whore' can spice up the dullest book or the most insipid party; it breathes exoticism and titillation. We hear more and more talk of 'reclaiming' the word. Everyone should dare to call themselves whores, says one journalist. Elsewhere, five women who blog about literature call their blog 'Bokhora' ['Bookwhore']. When the organization Prostitutes' Revenge in Society (PRIS), asked the bloggers why they chose this name, they answered: "'whore' simply means 'one who desires' and that 'whore' in the sense of 'prostitute' is nothing more than a transferred meaning, a 'dysphemism'."[7] But if it were only desire for books they wanted to convey, why didn't they just call themselves 'The book lovers'? No risk of confusion there. Obviously, the word 'whore' is titillating—and when those five

---

7   'Brev till bokhora.se – och deras svar,' <http://www.nätverketpris.se/bokhora. html>.

literature-loving women call themselves 'bookwhores' and print T-shirts screaming 'bookwhore', it is exactly the loaded meaning of the word 'whore' they are alluding to.

They call it paying homage: the whore has been scorned by society—now we must elevate her! But when a male journalist encourages women to dare to let themselves be called 'whores' and literature bloggers call themselves 'bookwhores', the point is that they do so because they have clearly *not* prostituted themselves. That is why they can use the word as an accessory—because it doesn't affect them, because it doesn't threaten their humanity. The gesture is, in fact, a way of dissociating themselves from prostituted women. They wear the 'whore' like a necklace: 'I wear her as an accessory, and thus show that I am not her'.

'Whore' is more than just a pejorative; it is a cultural fantasy. With the word 'whore', a male desire is transformed into a female characteristic. When we say that a man 'goes to see a whore', it sounds as if he does so on impulse, stopping by in all innocence. In spite of the fact that it is the man who creates the demand for prostitution, no label adheres to him. The woman, on the other hand, *is* labeled something: a 'whore'. The entire sex trade rests on this fantasy: that women can be whores, and that the whore is a particular type of woman who is perpetually available to men. The word 'whore' is a male invention transferred onto the woman and *transformed into an attribute that adheres to her*. Thus it differs from, for example, the word 'gay', which, although it can have a pejorative tone, alludes to something emanating from a person. It can therefore be transformed into a neutral or even a positive word. The whore, on the other hand, is not a female construct, but a male one.

"No women are whores," wrote Hanna Olsson in the 1977 Prostitution Inquiry (in Borg *et al.*, 1981). Good grief! A cultural archetype is being threatened! And so a whole society quickly rushed to restore the whore. She must not disappear! So people insisted: we are all whores, whores are good, whores should be proud, we will abolish the stigma of the whore; or even: the word 'whore' doesn't signify anything at all—in other words,

Being and Being Bought

people rushed to reclaim the word but simultaneously denied its significance, just like the book bloggers.

In reality, the admiration is nothing but scorn from a different perspective. It still fails to acknowledge the humanity of women in the sex trade; instead, it promotes a love of the 'ugly' and 'base' qualities with which prostituted women have frequently been associated. False admiration of the prostitute has a history as a means for male artists to position themselves against the hypocritical morals of the bourgeoisie. Bohemians and *flaneurs* have used prostitution as a backdrop against which the male ego tests its freedom. Prostituted women are seldom portrayed as individuals, but instead used as a key feature of a bohemian background. As Swedish author Peter Cornell has shown in his book *Mannen på Gatan* [The Man on the Street], the prostitute plays one of the key roles in modernity (2009, p. 13). Baudelaire, Degas, van Gogh—an endless number of authors and artists have searched for the 'sacred' and 'beautiful' in the 'ugly' and have therefore declared prostitution to be a sacred art form—without ever getting beyond the superficial. In the Swedish novel entitled *Siki* [Siki] by Torbjörn Säfve, the protagonist walks around in the city's less affluent neighborhood where garbage and women merge into a tasty brew (1987, p. 109):

> The gutter ran across the middle, like a little stream with narrow, sloping banks. Everything flowed down the river: refuse, excrement, dishwater ... In the doorways of houses stood the women, selling themselves cheaply. They fanned their robes open and shut to air out the stink of last night's sailors. I found myself right in the midst of this life, and I couldn't dislike it.

He is visiting the Red Light District, and everything he describes— the gutter, the refuse, the excrement, the stink of sailors and the women "selling themselves cheaply"—becomes united in a full-bodied soup. By rubbing shoulders with the people of the street, he thinks he is dissociating himself from the bourgeois life and becoming a man who is 'in' with the 'whores'. Unexpectedly often, the reader notes, they give themselves to him for free—only *he* enjoys this benefit, of course. But in spite of his diatribes against snobs and puritans, in spite of his bellowing in the salons, and in spite of his fashionable flirting with prostitutes, he forgets that they are human beings. Or, more correctly, he takes pleasure in the idea the *he* becomes more of a human being than ever in their company. Often, his love for the women who sell themselves cheaply goes hand-in-hand with an unreasonable hatred for the kept women of wealthy men: how dare they be 'whores' without being available to *me*?

The *flaneur* is a precursor to the sex radicals of our time. In *flaneurs* we see the same search for the picturesque and the same admiration for everything that upsets prudish bourgeois respectability. They love the 'ugly' (always within quotation marks): 'ugly' is beautiful! Swedish queer theorist Ulrika Dahl describes a visit to Amsterdam:

> My feet ache after days in tall black boots on the streets of Amsterdam, the city we travel to in order to lose ourselves in something. In the symbolic heart of Western Europe's sexualized public, working girls sit in the row of windows, lit by red lights, night after night, posing mostly for curious tourists and hordes of British working-class blokes at stag parties (Dahl, 2007, p. 18).

The Red Light District is described as a "marshland of whores" and a "hotbed of sin" that "is inhabited by and visited by the wrong sort of people: the drunk, the drugged, the idle, the people who don't give a crap about van Gogh ..." Now, Dahl regrets to inform us, the district is going to be redeveloped. "So the junkies, queers, wogs and whores will be deported to the periphery." It is a reenactment of the habits and viewpoints of *flaneurs*, but this time by a female ego that tests *her* freedom with 'whores' as the backdrop. She comes no closer than anyone else, though: she "looks at the girls," but as usual, "they don't look at me." A picture window separates them, and the prostituted women remain distant. She seeks a connection anyway: "those of us who walk the streets in this hotbed of sin ... are all marked as different types of public women." What Säfve and Dahl have in common is that the metaphors of the 'hot bed of sin' and 'garbage' are more real to them than the people who live there. Identifying with addicts and prostitutes remains simply a tool for dissociating from mainstream bourgeois tourism.

In Dahl's article, bourgeois respectability is symbolized by a young American tourist. The American "wrinkles her nose, in her comfortable shoes and with a backpack over her brand-name jacket" and says that she "never thought sex could be such a turn-off; it's disgusting," she has "had enough" and looks for a Starbucks. Dahl intends the reader to understand it is she, Dahl, dressed in tall black boots, who melts into and belongs in this 'hotbed of sin', in contrast to the disgusted American.

Ulrika Dahl was one of the first to introduce the concept of the 'femme' identity to the arts and academic scenes in Sweden. In a 2006 article entitled 'Femme-inism' in *Arena*, Dahl defines 'femme': "Femmes seldom sit in the fine salons" (p. 15), femmes are "bad girls" (p. 14)—they can be "queer girls, whores, sluts and lesbians" (p. 14). Femmes are also working-class women and transsexuals, and the word has come to be understood more broadly in racial terms, including African-American and Latina femmes. But what does all this mean in relation to prostitution? Hardly that all 'femmes' sell sex for money—no more than the blogging book lovers. Instead, it has to do with a desire to absorb the 'whore' and use her as an accessory.

White 'wiggers' absorb hip hop; backpackers and vagabonds absorb so-called Third-World culture; male transvestites and drag queens absorb the woman; and 'femmes' absorb the prostitute. The transgression of boundaries presupposes the preservation of boundaries. When whites play blacks and academics pretend they are 'whores' and 'junkies', they deride the *humanity* of the black person, the junkie and the whore. There's a slogan printed on T-shirts in Barcelona distributed by a 'sex worker' group: "Yo també soc puta" ["I'm a whore, too"]. This shirt is proudly worn by radical youths and other daring souls who believe that, by wearing this silkscreened T-shirt, they have transgressed the boundary that separates people. "We are all whores," they think. What they don't get is that the whore isn't just a whore. She is a person, just like they are.

People who feel marginalized by bourgeois society seek to identify with prostitutes, but they don't see that it is precisely this false identification that confirms the label of 'whore' and its corresponding objectification. When the 'whore' is fetishized, she gains mythical powers. She becomes an oracle. In her presence, people become breathless and tongue-tied. They are suddenly unable to look rationally at things, they tremble, they are wracked by nerves, they are ready to agree with anything she says, they hardly hear what she says because they are so busy nodding frenetically: yeah, *I'm down with that.*

This admiration of the whore is no vaccine against contempt— it is exactly the opposite. It goes hand in hand with scorn, overt or covert, for her humanity and a lack of insight into her actual living conditions. A 'femme' can repeat all day long that she is a 'slut' and a 'whore' and simultaneously have a blasé attitude towards prostitution. A transsexual can demand that everyone call him a woman and at the same time have absolutely no understanding of women's issues. The vagabond wears a Mexican poncho but does not forget to haggle over the price. A man who romanticizes the working class applauds the physical laborer and hopes that he has some of those attributes, but it is stereotypical masculinity he admires, not a living person trying to survive under difficult conditions. The 'wigger' feels like he is part of the black community, but is not upset about violence in the ghetto—in his mind, it is part of the draw! What he fails to understand is that by fetishizing someone's everyday life, he shows how distant he is from it. Living conditions become an identity, and then a fetish. An American joke shows the difference between the fetish and the reality:

> Wigger: Yo, wassup my niggas, how's it hangin', black?
> **BLAST**
> Black Man 1: Yo, you just shot the Wigga, cuz.
> Black Man 2: A white boy. He wanted equality. I gave it to him. Now he's just a statistic like the rest of us.

A 'wigger' comes along and wants to be one of the gang, but of course, he doesn't understand the actual living conditions. As a result, he is despised by those he imitates, even if they don't openly show it as they do in this joke. The oppressed is keenly aware of the humanity of the privileged. For the privileged, on the other hand, the oppressed is an enigma living in a magical, half-human world. The fantasy of the privileged is having the ability to wallow in this world. He wallows around and shouts: I am just like you! I am the slut, the junkie and the factory worker! He buys the same clothes at the same shop but wears them wrong, he picks up a few slang words but says them at the wrong times, he thinks that everything is a festive orgy. It is so embarrassing to watch that you have to look away.

In the *El Raval* district in Barcelona, this phenomenon plays out every evening. *El Raval* is a prostitution-dense, bohemian quarter that is both home to many immigrants and a destination for certain types of tourists. Some people who live there like to think that they live in the midst of a crowd, a carnivalesque melting pot, but the boundary is razor-sharp. On the narrow street *Carrer d'en Robadors*, African women with tired eyes and fanny packs stand selling themselves while a sour-faced pimp hiding in a doorway supervises everything. This goes on all day and all night, with only a short break between seven and ten in the morning. In the pubs, 'alternative' people party. They love prostitution and filth, despise authorities and censorship, speak adoringly of the quarter's charming character and pretend that some of it has rubbed off on them. The existence of prostitution is important to them. But people never exchange places: the African women never go into the pubs, and the pub patrons never go out and prostitute themselves. They pass each other every day, but the crowd is only an illusion—there is no common, shared experience. Everyone has an established role and no one speaks to anyone else.

The important thing for those who glorify the prostitute is to enact the erasure of boundaries at the same time as they are upheld: the other is not me, but someone I can dress up as. In this way, prostitution is simultaneously normalized and held at arm's length. Frantz Fanon wrote:

> In our view, an individual who loves Blacks is as 'sick' as somebody who abhors them … The black man is not more inherently amiable than the Czech; the truth is that we must unleash the man (Fanon, 2008 pp. xii–xiii).

In an absolute sense, whores do not exist. People end up in prostitution for a number of reasons; some for a shorter time, others for longer. They are not 'types', not characters. They are people who end up in this particular situation. The fetishized *transgression* of boundaries is hailed as subversive, but it reduces people to objects. The *dissolution* of boundaries, on the other hand, has revolutionary potential. Dissolving boundaries means recognizing humanity in every person; recognizing that each and every one of us is a human being. There is nothing exploitative or slimy about this; it is objective solidarity founded on subjective understanding. I observe another person in the flesh and realize that this other person is simply *me in a different situation*, under other life circumstances. It is looking into another's eyes and seeing yourself. With this insight comes the recognition of the cruel system that has reduced a 'whore' to a 'type'.

The World's Oldest Profession: Regulation

One hundred years ago, when prostitution exploded in European cities, it followed another storyline. Prostitution was said to be not only natural but also a necessary component of civilization, and prostituted women were said to be biologically inferior. The Italian *fin-de-siècle* doctor Cesare Lombroso, known as the first criminologist, claimed that prostitutes were the female equivalent of the male criminal (Lombroso and Ferrero, 2004, p. 37). But prostitution was better than crime, because "while every crime involves calamity, prostitution can be a moral safety valve." Prostitution had, according to Lombroso, "been a normal fact of life from the dawn of evolution" (p. 100). Although *prostitution* was normal, *prostituted women* were not like other women. They had darker hair than 'honest' women, larger thighs, smaller heads. They were, Lombroso stated, free from wrinkles and were overweight, had large jaws and odd teeth, monkey-like feet, wild eyes, disturbed facial expressions and asymmetrical faces (pp. 123, 132, 140). According to Lombroso, they were vain, lazy, greedy, thoughtless, dishonest and had a weakness for alcohol (p. 218). In other words, prostitutes were almost another race entirely.

The Drainage Model

The foremost hygienist of the 1800s, French physician Alexandre Parent-Duchâtelet, created a model for regulated prostitution that was exported to the rest of Europe and the French colonies. Called the 'Drainage Model', it was based on the idea that prostitution was necessary for channeling the unhealthy urges of men. Prostitution was like a drainage pipe that had to be installed to prevent the whole system from clogging up and beginning to stink. In Parent-Duchâtelet's monumental 1836 study of prostitutes in Paris, however, he did not even mention men or money. Prostitution was synonymous with the prostitute. He did perceptively identify poverty as a primary cause of women entering prostitution, stating that in the women's backgrounds, "one sees nothing other than laborers and people of less-than-fortunate lots." None of the women had any education whatsoever, and poverty was "one of the strongest motives for prostitution" (Parent-Duchâtelet, 1981, pp. 82, 88). But Parent-Duchâtelet also believed another cause was the women's characters. He described them as vain, lazy, generally listless in the morning, and restless. He wrote that they got up late, had a weakness for dancing and gambling, ate and drank voraciously, lied, were irascible and as childish as 12-year-olds. But he also noted that they were loyal to each other, were motherly and loved children (pp. 98, 104–106).

Other doctors and scholars measured the bodies of prostituted women and investigated their psyches and came to the same conclusion: something was wrong with these women. German psychiatrist Karl Bonhoeffer calculated that 31% of the prostitutes were 'feeble-minded' and that over half of them suffered from a genetic defect. Another psychiatrist, Kurt Schneider, arrived at even more dramatic numbers, finding that half of all the prostitutes in Vienna were 'feeble-minded'. And one more early German researcher claimed that 35% of prostitutes were oligophrenics (imbeciles). Psychiatrist Max Sichel from the University of Frankfurt said that 36 of 152 prostitutes were psychopaths. They have large heads and small faces, typical of a lower order of people, declared the Italian researcher Ettore Fornasari (in Ellis, 1927, p. 198). They are ugly and repulsive, wrote the American physician Woods Hutchinson (p. 199). Again and again, male doctors and scholars explained that prostitutes were an inferior order of people. One is inclined to ask why on earth men all over the world, and especially men of the upper echelons of society, would be interested in sleeping with such ugly and horrible women. But even so, doctors and criminologists believed that society could benefit from these inferior women. The defect was, therefore, for the greater good: "One might say that the more women degrade themselves and the more they sin, the more they are helping society," Lombroso wrote (2004, p. 37). For as the women 'fell', the men could take out their urges on them: brutality and repressed desires could be relieved by this lowest class of women who were not good enough for anything else.

Between 1859 and 1918, for almost 70 years, Sweden had a regulated prostitution system. In Stockholm and other larger cities, prostituted women were forced to register at municipal offices (Svanström, 2006, p. 12). Nor did Scandinavia lack its share of Lombroso and Parent-Duchâtelet imitators, either. Tage Kemp, founder of the Danish Institute for Human Genetics, published a study in 1936 in which he proved that prostitution was a genetic defect. Kemp studied 600 prostituted women and presented the results in *Prostitution: An investigation of its causes, especially with regard to hereditary factors*. In his Foreword, he explained that it had nothing to do with morals but was instead pure biology: "In these pages, prostitution is regarded from a purely objective standpoint and is considered a biological phenomenon, neither

43

moral nor political prejudice being harboured." That it was a "biological phenomenon" meant that the reasons for it were to be found in the woman's body alone. To reveal them, Kemp studied the body and brain of each woman. He conducted an intelligence test, a personality test, an interview about the woman's family and possible psychological illnesses in the family, and ended by examining her body for "physical abnormalities." Then he made his diagnosis, which almost always read 'feeble-minded', but was nuanced with labels ranging from weak character to 'psychopathic constitution', 'retarded', 'imbecile' or 'chronic alcoholic'.

Virtually all of the women Kemp examined were living in abject poverty, and almost all of them could tell of mothers who drowned themselves, parents who disappeared, brothers in prison, illegitimate children who had to be taken care of, and stillborn babies. Many of the women were adopted and several had bruises and scars on their bodies—one Russian woman's head and body were covered with wounds from daily beatings by her pimp. In Kemp's mind, this was all further proof of their mental weakness. Of the Russian woman who was covered with wounds from abuse, Kemp wrote: "She can, without a doubt, be seen as one of the most inferior women of all who have been studied in this book" (p. 112). On the mother who committed suicide, he stated that she should have been sterilized because it was clear that she suffered from a psychological illness. Often, he recommended sterilization of those women who had a serious mental disturbance so that the illness would not be passed on. Kemp's conclusion was that over 70% of the women were, "in one way or another," psychologically abnormal. "These women's fate is, to a great extent, a consequence of mental weakness," Kemp wrote (p. 14). It was futile to attempt to cure this weakness, because, as he stated, "the general understanding now is that 90% of all mental defects are hereditary" (p. 55).

Consequently, prostitution was not something one *did*—a prostitute was something one *was*. The doctors' and criminologists' studies display a belief in the constructed view of 'the whore as other'. The studies represented massive stigmatization of prostituted women. The recurring theme was that the prostitute is defective, feeble-minded and degenerate.

Although regulation aimed to limit and control prostitution, the sex trade continued to expand. In the early 1900s, the so-called white slave trade thrived in Europe. European women were transported to America, Egypt, Turkey and Tunisia and sold into prostitution (Jeffreys, 1997, p. 15). A report from the League of Nations already in 1927 implicated regulated prostitution as facilitating and encouraging slave trade (p. 15). In Europe, organizations held conferences with the goal of halting the increasing prostitution and slave trade—a mission that was interrupted by World War II but in the end resulted in the UN Convention for the Suppression of Traffic in Persons in 1949 (p. 12).

Holland was quick to discover the connection between regulated prostitution and the increased trafficking of women, and became the first country in Europe to abolish regulated prostitution in 1910. Sweden followed suit after a parliamentary decision in 1918. After regulated prostitution was abolished in 1918, prostitution decreased in Europe. The decrease can also be attributed to the rise of the welfare state. This applied to Sweden as well, in spite of mass migration from rural areas to the three large cities (Borg *et al.*, 1981, p. 108). In the 1950s, many people thought that prostitution was heading for extinction, along with other traces of bygone eras of inequality.

But today it is again on the rise—with the potential of reaching gigantic proportions. The UN and ILO estimate that between 2 and 4 million people are victims of trafficking for sexual purposes (Marcovich, 2007, p. 331). And, moreover, it is important to note that the basic structure of prostitution has not changed appreciably in over 100 years. It is still overwhelmingly men who pay for intercourse with women, and prostitution still takes place on streets, in apartments and in brothels. It involves the same poverty and the same violence. Poor women are still trafficked to other parts of the world and sold in brothels. The trade is still controlled by pimps and organized crime. More countries have reverted to forms of regulated prostitution.

What *has* changed, on the other hand, is the manner in which prostitution is defended—the arguments now are *exactly* the opposite of what they used to be! Back then, it was said that prostitution was natural and necessary to preserve marriage and civilization—now it is said to be a free choice and a rebellion against traditional gender roles. During the nineteenth century, brothels were said to preserve order; the same brothels are now claimed to be a revolt against the existing order. In the past, people claimed that the prostitute was biologically inferior. Today she is held up as the ultimate feminist. Then, she was 'feeble-minded'—now, she is strong. Then, prostitution was an inescapable fate—now, it is a completely free choice. Then, it was shameful but preserved social morals. Now, it is honorable and rightfully calls 'morality' into question. Then as now, however, prostitution is presented *as a characteristic of the woman.* Then as now, the man is left out of the story, as is the question of why he purchases sexual services. And then as now, people subscribe to a story that allows them to speak out in favor of regulated prostitution. Today it is called 'legalized' or 'decriminalized', but it is largely the same system by which prostitution is guaranteed a lawful place in society.

How, then, was prostitution successfully reinstated in society? How was this outdated, slavery-like industry made to look modern?

CHAPTER TWO
_____

An Industry is Born—1970 to present

The 1970s: The Sex Industry Expands—and Gets into Trouble

In the mid-1970s, the contemporary sex industry began to take shape. During the Vietnam War, the USA had opened mega-brothels for its soldiers in the Thai cities of Pattaya and Bangkok. Built in 1967 in compliance with an agreement between the Thai government and the US army, they were called 'rest and recreation complexes' (Truong, 1990, p. 161). After the war in Vietnam, the brothels stayed open and soon received the first waves of male tourists. Former American soldiers took over cafés and teahouses in Bangkok, turning them into nightclubs and brothels (p. 162).

Laws against pornography were repealed in much of the capitalist world, opening up an enormous market. At the same time, prostitution districts like the Red Light District in Amsterdam and the Reeperbahn in Hamburg were transformed from shabby street corners into entire neighborhoods replete with strip clubs, sex shops and porn movie theaters.

This was a turbulent time of powerful social contradictions. Prostitution was attacked by the women's liberation movement, which described it as one of the worst possible expressions of women's oppression. It was also attacked by social justice movements and, to some extent, by proponents of the sexual revolution who

47

believed that if people felt free to have sex with whomever they pleased, prostitution wouldn't be necessary. The 1970s saw the publication of many groundbreaking works analyzing the sexual oppression of women, such as Kate Millett's *Sexual Politics* (1970), Susan Brownmiller's *Against Our Will* (1975), and Kathleen Barry's *Female Sexual Slavery* (1979). Women's rights groups demonstrated against, criticized and blockaded porn clubs all over the world. In Lyon, France, prostituted women protested against police brutality and double standards by occupying a church. This action sent shock waves around the world, and several of the women involved later composed an anthology of their stories called *Prostitutes: Our life*, edited by Claude Jaget. In 1977, the Swedish women's liberation movement staged massive protests and successfully put a stop to the recommendation from the Sex Crimes Inquiry to reduce the legal sanctions for rape in Sweden.

In the same year, the paradigm of Swedish prostitution research shifted. Previously, such research had been carried out by doctors and focused primarily on theories of deviance and aberrant behavior. Now, researchers began to seek their knowledge from the reality of prostitution. The 'Malmö Project' was the first outreach-based project in Scandinavia to do social work among prostitutes. The same year, an investigation of prostitution was launched in Sweden in which hundreds of women in prostitution described the reality of their everyday lives. New knowledge about prostitution was gathered through a combination of academic research, governmental investigative work and fieldwork. At the core of all this effort lay the conviction that the truth had to be sought at ground level, in people's own stories. By living in the same environments as prostituted women and listening to the women, johns, pimps, and others involved in prostitution, researchers were able to reach a whole new understanding of prostitution. They began to understand that it was not a subject of countless racy jokes, not a taboo subject, not the result of congenital defects in women, but something that men did—with terribly tragic consequences.

The old arguments for the preservation of prostitution—a biological urge in the man, a mental defect in the woman, a necessary evil to preserve the institution of marriage—were exposed in all their absurdity.

It suffices to say that, as a result, the sex industry had a serious image problem on its hands. What happened next was not a result of a conspiracy but rather the result of collaboration among various interest groups. During the sixties and seventies, myriad political advocacy groups were founded, including groups for equality between the sexes, groups for homosexual liberation, groups for rent-free housing, groups for legalizing drugs, and communist groups. Groups that took a stance on prostitution were not absent from the list. But there was one group, possibly the only one, that was able to gain financial support from both churches and porn magazines simultaneously: the American group Call Off Your Old Tired Ethics (COYOTE). COYOTE was founded in 1973 by a liberal faction of the hippie movement, and their central belief was that prostitution was an expression of sexual freedom. COYOTE was comprised of a mix of sex liberals, beatniks and women who had experience with prostitution, but the leaders of COYOTE also included known pimps who used the organization to gain access to a new market (Oriel, 2006, p. 97).

COYOTE was marketed with a spectacular media strategy: they organized gala dinners, called 'Hookers' Balls', and invited journalists to rub elbows with 'real whores'. Another highlight was the auctioning-off of a night with a prostituted woman. The slogan of the first ball was 'Everybody Needs a Hooker Once in a While'.

The Methodist Church in California and *Playboy Magazine* were two of the early donors to the rapidly growing COYOTE— after eight years the organization reported having 30,000 members, of whom only 3% were prostituted women. Despite its small percentage of prostitutes, the group was repeatedly labeled the first national organization for prostitutes, a union for whores, and later, simply 'the hookers' union' (Jenness, 1993, p. 114). Scholar Valerie Jenness, who has studied the rise of COYOTE, points out the fascination of the American press with the idea of the 'organized whore'. Newspaper articles ran headlines such as 'Hookers arise!', 'Hookers of the world unite', 'Love's laborers organize', 'Hookers

stand up for rights', and 'Organizing the oldest profession' (p. 115).
But as Jenness explained in her study, "[c]ontrary to COYOTE's
public image, only a small percentage of its members have worked
as prostitutes, and an even smaller percentage are active prostitutes
who are also active in the organization" (p. 114). Because the
success of COYOTE hinged on the sensationalism of the fact that
women openly called themselves 'whores' and that prostitution was
seen as the essence of women's liberation, advocates of COYOTE
increasingly presented themselves as prostitutes. Dorchen A.
Leidholdt (2004)—co-founder, with Kathleen Barry, of the
Coalition against Trafficking in Women (CATW, <http://www.
catwinternational.org>)—describes how COYOTE spokesperson
Priscilla Alexander flirted with the idea of being a sex worker:
"The term sex worker was coined by COYOTE stalwart Priscilla
Alexander, who argued, with a straight face, that her four years at
Bennington College qualified her to claim that label." With a death
grip on the 'whore' image, Priscilla Alexander and Margo St. James
traveled around the world, marketed their ideas and gained political
power by creating diverse organizations such as the National
Task Force on Prostitution, and California Prostitutes' Education
Project (Pheterson, 1989, p. 5; Oriel, 2006, p. 89). Alexander was
later hired by the World Health Organization (WHO) as adviser
for their HIV/AIDS program and helped to develop their policy
on prostitution (in Oriel, 2006, p. 89). Although COYOTE was
successful in carrying out some positive changes for women in
prostitution, such as abolishing the forced quarantine of prostituted
women waiting for the results of gonorrhea tests (Pheterson, 1989
p. 5), its emphasis lay squarely on legitimizing prostitution as work
(Jenness, 1993, p. 67). COYOTE did so with empowerment-
themed slogans such as "sex work—female labor that must be
recognized" and "to sell your body is a human right." From now on,
'feminist' arguments were increasingly used to *promote* prostitution.

The 1980s: Holland Takes Up the Thread

The governments of numerous countries saw great potential in COYOTE's argument. Looking back at the history of the word 'sex-worker', we find ourselves time and again in Holland. Since the early 1980s, the Dutch government has invested in multiple projects aimed at normalizing prostitution. The process culminated in 1999 with the legalization of all aspects of the sex industry. That Holland has been at the forefront of legalizing prostitution is, as Swedish lawyer Gunilla Ekberg (2009) has pointed out, a historical irony: Holland was the trailblazer in abolishing brothels 100 years earlier, upon the discovery that they contributed to the white slave trade.

One group that played a central role in the legalization of the sex industry in Holland was the Mr. A. de Graaf Foundation (Marcovich, 2007, p. 349). In the early twentieth century, this was an independent foundation dedicated to ending slavery and to helping prostituted women get out of prostitution. In 1976, however, the foundation changed its stance, becoming a pro-prostitution organization (Wijers-Hasegawa, 2002). Today, the foundation has official status as the Dutch Institute for Prostitution Issues in Amsterdam and, with this designation, has become one of the most important sources of propaganda for prostitution.

One of the achievements of the de Graaf Foundation is the founding of what is possibly the world's best-known 'union for prostitutes', *de Rode Draad* [The Red Thread]. In tourist pamphlets and guidebooks, articles about Holland, and anthologies about sexuality, *de Rode Draad* is touted as a model for the organizing of prostitutes. The official story is that *de Rode Draad* originated from "the prostitutes' liberation movement" (Altink and Bokelmann, 2006), but it is clear from their website that the trade union was founded in 1985 by the de Graaf Foundation and was initially fully funded by the state. *De Rode Draad* was one of de Graaf's many projects that attempted to give prostitution the status of 'work'. The founder was sociologist Jan Visser, who worked at de Graaf and later chaired *de Rode Draad*. He has held a variety of positions at *de Rode Draad*: chairman of the board, policy adviser, and director, and today serves as its part-time administrator. In 2002, after the entire Dutch sex industry was legalized, *de Rode Draad* became an official trade union under the name *Truss*. *Truss* then joined Holland's largest federation of trade unions, the FNV, thereby gaining access to resources for printing brochures and organizing continuing education. But the state contributions stopped in 2004, and today *de Rode Draad* is languishing.[8] They report having only about 100 members in their union and have still never dedicated themselves to any trade union battle.

When I meet *de Rode Draad's* representative, social worker Sietske Altink, she describes the work of the organization as somewhere between an outreach project and an information center about prostitution. When I ask about the trade union, she says that this is another part of the organization, adding that membership numbers are confidential. When I ask if *de Rode Draad* has ever pursued a trade union issue, the only thing she is able to show me is a document claiming they have achieved two things: argued successfully that prostitutes should have the right to open bank accounts, and prevented the municipal council from instituting closing times in the Red Light District. However, neither of these campaigns can be described as union-related, and the latter could just as well be to the advantage of brothel owners and the landlords who own the display windows. I have yet to see any evidence of a *legitimate* trade union under the name *de Rode Draad*. The Dutch Brothel Owners' Association (VER) does not seem to feel threatened by this supposed union—on the contrary, they proudly provided a link (now defunct) to *de Rode Draad* on their website.

In spite of low membership numbers and the lack of union-related activities, the idea of the 'trade union for prostitutes' continues to live a life of its own. The story spreads via anthologies about prostitution, on the internet and not least through the tourist industry. In Amsterdam's tourist magazine *Boom!*, the article 'Not a

---

8   Ministry of Health, Welfare and Sport (1 September 2004) 'Antwoorden Kamervragen over voortbestaan stichting de Rode Draad' <http://www. nieuwsbank.nl/inp/2004/09/01/R221.htm> accessed 26 April 2013.

bad solution for the world's oldest profession ... Red Light District: Sex!' informs the reader of where the brothels and strip clubs can be found. The sex tourist with a guilty conscience receives absolution in the article: "Some prostitutes are trapped in debt and drugs, but many are in control of their destiny. Some fill out tax returns and many belong to a loose union, the Red Thread" (*Boom!*, 2008). It does not seem to matter that *de Rode Draad* barely exists in reality. One hundred people—if they even are a hundred—out of 25,000 does not justify a claim of 'many'. But the *actual* existence of labor unions isn't important; it's the *idea* of them that counts.

The de Graaf Foundation, together with the Dutch Ministry of Social Affairs and Employment, also provided financial backing for the World Whores' Congress, held in 1985 in Amsterdam and in 1986 in Brussels (Pheterson, 1989 p. 26). Initiators of the conference were COYOTE's Margo St. James, Priscilla Alexander, and professor of psychology Gail Pheterson. Prostitutes' travel expenses were covered, and according to Pheterson half of the participants were prostitutes and half were prostitution advocates: academics, sex liberals, government representatives, the police and other representatives of the sex industry (p. 35). The record from the Congress reveals a frank and open discussion in which people in the sex industry, from performers to ex-child prostitutes from Thailand, exchanged experiences and opinions. Some supported prostitution, others wanted to get out of the industry, and still others considered prostitution a necessary evil. Many of the testimonies are very upsetting. One woman described being raped and beaten by a pimp when she was only 13; another talked about how her ex-boyfriend abused her twice a week until she agreed to become a prostitute (p. 162).

But in spite of these negative testimonies, the agenda had already been set: prostitution was to be seen as a profession and had to be recognized as such. The organizers didn't hesitate to speak for prostitutes; Pheterson declared that

> the word 'whore' is used to stigmatize women, the word 'prostitute' is used to criminalise women. Rather then [sic] disassociate from

the social or legal labels used against us, we identify with both, and we demand our rights as whores, as prostitutes, as working women (Pheterson and St. James, 2005, p. 162).

Pheterson herself appeared at the conference dressed up as a 'whore', with a pale powdered face and sultry, raven-black eye makeup.

The congress resulted in the adoption of a manifesto demanding the decriminalization of both prostitution and pimping. This document has since spread over the entire world. It is ubiquitous, appearing in everything from reports by the ILO to photocopied punk fanzines. It proves an easily accessible alibi for anthologies about sexuality in which the editors realize at the last moment that they should have included something about prostitution. In academic texts about prostitution, a reference to the manifesto is virtually obligatory. But such references are seldom, if ever, followed by any critical examination of the Congresses in Amsterdam and Brussels. Who took the initiative of organizing them? Who sponsored them? Who was invited and who spoke? In terms of the story of the sex worker, both *de Rode Draad* and the manifesto were brilliant marketing ploys, as they both became synonymous with the voices of prostitutes. Yet the manifesto is considerably better known in academia than in the world of prostitution.

The 1990s: HIV/AIDS—Money Comes Through

As Jennifer Oriel points out in her doctoral dissertation, it was the HIV/AIDS epidemic that transformed the 'sex worker' movement from an underground phenomenon into a major international force (2006, p. 79). In the late 1980s, when the gravity of the HIV/AIDS epidemic had become clear and solutions were desperately being sought, governments and international organizations made large sums of funding available for HIV/AIDS prevention projects. With this money, pro-prostitution groups were able to grow from small coalitions to international networks (pp. 88–89). The funded projects ranged from networks of volunteer social workers to charity projects and support groups for prostituted women. COYOTE promptly received 50,000 dollars for its project of educating prostitutes about what it called 'safe sex' (Jenness, 1993, p. 113).

In 1993, the world's largest network for 'sex workers', the Network of Sex Work Projects, was established with funding intended for HIV/AIDS prevention projects. The money came from a number of governments, including Sweden, as well as the EU and the Rockefeller Foundation (in Oriel, 2006, p. 90). Today, the Network of Sex Work Projects can be found in 40 countries. In addition to teaching prostitutes about condom use, one of its goals is to normalize prostitution in terms of 'work'.

In the same year, the de Graaf Foundation established TAMPEP, a network for HIV/AIDS prevention work in the "migrant sex worker" sector (Wennberg, 2002). The organization has received increasing support from the European Commission, totaling 600,000 euros in 2006.[9] Although this funding comes from the budget for HIV/AIDS prevention projects, TAMPEP works on other issues, too; for example, a significant portion of their effort goes toward campaigning for regulated prostitution. For its first five years, TAMPEP's leader was none other than de Graaf's house sociologist Jan Visser, a spider in the web of Dutch 'sex worker' politics.

I visited TAMPEP at their office in Amsterdam in 2009 and spoke with philologist Hanka Mongard, who works in street outreach. She shows me a number of four-spot color brochures distributed by TAMPEP. Some are directed at the general public and politicians, with phrases like "harm reduction," "a holistic strategy" and "innovative health work." Others are directed at people in prostitution, informing them about the Dutch universal health care system and offering tips about protection against sexually transmitted diseases. TAMPEP can arrange medical supervision for prostitutes and has a telephone hotline as well. Their foremost activity, however, is distributing condoms. 'Harm

---

9   European Commission, Executive Agency for Health and Consumers (EAHC) Grants for Projects, Project No. 2006344.

reduction', in practice, often comes down to one thing: condoms. Mongard's work consists of walking the streets in Amsterdam's prostitution districts, equipped with condoms. She says her Polish background is a big help: "[T]here are streets here on the outskirts of Amsterdam with 140 shop windows, and 99% of the women are from Eastern Europe." The brothel owners call her 'the condom lady' and are eager to invite her in to show the women and girls how to put them on the johns. Mongard sees her work as a kind of training for prostitutes in how to stop the spread of HIV/AIDS and other sexually transmitted diseases. TAMPEP has the reputation of being a charity organization that helps poor, foreign prostitutes in Europe, many of them trafficked. But when I ask if she can help women to get out of prostitution, she answers bluntly: "Why? Our goal is to teach them to be better prostitutes."

The EU spends millions of dollars each year toward this aim of teaching Eastern European women to be better prostitutes for Western European men.

When HIV/AIDS was spreading like wildfire in the 1980s and prostitution was identified as one of the sources of infection, groups like COYOTE and TAMPEP offered a solution: teach prostitutes about condom use. Instead of questioning the existence of prostitution and turning the focus onto the buyers, governments and international organizations opted to preserve the institution of prostitution. Groups with a prostitution-friendly stance received millions to teach what they call 'safe sex', but they were also not restricted from spending some of this money on lobbying.

In her 2006 dissertation on funding for pro-prostitution lobbying and HIV/AIDS prevention, Jennifer Oriel states that "worker peer education" became a 'buzz-word' that opened doors for HIV/AIDS prevention grants in South-East Asian countries (Oriel, 2006, pp. 92–96). In short, prostituted women would help other prostituted women by teaching them how to practice safe sex. Safe sex, though, is mainly aimed at preventing the spread of HIV/AIDS. It does not refer to the psychological well-being of the woman. The HIV/AIDS money goes in part toward printing brochures that, as TAMPEP's Mongard says, teach women to become better whores. For example, we read in one Australian state-sponsored brochure the advice to "always act like you enjoy it" (Oriel, 2006, p. 92), and in one financed by the European Commission, we see an upbeat description of how to disinfect a whip (in Marcovich, 2007, p. 349). In a brochure from the Scarlet Alliance, Australia's national sex worker organization, we read the advice to stay and keep arousing a violent man: "If a client has gone past your limits, you need to be able to bring him back without causing too many issues such as him losing his momentum (or hard on)" (in Malarek, 2009, p. 210). If this doesn't work, she should pull back—not to prevent violence and harm to herself, but because bruises "can force you into having time off work, in turn losing more money" (p. 211). To avoid STDs, the advice is to "inspect the man's pubic hair and look for insects and eggs. Comb carefully through the hair with your nails and look for lice or anything else that moves" (p. 209). One South African sex worker organization advises women to 'accidentally' toss a shoe under the bed so they can check for weapons (p. 211). Peer-taught safe sex education, however, has its downsides. As TAMPEP writes in its educational materials, sometimes teachers exploit their dominant positions to take advantage of their students—in short, to become their pimps (in Oriel, 2006, p. 92).

This approach has also reached Sweden. The advice to prostituted women from the City of Malmö is strongly influenced by the 'harm reduction' perspective. The city offers a prevention kit for 'sex workers' that contains, for example, a personal alarm, condoms, lip balm, lubricant and breath mints, all with the purpose of "contributing to better quality of life for people who sell sex." The message is that men can be so dangerous for these women that they might need an alarm[10]—but this risk shouldn't keep them from having fresh breath and soft lips for the benefit of these same men. After protests from the network Prostitutes' Revenge

---

10 In her 2007 book *Making Sex Work* about the legalization of prostitution in the state of Victoria in Australia since 1984, Mary Lucille Sullivan discusses similar 'strategies' (pp. 272–274).

in Society (PRIS), the city stopped distributing condoms to johns (Larsson, 2009).

What again rears its head here is nothing but good, old-fashioned regulated prostitution, where prostitution is legal and prostituted women are responsible for preventing the spread of disease. As human trafficking expert Malka Marcovich has pointed out, this means a return to nineteenth-century ideals of hygiene, where the onus was "primarily on the women to take responsibility for the health of 'the customer', so diseases would not be spread to their families" (2007, p. 347). In many European countries, however, condoms are not hard to get, and prostituted women already know how to use them. The 'safety' aspect of handing out condoms is more about the psychological, placating effect it has on society at large. The surface of a condom forms an imaginary barrier, protecting society against the qualitative effects of prostitution: misery, violence, oppression of women and inequality. It is an insurance policy: we guarantee 'safe sex'.

As a result of the sudden increase in HIV/AIDS funding, the story of the sex worker started gaining serious ground. In 1998, the ILO recommended the legalization of prostitution so that national governments could also profit from it, and in 2001, the WHO offices in South-East Asia spoke out in favor of the decriminalization of the sex industry (Marcovich, 2007, p. 349). Both organizations used the arguments "she is an agent, not a victim," and prostitution is "female labor that must be recognized" (as COYOTE demanded). This story has also made a strong mark on international organizations such as UNAIDS. As Malka Marcovich writes, "the prostitution-friendly groups have been able to place some of their representatives in national, regional and international institutions" (p. 352). The first UN Special Rapporteur on Violence against Women, Radhika Coomaraswamy, made a clear distinction between "sex workers" and women in "forced prostitution" (in Marcovich, 2007).

The New Millennium: 'Unions for Sex Workers'

At the beginning of the twenty-first century, 'trade unions' became a magic word in the debate about prostitution. Whenever opponents of prostitution pointed to the violence and misery, the proponents pulled the term 'trade union' out of their back pockets: certainly everyone knows about prostitution's seedy underbelly, but the problems can be fixed without abolishing the whole system! The idea of trade unions fascinated people and provided a perfect argument for legalizing prostitution. It appealed to the Left, it suggested that prostitutes would get organized for fair conditions, and it assumed that prostitution would remain intact. But the larger impact was that people began to speak regularly of prostitution in terms of 'work'.

The positive associations with international trade unions excited many people. An article appeared in the Swedish liberal weekly *Kristianstadsbladet*, for example, claiming:

> There is a sort of revolution in the works … an organized sexual revolution that is being talked about more and more, spreading throughout Europe with countries like Great Britain, Denmark and Germany in the lead—as well as in the rest of the world. *The International Union of Sex Workers* (IUSW) is here to stay and is a force to be reckoned with (Andersson, 3 January 2003).

Andersson, a Swedish journalist, was so impressed by this 'organized revolution' that he became an associate member of the IUSW and wrote a flashy appeal to all sex workers: "Let us know when you are ready to meet us on our terms—Sex workers of the world—Unite!" But who 'we' were and what he meant by 'sex workers' meeting them on *their* terms remained a mystery.

Talk of trade unions also hit home with extreme left-wing revolutionary groups. In the early 2000s, mention of the IUSW even appeared in the newsletter of the communist Swedish group *Arbetarmakt* [Workers' Power], otherwise hardly known to be compromising of its ideals:

In early March, GMB, a general labor union in Great Britain introduced a section for sex workers in London. This is an important step forward in the fight for workers' rights in this large and expanding industry.[11]

Arbetarmakt was so enthusiastic about the IUSW that they demanded the legalization of the whole prostitution industry: "The answer to this exploitation is to decriminalize prostitution and give sex workers the same rights as other workers. The best way to reach this goal is through organizing and union association."

The term 'trade union' lent respect to advocates of prostitution who thus appeared engaged in the fight for the rights of prostituted women. It had a titillating effect, capitalized on by the Swedish theater group Arena Baubo in their performance *A Union Meeting for Prostitutes* (Arena Baubo, 2007). It had unbelievable power to open doors to both the political Left and feminists who promoted legalization of all aspects of the sex industry. But even the political Right applauded this move. In the Swedish tabloid *Expressen*, Leo Pierini, secretary of the youth movement of the conservative Centre Party, applauded the idea of trade unions for prostitutes, saying: "If prostitutes had unemployment insurance, trade unions, collective bargaining and the like, their situation would surely become better and they would be able to make legally binding contracts with their pimps" (10 May 2007).

A member of the Centre Party, which is historically in favor of decentralized government, applauding labor unions and collective bargaining? Not to worry! This support was exclusively for prostitutes. A few months later, the same Leo Pierini wrote on his blog: "The time has come to abolish collective bargaining, the Employment Protection Act and all other exclusive rights of trade unions, now that we know what a disabling effect they have on the Swedish market" (18 December 2007).

Suddenly, collective bargaining had to be abolished—for everyone *except* prostitutes! This reminds me of Bert Karlsson,

11 *Arbetarmakt Nyhetsbrev* [Workers' Power Newsletter] (2002) No. 115 (04/02) – 020322.

founder of the right-wing, populist New Democracy party that went bankrupt in 2000, who wanted to minimize the power of the state at the same time that he demanded that Sweden establish state-run brothels. Here, the same duplicity as Pierini's is at play: special rules for prostitutes, yet based on the argument that prostitutes are just like everyone else. The contradictions in this argument show that few people who engage in this debate take the idea of trade unions seriously. For what is the real goal of this 'organized revolution'? The proponents never enumerate what demands these unions should make or what conditions they think should apply to prostitution. Is it a reasonable expectation that a woman should have intercourse with 10 men per day, or should the line be drawn at 5? What is one act of intercourse 'worth'—15 dollars or 1,500 dollars? How do you enforce legally binding contracts with the heavily armed mafia? Is 'sex work' where women and girls are hit and urinated on in compliance with legislation for safe work environments? And what about the law against sexual harassment? How does that fit in?

Instead, discussions of trade unions remained on a very abstract level. They were always followed, however, by a highly concrete demand: prostitution must be decriminalized, proponents said, or trade unions can't do their job. This argument was used in spite of the fact that prostitution was already legal in many of the countries concerned. In Great Britain and Denmark, it is not a crime to buy or to sell sex. In Sweden, as described earlier, the prohibition focuses on the person purchasing what it terms 'sexual services'. There is no legal obstacle to prostituted women organizing in trade unions or paying income taxes. The demand for legalization, therefore, only concerns its 'industrialists'—the brothel owners, the procurers and the pimps.

Few of the people who were vocal in this debate attempted to find out if there really were any trade unions for 'sex workers', what they did and who their spokespeople were. It was enough for them to know that trade unions *might* exist. The heated debate among Swedish anarchosyndicalists in 2002 about organizing 'sex workers' fell apart when it was discovered that the only two women who had requested membership in this supposed trade union were self-employed strippers—but then who was sitting on the other side of the negotiating table? This demand was revealed as simply a platform from which to promote prostitution as work, and after it had gone back and forth a number of times, the debate faded into oblivion. So what happened to the revolution that was supposed to unite the 'sex workers' of the world?

To understand this, I spent two years meeting with representatives from various European organizations. I traveled throughout Holland, Spain, and France. Some organizations were called 'trade unions for sex workers'. Others were 'support groups for sex workers'. What they had in common was that they all promoted legalized prostitution and presented themselves as representatives of people in prostitution.

The International Union of Sex Workers—Pimps

The British International Union of Sex Workers (IUSW), which, as we have seen, quickly gained international fame, was launched in 2000 with a Pride-inspired carnival demonstrating the joys of being a prostitute. The party included a samba band, plenty of sex radical activists, banners with silhouettes of strippers; it succeeded, as one might imagine, in attracting immediate attention to the IUSW. The group was subsequently invited to assist the British Green Party in forming policies on prostitution, to speak at the LGBT conference of the Labour Party and, only a few years later, to join the National Union of General and Municipal Workers (now part of the GMB). Although their website claims that the group was established by "sex workers and some support members," the IUSW is not a massive movement. In 2003, it had only 150 members—while at the same time there were over 100,000 prostituted people in Great Britain (Gallin, 2003). The organization's founder was Ana Lopes, who had worked as a telephone sex operator while she was completing her doctorate in anthropology (Lopes, 2004; ProCon.org). At the time of writing, the most active member of the IUSW is a man by the name of

Douglas Fox. He writes nearly all of the articles on the website, which are mainly about the pleasures of being a 'sex worker' and the horrors of feminism. He often appears in the media claiming to represent both the IUSW and sex workers in general. Saying he is an independent homosexual male escort, he launches appeals and initiates petitions protesting sex purchase laws, as in a *Guardian* article 'Don't criminalize our clients' (19 November 2008).

But Fox isn't an escort. He is the founder and co-owner of one of England's largest escort agencies. His company, Christony Companions, supplies men with women to have sex with in exchange for payment (Foster, 7 August 2006). In the magazine *The Northern Echo*, Douglas Fox describes his flourishing business, saying that the agency has a register of hundreds of girls and advertises in countless daily papers. Fox and his partner, John Docherty, take calls, book appointments, and find buyers, and the two men thrive on the work. Fox believes he is doing the girls a favor: "Girls working alone like to know that there's someone who knows where they're going, what time they're due to arrive and what time they're due to finish an appointment." He also thinks that the English National Health Insurance should step in and pay for the services as it is really about a "human need for companionship." Sex, he says, is never discussed with the customers over the phone. He states, without the slightest touch of irony regarding his profession, that "it would be very prurient delving into people's sex lives" (19 November 2008).

Douglas Fox is, in other words, a pimp. He and his partner continued with their agency at the same time as he was founding trade unions. On the one hand, he does television commercials for his agency—for which one marketing method is offering 'free sex' as a contest prize—on the other, he writes articles as an 'independent male escort'. Few people seem to be interested in revealing the relationship between the two Douglas Foxes. Although the conflict of interest here would be easy enough to discover—and indeed, active unionized feminists such as Cath Elliot have pointed it out—neither the GMB nor the parties that have welcomed the IUSW with open arms have addressed the issue

(Elliott, 2009). Furthermore, it is difficult to ascertain who actually comprises IUSW's membership base, in part because anyone can become a member, even brothel owners and the general public. Founder Ana Lopes believes pimps are not necessarily the enemy, "pimps may be necessary for protection since most of the police fail to do this for sex workers" (in Bindel, 2003). IUSW encourages buyers, sympathizers and escorts, to become members and donate money (Elliott, 2009). Against this background, it is not strange that this alleged trade union doesn't make any demands on the sex industry. On the contrary—the IUSW defends the industry. In an open letter to the Secretary of State for the Home Department (commonly known as the Home Secretary), the IUSW lobbied to reject the campaign against trafficking: "Government plans aimed at curbing exploitation in the sex industry will imperil workers' lives and human trafficking victims' chances of rescue, warns the International Union of Sex Workers."[12] A trade union that not only is led by a known pimp but also fights measures intended to prevent exploitation should cause most people to raise an eyebrow but seems to have gone unnoticed.

Les Putes/STRASS—The Men

In France, the purchase of sexual services is legal, while brothels are illegal. The country tends to side with Sweden in the international debate, but their domestic measures are, in contrast to the situation in Sweden, focused on both buyers *and* prostitutes. In 2003, when Nicolas Sarkozy was Minister of the Interior, he instituted *la loi sur la racolage*, according to which prostitutes could be fined for picking up buyers on the street.

Les Putes [The Whores], a Paris-based group, calls itself a separatist organization solely for prostitutes. The goal of *Les Putes* is to introduce a system similar to the one in Holland and Germany in which prostitution is regarded as work. In the

---

12 'Thousands of sex workers could be endangered by the Home Secretary's proposed changes in the law' (2009) <http://www.iusw.org/2009/03/thousands-of-sex-workers-could-be-endangered-by-home-secretarys-proposed-changes-in-the-law>.

manifesto 'Proud to be whores', they write: "No, we don't have pimps. No, we were not raped as children, nor later in life. No, we are not drug addicts" (Maîtresse Nikita and Schaffauser, 2008). They have received an immense amount of attention in the French media by writing polemical articles in which they call well-known feminists 'whoreophobes'. They've also been interviewed in English newspapers. When you encounter such articles and interviews, you could easily get the idea that they are part of a much larger movement, and they're doing everything they can to encourage this interpretation. They talk in collective terms, about 'us', and claim to represent prostitutes as a whole. This façade has been accepted without anyone attempting to find out who is behind this organization.

In January 2007, I met three representatives of *Les Putes* at a café in Paris (Ekman, 2007). The spokesperson was a man who called himself Maîtresse Nikita. An older woman and a younger male transvestite also attended the meeting. They confirmed that *Les Putes* was, at that time at least, basically comprised of these three active members. The website and articles were all created and written by Nikita himself. These three were completely convinced that all the consequences of prostitution—violence, shame, fear and social alienation—would disappear if only prostitution were legalized. They were very friendly, and I am sure they could be of great help for the occasional prostituted person who seeks them out for support and guidance. There are few support groups for people in prostitution, and speaking to people with similar experiences can be very helpful regardless of whether or not they share the same opinions. But three people, two of whom are men, are not what we imagine when we read a manifesto with the words "The whores' fight is the fight of every woman" as appears on the *Les Putes* website (now defunct). Actually, by saying they don't have pimps, these three prove they are *not* representative of most prostituted women, for prostitution in France is more pimp-driven than in most other European countries. According to a study from the NGO *Mouvement du Nid*, 95% of the prostituted women in France have pimps (Rapin, 2002).

In March 2009, the French 'trade union' *Le Syndicat de Travail Sexuel* (STRASS) was established. They, too, have received a great deal of coverage in the media, and they state they have approximately 100 members. Looking a little more closely at the operation, however, we note that STRASS is largely nothing but *Les Putes* in a new guise. The very same people appear on the websites of *Les Putes* and STRASS. In establishing STRASS, the trio I met with in Paris joined forces with well-known social commentators and advocates of prostitution who applaud the idea of the 'trade union for prostitutes'. And the same pattern repeats here as with *de Rode Draad* and the IUSW: STRASS calls itself a trade union but doesn't engage in union-related activities.

The International Committee of the Rights of Sex Workers in Europe—The Researchers

The International Committee of the Rights of Sex Workers in Europe (ICRSE) is an umbrella organization established in Holland in 2003, claiming to be comprised of 'sex workers' and their allies. They do not specify any particular number of members, but on their website they write that they organize 'sex workers' all over the world. According to the ICRSE, prostitution is a job and should be acknowledged as such.

The board of the ICRSE consists of five women: the first is historian Marieke van Doorninck, who previously worked at the de Graaf Foundation and as a lobbyist for the organization *La Strada* (which works with prostituted women in Eastern Europe) and is currently leader of the *Green Group* in the Amsterdam City Council. Next, there is sexuality researcher Marianne Jonker, the former managing director of *de Rode Draad*. Thirdly, there is Marjan Wijers, who was the chair of the European Commission group of experts on trafficking. Fourthly, there is Licia Brussa, coordinator at TAMPEP and editor of the magazine *Research for Sex Work*. And the fifth member, Ruth Morgan Thomas, is a project leader at the Scottish Prostitutes Education Project (SCOT-PEP), which advocates legalized prostitution and works within the ideology of 'harm reduction'.

These people pop up time and again. They reappear at the heads of organizations such as TAMPEP, *de Rode Draad*, the de Graaf Foundation and *La Strada*. They travel to conferences, express themselves in the media and write reports promoting legalized prostitution. They apply for EU funding and create websites and new groups over and over again. They comprise a very special group of entrepreneurs: researchers, politicians, lobbyists and social workers who have all found their niche in the question of 'sex workers' rights'. The deluge of activity they create generates a smokescreen, giving the uninitiated the impression that there are lots of groups working for the rights of prostitutes.

The heart of the ICRSE, though, is actually not one of these reappearing people but Petra Timmermans, who herself has experience with prostitution and who also works at the Prostitution Information Center in Amsterdam.[13] She coordinates the ICRSE's activities from her home computer. Often, this means being interviewed by media outlets. In an interview with Timmermans on Swedish Radio channel P3, the organization was described in the following way:

> ICRSE's goal is that prostitutes should receive the same rights as other workers, regardless of occupation; that is, the right to health care, trade union membership, unemployment benefits and so on.[14]

But when I met Timmermans in Amsterdam, she said that the ICRSE doesn't even attempt to fight the industry: "[W]e have our hands full fighting the abolitionists, feminists who want to abolish prostitution." The ICRSE fails to act as a union at all, even in those countries in which the sex industry is legal. Instead, their operation aims to convince politicians across the globe to legalize the sex industry.

---

13 Sex Worker Internet Radio Library (November 2007).
14 *Sveriges Radio P3* (27 June 2009) 'People like sex, this is Amsterdam'.

Ámbit Dóna—The Social Workers

In Spain, I met with representatives of *Ámbit Dóna*, a Barcelona-based group described in the media as "defenders of sex workers' rights."[15] They run a center where prostituted women can get free condoms, showers and HIV/AIDS tests. They also do outreach work and distribute condoms to prostituted women around the city. *Ámbit Dóna* receives both public and private funding for their two primary aims: the first is the practical work, the other is the campaign for the legalization of prostitution. They are often found in the media promoting a view of sex as work, and they tell me that "this is what the women want for themselves" (Ekman, 2006). No member of the *Ámbit Dóna* staff has been in prostitution; all of them are volunteers or social workers. Through their practical work with women in prostitution, they seek to gain the legitimacy they later use to advance their opinion that prostitution is work. They devote no resources, however, to helping anyone get out of prostitution, in spite of the fact that some women ask them for exactly this kind of help.

The Industry

Of course anyone has the right to form a support group with people in similar situations and to promote their own ideas about prostitution. But for a group to be a trade union, their union counterpart has to be an employer. Neither STRASS, nor the IUSW, nor *de Rode Draad* takes up the struggle against the employers—on the contrary, the IUSW *promotes* the interests of pimps and works against the passage of bills intended to help victims of trafficking. *De Rode Draad* was founded by the Dutch state as part of the legalization of the sex industry and is not involved in union-related struggles. *Les Putes*/STRASS, on the

---

15 'Aqui trabajamos con otra realidad, trabajamos con la historia de vide de las mujeres' (19 February 2009) Entrevista a Constanza Jacque, psicóloga de Ámbit Dóna, <http://grupos.emagister.com/documento/entrevista_a_ambit_dona_/1017-111657>.

other hand, *are* comprised of people in prostitution, but still fail to engage in labor disputes.

The picture of trade unions for prostituted women looks the same in other parts of the world. In Germany, where the sex industry has been legal for over a decade, there is only one trade union confederation, called ver.di, that organizes sex workers. But when I ask a representative of ver.di about the matter, she answers that they "do not have a list of sex workers in our organization, but we know there are only a few."[16] They confirm that they have never been involved in a labor dispute in the sex industry, nor have they ever heard of one.

The Spanish labor confederation *Comisiones Obreras* (CCOO) decided to organize sex workers in 2006. They have printed brochures and arranged conferences, but four years later, in 2010, not even a single prostitute has joined. A representative of the CCOO told me that as of yet, they have not heard of any labor dispute in the sex industry.[17]

In spite of my efforts, I was not able to find any group that functions as a trade union in the true meaning of the term: an organization run and financed by its members, negotiating with employers to promote the best interests of workers. Although there may be or may have been such groups, I still draw the conclusion that the majority of groups calling themselves trade unions for prostituted individuals are mislabeling and misrepresenting themselves. Instead, most of them are interest groups using the term 'trade union' to make prostitution out to be a job like any other. If the goal is to improve conditions for prostituted women, these groups are a complete fiasco. If, on the other hand, the goal is to encourage the view that prostitution equals work, it seems to be advantageous for them to *call* themselves trade unions.

For when the term 'trade union' is introduced, people begin to think in terms of work. It shifts the discussion from being about what prostitution is—inequality between men and women,

---

16 E-mail from Emilija Mitrovic, ver.di, 7 June 2010.
17 E-mail from Secretaría Confederal de la Mujer de Comisiones Obreras, CCOO, 24 June 2010.

the fulfillment of men's sexual demands, and the vulnerability of women who were sexually abused as children (to name just one known reason why women are in prostitution)—to a conversation about work, salaries, unemployment benefits, working conditions, pensions, union organizing. But these words have no equivalents in the real world of prostitution. They have only one function: to legitimize prostitution as work.

These groups have proven very useful to the lobbyists working for the sex industry, because the sex industry thus no longer needs to speak under its own name. Since the late 1980s, the sex industry has joined forces with lobby groups. The Australian Eros Foundation, an association of brothel owners, for example, has a profile reminiscent of the hippie era and touts slogans like "sex is not harmful" and "more sex for all." A person could easily mistake them for a tantra center. By organizing presentations in which female sex shop owners appear under the banner 'Our Bodies Our Rights'[18] and claim to give a 'feminist perspective' of prostitution, brothel owners can speak in places where the sex industry is not usually welcome, such as internal Labor Party Conferences (Wu, 2007, p. 208). Representatives of the Eros Foundation have positions in official organizations for the prevention of HIV/AIDS and had connections to the Australian Democrats (now a defunct party), and some leaders from Eros have even stood for election to parliament (Sullivan, 2007, pp. 168, 169). In Australia we also find a political party called The Sex Party, whose aim it is to promote the demands of the porn industry; their populist rhetoric is directed with a randy wink at the beer-guzzling male. Their female party leader Fiona Patten—also CEO of the Eros Foundation—appears scantily clad on stage and in magazines, speaking about sexual freedom.[19] The British Adult Industry Trade Association (AITA) strives to give the porn industry legitimacy with banks, the EU and governments. One of their concrete goals is to have pornographic products approved alongside other commodities, without the

---

18 This is an appropriation of the classic feminist text, *Our Bodies Ourselves*, Boston Health Collective.

19 Australian Sex Party <http://www.sexparty.org.au> accessed 26 April 2013.

warning label of 'offensive' material. The American equivalent, the Free Speech Coalition (FSC), boasts the membership of all of the larger groups within the porn industry. With a budget of 3 million dollars per year, the FSC pays researchers and other experts to 'prove' that pornography is not addictive. The FSC has also succeeded in taking the sting out of American legislation against child pornography by claiming that child pornography is protected by freedom of speech. These three lobby organizations—in Australia, the UK and USA—have female CEOs. And to some extent, all three use the myth of the sex worker to advance their own interests.

The growth of the sex industry is incredibly dependent on social attitudes. IBISWorld, a think tank that develops reports for Australian companies, completed a study in 2006 of opportunities for growth in the sex industry. The study talks of sex as if it were just another commodity to be bought and sold. You can find it on their website along with reports on nickel ore mining, cotton growing and private equity. With the help of diagrams and statistics, it shows growth in brothel operations, street prostitution and escort services. And there is no doubt as to their goal: increasing profits. This means getting more and more people to pay for sexual services in different forms. More men should be going to brothels. More men should be paying for sex on the phone, online and at strip clubs. The report verifies that the future looks hopeful, in spite of competition from "unpaid sex." Success depends on the fact that "sex work is better accepted by modern generations" which is "due to the prevalence of pornographic material that normalises sexual services ..." (IBISWorld 2006/2009, p. 18). What will determine the future of the sex industry, the report says, is people's attitudes. If we normalize the porn industry, we will see an increase in prostitution. The report recommends conspicuous advertisements for strip clubs, because visibility will "normalise sexual services in the eyes of many." One particularly highly recommended strategy is to have strip club advertisements pasted on the sides of cars driving around the city. Such porn-promoting cars appeared around Swedish cities in the late 1990s, but this advertising campaign was halted when girl-power groups took to throwing Molotov cocktails at them.

Australian feminist and professor of political science Sheila Jeffreys cited this report when she was invited to address the Finnish Parliament in 2006, pointing out quite correctly what ought to be easy to see: the greater the presence prostitution has in society, the more men will buy sexual services. Jeffreys told the Finnish Parliament of IBISWorld's recommendation for large, conspicuous prostitution zones to encourage men to pay for sex, and stated that 1 in 6 Australian men admits to having purchased sex (Jeffreys 2006). (In Sweden, the corresponding figure is 1 in 12, which is a marked decrease from before the Sex Purchase Act was introduced, at which time it was 1 in 8.)[20] In 2007, Australia had over 5,000 legal and 2,000 illegal brothels.[21] According to IBISWorld 2006/2009, acceptance of the sex industry has increased, but the industry "still has a negative image, largely due to the moral, health and safety issues associated with it" (p. 15).

This is where the story of the sex worker enters the discussion. It is exactly the lubricant the industry needs to gain greater acceptance. No other story could help the sex industry as much as the one claiming that 'sex work' is a question of *women's rights*, with the additional aid of the handy smokescreen provided by the idea of trade unions.

False Façades

A great many things in this story are not what they seem to be. Trade unions aren't trade unions. Groups for prostituted women are simultaneously groups for brothel owners. The most central deception is that the propaganda promoting the rights of 'sex workers' isn't intended to transform the institution of prostitution *in itself*. It isn't directed towards men who buy sex to make them see that women in prostitution are independent individuals who deserve our respect. On the contrary, it is strictly about changing

---

20 Nordic Council of Ministers (2008) 'Prostitution in the Nordic countries', Conference Report, p. 756.

21 IBISWorld (26 July 2007) 'Boomers put boom back into sex industry'.

the *image* of prostitution. The key word in the sex worker narrative is how we ought to *view* prostitution—not what we should *do* with it. Prostitution must be viewed as an active choice by a willful individual, a free choice, even a sexual orientation as British gay historian Jeffrey Weeks claimed (1981), and certainly as a legitimate job. In other words: no *real* transformation is necessary.

This image is achieved by presenting a dramatic tale of good vs. evil. On the good side is the prostitute, euphemistically re-labeled as the 'sex worker'. On the same side we find liberated sexuality, free will, the right to work, and the right to make choices about one's own body, as well as the rights of oppressed groups, homosexuality, the market economy, progress and norm-breaking behavior. On the other side are feminists and politicians. Along with these groups we find the stodgy, oppressive characteristics of morality, duplicity, stigmatization, sexual hostility, essentialism, state control, victimization and, as Wigorts Yngvesson (2006) writes, "thousands of years of Western modes of thought in which the woman has been considered the property of the man." All of the categories that have a positive, timely significance are on the side of prostitution, while the feminists are placed on the negative side. Importantly, however, this categorization is not achieved via critical analysis; it is done by crass association.

The most remarkable thing is how the story of the sex worker comes to appear as a *feminist* story. The 'sex worker' is presented as a feminist heroine who smashes to pieces outdated expectations of women's behavior and has a well-developed sense of power relationships. All the classical concepts of feminism are included, but something is completely missing: the men. Men have been replaced by feminists, who thereby become representatives of a punishing, censuring, stigmatizing, accusing patriarchy. So what we have at hand is, in fact, the feminist story ironically directed against feminism itself.

One consequence of this attractive façade is that prostitution becomes romanticized. Another is that feminism is demonized and presented as if it contradicts itself. No wonder, then, that this story has been so successful in confusing feminists and non-feminists alike. Some have even felt pressured to surrender their long-held opposition to prostitution. When Petra Östergren's book came out in 2006 in Sweden, many feminists fell into a quagmire of doubt: might prostitution actually be liberating? Many writers claimed that they personally didn't like prostitution, but didn't feel that they had the right to question it since the 'sex workers' themselves seemed to think it was just fine.

"Is it really so easy?" Caroline Matsson (2006) asked hesitatingly in the cooperatively organized weekly *Stockholms Fria Tidning*, adding that "the debate Petra Östergren is calling for is urgent." Dilsa Demirbag-Sten (2006) called Östergren "an important voice in feminist Sweden" for her ability to "think outside the box, daring to depart from the stodgy thought patterns of others." She continued: "unlike many other social commentators such as myself, Petra Östergren has actually read porn magazines" as if that were a heroic act in itself (Demirbag-Sten, 2006). Others felt uncomfortable with the thought that prostitution could gain status as a profession, but accepted Östergren's claim to speak for prostituted women. Many wavered, not knowing what they should believe, and landed in a liberal quagmire: anyone who wants to prostitute herself should be able to do so, and anyone who doesn't, shouldn't have to—which, apart from being a completely irresponsible attitude, is as close to silencing intellectual debate as we can get. Some who were convinced that prostitution was detrimental decided to keep quiet so they would not be painted as self-righteous hags or patriarchal fogeys. I, too, was hesitant when I first happened upon this type of rhetoric. On the one hand, supporting prostitution contradicted my gut instincts and felt wrong; on the other hand, it truly sounded like there was a global movement of prostitutes fighting for their own rights. And fighting for rights can't be wrong, said a voice inside me. The more involved I became in this issue, however, the more obvious it became to me how shallow this movement really was and how many facts it was intentionally covering up.

Among both those who promote this story and those who let themselves be fooled by it, we see an unwillingness to take responsibility for the very real consequences of legalized prostitution.

There is one fact that the story of the sex worker will never point out: prostitution is by far the deadliest situation a woman can be in. For women and girls in prostitution, the death rate is 40 times higher than the average.[22] No group of women, regardless of career or life situation, has as high a mortality rate as prostituted women. The research is irrefutable: the pattern repeats itself in studies from Canada, USA, Kenya and England. The causes of death vary from murder to accidents, drug abuse to alcoholism. In a study from 2004, American researchers state that women have a greater chance of staying alive if they are 'just' drug addicts, homeless, or alcoholics rather than if they enter prostitution. The same study shows that women in prostitution run an 18 times higher risk of being murdered than other women (Potterat *et al.*, 2004). The researchers summarize: "Thus, the vast majority of murdered women in our sample were killed as a direct consequence of prostitution" (p. 782). Nor does legalization provide protection for prostituted women in this respect. The studies show no difference in mortality rates between countries in which prostitution is legal compared to those in which it is not, in spite of the fact that increased safety is one of the most common arguments used by advocates of legalization. Amsterdam's tourist information center proclaims, for example: "Also, contrary to popular belief, the RLD [Red Light District] is actually the safest area in Amsterdam as clusters of policemen, and private bodyguards employed by the girls themselves are always on duty." Yet, since the legalization of the sex industry, Amsterdam's display windows still see one woman murdered each year, often in the adjoining room (Klepke, 2007). So my question is: In what other legal profession would this be accepted? Police officers and military personnel, who also risk being subjected to violence, are generally equipped with firearms,

---

22 'Pornography and prostitution in Canada: Report of the Special Committee on Pornography and Prostitution' (1985) Minister of Supply and Services Canada, p. 350 <https://www.ncjrs.gov/pdffiles1/Digitization/131616NCJRS. pdf> accessed 26 April 2013.

batons and bulletproof vests. Postal workers and bank tellers have bulletproof glass windows to protect them against armed robbery. But prostitutes stand in their underwear, if that, and have direct physical contact with their potential assailants. Never do the police officers or private bodyguards enter the rooms where prostitution happens. Not to mention that often, the 'private security guards' advertised by the tourist center are actually the women's pimps. Can it be any more clear that a man's privacy is still regarded as more important than a woman's life?

While the story tells of 'work' and 'job positions', it disregards the fact that, in legalized prostitution, prostituted women are seldom formally employed. When Germany evaluated its legislation in 2007, it turned out that less than 1% of prostitutes were registered as employed.[23] Only 5% wanted any sort of registered employment in prostitution while over 60% would not even consider being registered with their profession listed as 'prostitution'. One reason was that the women were scared of losing their anonymity; another, that they preferred to see prostitution as a temporary occupation (p. 19). Although the majority of prostitutes did have health insurance, they did not get it through their 'work' in prostitution, but through other work or social security (p. 24). The report states that legalizing prostitution did not give prostitutes a better safety net, it did not lead to improvement of work conditions, it did not decrease the number of prostitution-related crimes and it did not lead to prostitution truly becoming a job like any other (p. 79). On the other hand, legalization made it harder to get out of prostitution. According to the German lead investigator from the 2002 investigation, many "stay in prostitution although they long ago pushed themselves beyond their personal limits" (p. 38).

The common practice in Germany, Holland and Australia is to regard prostitutes as self-employed. They are not hired by brothels but instead rent a room or a display window. For the brothel owners, this is a very comfortable situation; they simply assume the role of

---

23 'Report by the Federal Government on the impact of the Act Regulating the Legal Situation of Prostitutes' (2007) Federal Ministry for Family Affairs, Senior Citizens, Women and Youth, BMFSFJ, p. 17.

landlord. They have no obligation to take care of the women or any responsibility for what happens, and no matter what goes on in the rooms, they collect the same amount of rent each night.

For the women, it's not as comfortable. In the Red Light District of Amsterdam, for instance, rental of a display window costs 150 euros per night. This means that a woman has already invested a substantial amount of money at the start of the evening. Since according to the standard menu of Amsterdam, one act of sexual intercourse costs 60 euros, she will have to have sex with 3 men before she breaks even. Every single night. The first 3 only go to pay her rent; the next 2 might go to pay her pimp and, many times, she has children to support in her home country. A quick calculation tells us that this adds up to at least 5 men per day. Hanka Mongard from TAMPEP confirms that most women are there 7 days a week. This means that a woman will have sexual intercourse with a minimum of 35 men per week, and even if she takes days off when she has her period, it still comes to over 100 men each month. Even if she has a month-long vacation, the total is well over 1,000 men every year.

Physical violence, assault and battery, rape and brutality are an everyday part of prostitution. A significant study of individuals in prostitution was carried out in 2003 by a team of doctors and psychologists who interviewed 800 prostitutes in 9 countries: Canada, Columbia, Germany, Mexico, South Africa, Thailand, Turkey, the USA and Zambia. The results showed that

71 percent had experienced physical assault while in prostitution
63 percent had been raped while engaged in prostitution
89 percent said they wanted to leave prostitution and would if they had the possibility
68 percent met criteria for a diagnosis of posttraumatic stress disorder (Melissa Farley *et al.*, 2003, pp. 43–44).

There are no similar figures for any other profession, neither for men nor women. In no other situation are so many people raped, assaulted or murdered as in prostitution. How can this be accepted year after year? Why is prostitution an exception for so many governments, intellectuals and human rights activists who otherwise defend every person's right to a life with human dignity? Why do so many ignore or even glorify this existence? Is it because most of the people subjected to this violence are women? Is it because so many men give prostitution their silent approval? If some drug had caused such an early death in so many, it wouldn't be legal anywhere. But we're talking about prostitution, which Dodillet claims can show women 'the way', Östergren says is only for strong women, and Lundberg states is a radical choice. In light of the empirical facts of prostitution, these assertions appear both naïve and terribly cruel. Östergren's argument that many prostitutes enjoy their work should be dwarfed by the overshadowing reality of violence and premature death. No one who has dedicated time to studying prostitution could possibly have missed these numbers.

Rhetoric from the Left—Money from the Right

The story of the sex worker is mirrored by the strategy of Swedish right-wing politicians. Keep the same politics, but use the words of your adversaries. The Swedish Conservative Party calls itself the New Workers' Party; the Christian Democrats say that they represent "real people" and that left-wingers are "the elite." Following this strategy, advocates of prostitution call themselves 'feminists' at the same time as they paint feminists as the enemy.

This strategy becomes particularly clear when we read the social commentators who promote the story of the sex worker. Petra Östergren's background is in the women's movement where she taught feminist self-defense. Since Östergren published *Porn, Whores and Feminists* in 2006, her doctoral studies in social anthropology have been completely financed by the conservative Ax:son Johnson Foundation.[24] She has also received support from the right-wing industry think-tank Timbro.[25] Timbro has sponsored another prostitution-friendly publication as well

---

24 E-mail from Gunnar Andersson, Lund University, 29 March 2010.

25 Maria Rankka at Timbro confirmed in an e-mail on 10 June 2009 that "a few years ago, we supported Petra Östergren in a project that had to do with freedom and, most of all, what's happening with the Swedish left today. It

(Persson, 2006). The trajectory is clear: the arguments are gathered from the Left; the money comes from the Right.

But the story of the sex worker has a hold on more than just feminists. While resistance and trade unions appeal to the Left, the market economy speaks to the Right. In this way, the story finds inroads everywhere: to feminists it says that women must have the right to their own bodies; to liberals that it is a question of free choice and that every prostitute is an entrepreneur; to socialists that she is a worker who should join a trade union; to sex radicals, that prostitutes are a persecuted group like homosexuals. The story of the sex worker wants to put its mark on those who uphold the ideals of any and every ideology: on the workers of the socialist movement, the women of feminism, the individualists of liberalism, the pleasure-seekers of sex radicalism, the entrepreneurs of capitalism—in short, the twenty-first century human beings in general! The story of the sex worker borrows freely from a multitude of theories without feeling at all obligated to adopt their specific analytical methodologies. It also has the peculiar quality of uniting the idea of popular rebellion (the oppressed rising up against the powerful) with capitalism (the right to sell a commodity). Jenny Westerstrand calls this a "superdiscourse" in her 2008 dissertation 'Mellan mäns händer: Kvinnors rättsubjektivitet, internationell rätt och diskurser om prostitution och trafficking' ['Between men's hands: Women as judicial subjects, international law and discourses on prostitution and trafficking'] (pp. 127–128):

> For if we observe the prostitution debate from the perspective of classic feminist theories, we note that central elements from various currents have been incorporated under one and the same discourse— that of the sex worker. This development has taken place at the same time as the socialist understanding of prostitution has lost ground. The socialist understanding of prostitution as work—which, like other work, alienates the worker—has drifted in under liberal discourse and its way of speaking about the sex worker. Here, collective demands for trade unions are raised, but *without* socialist views of the harmful

will become a book, but isn't going to be published by Timbro. Petra received funding for that project."

alienation process present in all paid labor and without the original feminist socialist vision that prostitution—like all other paid labor—will disappear after the revolution ... In a similar way, the sex worker discourse has picked up central concepts of radical feminism, and the concept of the patriarchy is used repeatedly in descriptions of the society in which women in sex work assert their interests. But all this happens without the concept being given precise theoretical treatment.

And yet, at the end of the story nothing has been said about what prostitution is, why it exists, or how it works. Instead, we have heard a contemporary saga of progress, a romantic tale of how an old, decaying tradition long tried to keep people down and tell them how they should live—until some brave individuals rebelled in order to gain the right to live as they wanted, standing up for freedom and sexuality! It is a story we know all too well. It fits into an even larger story: the revolt of sexuality against morality, Romeo and Juliet against their parents' narrow-mindedness, romantic love against arranged marriage, lust against the church, and also the sexual revolution, the 1968 revolt, anti-establishment rock and hippie cultures and their accompanying promotion of freedom and sex. In just a few quick rhetorical turns, prostitution became a contemporary story. Voilà, the total makeover of prostitution: once considered the world's oldest profession, prostitution is now the world's most modern one.

Power Transformed—The Legacy of 1968

This shift in the story of prostitution teaches us how the defense of the status quo changes over time. The traditional model for legitimizing power was built on the idea that power was given by nature, while the oppressed were explained as being biologically inferior. Prostituted women, for example, were seen as defective and impaired, according to logic similar to that which was used to justify slavery, colonialism and the class society.

During the 1968 revolt, the people's movement deprived the powerful of their moral legitimacy. Power was no longer self-justified; it was no longer 'obey thy husband and master'—quite the contrary. "Rebellion is justified," echoed the voices of Mao Zedong, Jean-Paul Sartre and Jan Myrdal. All over the world, people rebelled against power—against capitalism, against patriarchy, against authority. These popular movements did not have the capacity to crush capitalism, but more importantly, they gave rise to the idea that 'power' is bad and 'rebellion' is good.

Since 1968, a very interesting process has been taking place in which those in power have redefined themselves according to the principles of rebellion. Institutions or phenomena that house power—the media, academia, political parties, male sexuality, capital, and upper class privilege—have had to redefine themselves to justify their continued existence. They can no longer claim that their authority is given by nature—in fact, they cannot even claim that authority is a good thing at all! Paradoxically, the only way to legitimize power has become to deny it. So everybody is the underdog, and any new product is 'revolutionary'. The right-wing Swedish Conservative Party rebranded itself the 'New Workers' Party' just like former French President Sarkozy's party, the *Union pour un Mouvement Populaire* (UMP) now wants to be known as the 'New Revolutionaries'. Companies, media conglomerates, best-selling authors—name one who doesn't pretend to be a norm-challenging, marginalized dissident.

The story of the sex worker fits right in. It unifies an old, gender-role-preserving practice with rebellious discourse. It becomes a symbiosis of the neoliberal Right and the postmodern Left. The neoliberal Right uses language that explains prostitution as a free choice on the free market. The postmodern Left, which loves language games and shuns political action, has an excuse not to fight the sex industry by claiming to listen to the voices of marginalized people. Both the neoliberals and the postmodernists relish the possibility of calling prostitution 'revolutionary'.

The postmodern Left is, as Terry Eagleton (1996) writes, a reaction to the neoliberal hegemony. After the fall of communism, when global capitalism completed its hegemony, parts of the Left reacted by masking their loss as a triumph. Eagleton says in this telling simile: "It is as though, having mislaid the breadknife, one declares the loaf to be already sliced" (p. 9). Instead of pointing out injustices, parts of the Left simply redefined the status quo as subversive.

When it feels overwhelming to question injustices, it becomes tempting to reinterpret them instead—perhaps the injustices are not injustices at all if we look more closely, but instead reveal themselves to be acts of rebellion? Immediately, pornography, prostitution and headscarves are declared to be 'marginalized phenomena', 'expressions of women's rights' or 'individual choices with subversive potential'. By calling itself 'feminist', the porn film *Dirty Diaries* (2009) succeeded in attracting funding to the tune of 500,000 Swedish kronor from the Swedish Film Institute, something that no other porn film can boast (Marklund, 2009). Critics wrote that *Dirty Diaries* "challenges the masculine hegemony and ridicules the patriarchal social order with pornography as its instrument" (Fagerström, 2009). In the same vein, gender studies scholar Maria Lönn (2008) calls Britney Spears and Paris Hilton heroines of the resistance, writing that "Britney, Paris and Lindsay shoot wildly from the hip at people's beliefs in 'right and wrong'" and that they "show that there is something self-chosen in a position that has long been reduced to alienation and victimhood" (Lönn, 2008). Magnus Ullén (2009) claims in his dissertation on pornography, 'Bara för dig' ['Only for you'], that pornography has the potential to transform society because "by showing us the shape of desire, [pornography] makes it possible for us to reshape desire in the long run." There is something very amusing about these writings. Apparently, we like pornography not because it is sexually arousing, but because it is 'revolutionary'! Porn, according to these writers, is not millions of internet pop-up windows of teens in underwear and the caption 'Fuck Me for Free'. No, we should rather think of political struggles, medieval sonnets, Baudry's ahistoricism and Western metaphysics—to quote actual examples from professor Linda Williams' book *Hardcore: Power, pleasure and the frenzy of the visible* (1989, p. 55).

The central issue is, as Janice Raymond pointed out already in 1989 (p. 139), that what is provocative, rebellious and subversive is now found *within* the status quo, not outside of it. And, more importantly, that the notion of *what* needs to be transformed is left out of the conversation (p. 142). Usually, rebellions are about saying: We are sick of the way things are—we want to create something new! What happens here, though, is: let's accept the prevailing order —since we have suddenly realized that it is already subversive. If you feel uncomfortable about the state of things— just keep quiet! As it turns out, things are organized so rationally that resistance happens to be built into the status quo—all we have to do is realize it! Accordingly, pornography will do its own fighting for us since, in and of itself, it challenges the masculine hegemony, transforms society and reshapes our desires! (We must read at least one academic dissertation in order to understand this, however.) The purpose is not to initiate a revolt, but to *legitimize* the status quo. Saying that something has 'subversive potential' in this context is to give it a stamp of approval—not to demand action.

Thus the postmodern Left and the neoliberal Right have entered into a tacit pact. The Right gains power, and in exchange, the postmodern Left saves face because the power is masked in their words. While the neoliberal Right attacks the welfare state and increases the gaps between socioeconomic classes, the postmodern Left costumes the attacks in the language of rebellion. They twist and turn the concepts and search for shreds of resistance in everything, they seek strength where others have seen vulnerability: in the abused woman's defiant glare before the blow, in the hysterical laughter of the victim of genital mutilation, in the curses of the prostituted woman—everywhere, we are now meant to see active agents. This is no easy task, and it also explains why contemporary discussions of feminism and the arts seem so 'academic' and opaque to many people. It is symptomatic of the ongoing struggle: on the one side a fight for women's rights; on the other, a legitimization of the status quo using exactly the same words.

One of the most cynical and unrealistic projects that fall under the heading of such horse-trading is the legitimizing of prostitution as 'work'—which, ironically, rears its ugly head in Sweden when prostitution has decreased considerably. The shift in the rhetoric of power is most evident in the story of the sex worker: prostitution is the same system, but its legitimacy is gained from the exact opposite reasoning. If the prostitute of the eighteenth century was feeble-minded, lazy, false and mentally retarded, the 'sex worker' of today is described as independent, strong, truthful and liberated—everything her earlier version wasn't. She is not a woman to be pitied—she is a role model for us all. With this image as a security blanket, both the neoliberals and the postmodern leftists sleep well, without needing to consult the murder statistics. There is a vast body of literature whose sole purpose is to create and uphold this image of the prostituted woman as a successful entrepreneur. She is certainly not being sold; she is the seller!

But there is something puzzling about this whole story. What we're hearing again and again is that the 'sex worker' does *not* sell herself. She is the *seller*—but what, then, is being sold? What, exactly, is the commodity being bought?

CHAPTER THREE

The Self and the Commodity in the Sex Industry

"My body is not my Self"

The commodity sold in prostitution is generally said to be 'sex'. People say the john is the 'buyer' just as the prostitute is the 'seller'. We read in a newspaper that a Russian gang has been selling sex in Finland for many years, but we learn nothing about what this 'sex' actually is and whom it belongs to (*Svenska Dagbladet*, 25 April 2009). Similarly, journalist Ulf Nilson writes with the indulgent tone of someone speaking to imbeciles that "sex always has been and always will be a commodity" (in Eduards, 2007, p. 156). And Petra Östergren writes in the same vein that feminists' opposition to prostitution has to do with an "antipathy about mixing sex and money" (2006a, p. 218). In other words, it is too self-evident to require further explanation that sex is the commodity in question. But what, really, is this 'sex'? Sex is at the core of the entire prostitution industry, and yet it is simultaneously the most mystifying component, the element that is never to be addressed no matter how many bookshelves are filled with volumes about prostitution.

The word is used in a way that makes it seem by nature an object, a noun. If you were to take the word 'sex' in the article about the Russian gang and replace it with 'cigarettes' or 'CDs', there would be no linguistic confusion. "The Russian gang sold sex in 26 districts for several years," the article states, and if we didn't know that people were involved, we could easily be led to believe that 'sex' is something manufactured in a factory. All this talk about 'selling sex' makes us think of it as something a person can carry around, hand over to somebody else or leave under the doormat if the recipient isn't home. "Here you go, ten pounds of sex. I'll send the bill." We don't say—though it is understood—that 'sex' is attached to a person.

If we look more closely, we see that the usage circles around what 'sex' *isn't*. The first thing we always hear is namely that it *isn't* the *Self*. "I sell part of my body, not my Self" is a constantly repeated phrase. In the French anthology *Prostitutes: Our life*, a woman using the pseudonym 'D' says:

> From the moment I decided to sell, or rather, rent out my body, I figured it's my own business and nobody else's ... My body belongs to me, and I do what I want with it (in Jaget, 1980, p. 117).

Prostitute Eva Rosta writes:

> You might sell your brain, you might sell your back, you might sell your fingers for typewriting. Whatever it is that you do, you are selling one part of your body. I choose to sell my body the way I want to and I choose to sell my vagina (in Pheterson, 1989, p. 144).

This is how the idea of prostitution is formulated today: a Self that sells her own body. What is most tangible about this notion is its dualistic character. In order to think of it as possible to *sell the body without selling the Self*, one must take Cartesian dualism for granted. In the sentence "I choose to sell my vagina," two roles are presented: the Self and the vagina. The Self is presented as an acting agent who chooses to make a sale: an entrepreneur, a clever businesswoman who has discovered a good product. But the vagina is clearly not a part of this active Self; *it* is no entrepreneur—it is the commodity being sold and bought. The vagina is described as an 'it', lying there passively and finding itself being sold without being asked. The prostitute is thus said to be one person comprised of two parts: the sold (the body) and the seller (the Self). She is called *the seller*, not *the sold*, to mark the difference: what is being sold is not actually *her*. This is supposed to convince the buyer that we are doing business with a human being, buying a commodity in a very normal transaction. The person we are buying from is an individual, a smart entrepreneur who is our equal, while *what* we are buying is a product that just happens to be her vagina, attached to the body of this entrepreneur. In other words, the prostituted woman is made up of both a being and a commodity. Her Self is a being like other people's Selves; her body is a commodity like any other.

For, as 'D' says: my body belongs to me and I do what I want with *it*. Her Self chooses—but her body has no choice. It has to go where the Self commands. Everything that characterizes the Self in the story of the sex worker—independence, strength and freedom of choice—stands in diametric opposition to the body. The body is presented as an object bending to the will of the totalitarian dictator, the Self. The freedom of the Self, so hailed in the story of the sex worker, stands in direct contrast to the lack of freedom of the body. In fact, the freedom of the Self presupposes the enslavement of the body.

This assertion stands at the core of the story of the sex worker. The idea of the 'sex worker' is based on the Cartesian concept of *the Split Self.*

This makes the story completely different from the traditional one. As we saw in the previous chapter, although the woman was, in earlier characterizations, feeble-minded and of restricted mental capacity, she was still considered a complete entity. There was no doubt that she was selling her whole Self. That this Self had shortcomings and was defective was what made the sale and enslavement possible. For that matter, the traditional defense of prostitution contains very little talk of 'selling' and 'buying' at all. The woman was referred to as 'immoral' or 'lewd': as Yvonne Svanström points out, it was a moral and sexual issue, not a commercial one (2006, p. 34).

Today, instead, the story is about a person who represents the ideal agent of our times, a commanding, rational individual who makes her own decisions: the free market agent in all her glory. Most of the story of the sex worker today presents her as fantastically strong, independent and invulnerable. But the story goes on to explain that what is being sold is, after all, not this independent agent herself. Her body has miraculously wrenched free and stepped onto the marketplace, becoming one out of many commodities for sale, while her Self remains in command, holding the reins, directing sales from a distance and raking in the profits.

At first glance, these two stories seem radically different. But their cores are essentially the same. The aim of each is to maintain prostitution by concealing its primary nature, but they do it in different ways. The traditional version admits that what is being sold is a Self, but a Self that is *defective*. This woman is stigmatized and labeled as 'feeble-minded', so all other women can breathe easy: the Self being sold is defective, so *our* Selves are not threatened. The story of the sex worker, in contrast, incorporates the prostituted woman's Self into the rest of society. We often hear of 'de-stigmatization'. The prostitute should no longer be seen as 'feeble-minded'; she is just as much, if not more, an agent as anyone else. Yet for this very reason she must be separated from her body: *it* must become an object, *it* must be stigmatized, because *it* is what is bought. While the prostitute as a *defective individual* was central to the traditional story, the *Split Self* stands at the center of the story of the sex worker. This echoes throughout pro-prostitution rhetoric: "But she's not selling her Self!"

Why is this statement so important? Because we are dealing with an ideology that tries to depict prostitution as *freedom*. The very same institution that was traditionally defended by describing the prostituted woman as *inferior* is now defended by asserting the prostitutes' *rights*. This falls perfectly in line with the prevailing free market ideology, a kind of liberalism for which 'the equal value of all people' is axiomatic. While it is totally alien to this ideology to allege that some people are biologically inferior, it is equally taken for granted that the free market must be defended at all costs. In this case, it is the free market that reduces people to mere commodities.

This is where dualism fits like a glove. Dualism, central to Western philosophy, offers a model that makes it possible to justify prostitution as freedom. Claims that the body isn't the Self have existed since Socrates and Descartes, not to mention in mainstream religions. Of course, this belief is not unopposed—Western philosophy is also replete with claims to the contrary. But the dualistic heritage is a part of our tradition of thought and can be actualized as needed, especially in the liberal market economy where an inherent antagonism arises: How can one *both* defend the equality of all *and* uphold a system in which women are sold in display windows?

With the help of dualism, this is perfectly possible. Since the idea *that a person is not a body* works so well, it can consequently be argued that the person is free to do the selling, while the body is sold. One can say: "Yes, she is standing there for sale, yes, men come and pay money—but they don't buy *her*." They buy something else—her *vagina*. *She* isn't the body to be fucked; *she* is a businesswoman.

Socrates spoke of body and soul as separate entities and believed that the soul was more beautiful than the body. Consequently, it was the duty of the soul to rule over the body; but irritatingly enough, in reality, the opposite would often occur. The body took over, weighed the soul down and led it astray with vanity and lustful acts. Socrates' conclusion—expressed so passionately in *The Apology*—was therefore that the soul could only be free if the body died. In life, it was impossible to free oneself from the prison of the body. Here we see, as Carolyn Merchant argues, an analogy to man's relationship to nature: in Socrates' time, the human being was still very much a part of nature and had not been able to dominate it, but not for want of trying. While the ideologically desirable relationship was that the soul (the human being) should dominate the body (nature), in reality, it was often the other way around (Merchant, 1994, p. 24).

Descartes' dualism was more far-reaching. For him, it was possible to separate the Self from the body even during one's lifetime. It was simply a matter of closing one's eyes and imagining that one didn't have hands, feet or a stomach. The body, according to Descartes, was nothing but a machine, and as such, it had no power over the soul.

> Thus this self (moi), that is to say the soul, by which I am what I am, is entirely distinct from the body, and is even more easily known; and even if the body were not there at all the soul would be just what it is (Descartes, 1971, p. 32).

This is exactly the underlying assumption in the story of the sex worker. The idea that the Self "is entirely distinct from the body" is the cornerstone of the whole idea that it is possible to sell your body without selling yourself. However, even if Descartes thought that the body, and all of nature, was a machine, he never went so far as to say that the body was a *commodity*. It had not yet become a saleable item.

"Sex is not the body"

In the story of the sex worker, something else happens as well. Sex becomes something separate from both Self *and* body. We still sometimes hear people say that a woman 'sells her body', but the expression is becoming passé. The most ardent supporters of prostitution will not be heard talking about selling the body; even this is too close to home, so we should be training ourselves to use the expression *sexual services*. Filip Wästberg and Per Pettersson from the youth section of the Swedish Liberal party wrote in a 2009 editorial: "What prostitution is fundamentally about is not, however, the sale of the body but commerce in services of a sexual nature. This is an important distinction that often goes unmentioned in debates." In a similar vein, Petra Östergren adoringly cites 'Lilian' as saying that "it is important, of course, to maintain the distinction that what we are selling is the service and not the body, and this is a service that can be carried out incredibly clinically and distanced … " (2006a, p. 160). Sex, it turns out, is neither the Self *nor* the body.

And so we move to another, even higher level of abstraction. First, the Self becomes the body. We're not selling our Selves— just our bodies! Then, the body becomes sex. We're not selling our bodies, we're just selling sex! At this new level, sexuality wrenches free from the body and constructs itself as a service. We thus have a threefold abstraction:

The Self becomes a body.

The body becomes sex.

Sex becomes a service.

When we speak of sexual services, we have moved several steps away from the human Self. We are no longer talking about Göran, 56 years old, who says to his wife and children that he will be working late but instead goes and solicits 17-year-old Miriam; we don't say that they sit in his car, that he reclines the driver's seat, that he has bits of toilet paper stuck in his pubic hair, etc. Instead, we have something abstract: a sexual service. Reflect on this phrase to describe what happens in prostitution: *she sells sex to him*. What does this tell us? Sex hovers in the air between two people as if it were completely unattached, a product that women happen to possess. And therewith the relationship between Göran and Miriam becomes veiled; the power differential becomes a static object, impossible to comprehend. The 'sexual service'—sex as a commodity—is convertible to currency, exchangeable in the marketplace and therefore socially accepted—without us having the chance to ask Göran what the hell he thinks he is doing.

Prostitution is, essentially, not a capitalist phenomenon but a patriarchal one. It did not automatically occur when people began to buy and sell but is instead rooted in the relationship between men and women. But when prostitution is incorporated into an advanced, highly developed market economy, this complex power struggle itself becomes a commodity. Sex is separated from the person and becomes supernatural. According to Marx, once something appears as a commodity it no longer behaves normally.

If you make a piece of wood into a table, even though the wood changes form, it is still wood:

> But, so soon as it steps forth as a commodity, it is changed into something transcendent. It not only stands with its feet on the ground, but, in relation to all other commodities, it stands on its head, and evolves out of its wooden brain grotesque ideas, far more wonderful than 'table-turning' ever was (Marx, 1915, p. 82).

When a person has sex, s/he is most certainly a person, and perhaps more than ever a body. But when sex becomes a commodity, it begins to act in all sorts of strange ways. It is wrenched from a person and seems to go around and exchange itself for other commodities. As Hilary Kinnell, British social worker at the Network of Sex Work Projects (the same organization as Laura Agustín's) asks rhetorically: "We accept the commodification of water and food, without which no human life would be possible, why not sex?" (Kinnell, 2002). The problem is that her question implies that sex is a thing, a material good like food and water, something that can be produced, delivered and walked away from.

Reification—When Sexuality becomes a Commodity

If we are made to believe that the sex sold in prostitution is something completely separate from the person herself, something that has wrenched free and walks around on its own two feet—what do we then become? We people of flesh and blood who, no matter what we say, have to be present in our bodies for there to be sex in the first place. How do we see ourselves? How do we relate to what we are doing?

I find a key to being able to answer these questions in the library stacks in the concept of *reification*.

Hungarian Marxist Georg Lukács coined the term in *History and Class Consciousness*, published in 1923 (republished 1971). In this work he discusses the psychological effects of capitalism on the human being. The word reification comes from *res*, Latin for 'thing', and literally means 'thing-i-fication'. Reification is a condition of disengagement and distance from the world so that we look at the economy as if it is not at all impacted by our behavior; objects seem to have agency and lives of their own, and people regard themselves as powerless. Reification occurs when a human creation or action is transformed into a commodity, a thing. This has already happened with work, housing, health care, education, and culture. Ever since its inception, capitalism has survived on the transformation of human needs, activities, and relationships into goods for the marketplace. This is in the DNA of capitalism: in order to continue, it must constantly seek new areas for commodification.

Human beings have always cultivated, built, created or invented, and these activities have become integral parts of our organic lives. But capitalism transforms our work into objects to be sold. We begin to see our ability to lift, carry, make, sew, think, convince, sing, write, or care for others as functions separate from ourselves.

Reification, Lukács writes, is a phenomenon particular to late capitalist society. A slave is not reified. Slavery is something else. It is the owning of another person and even if the methods of pressing out more work are "more obviously brutal than we see later" (Lukács, 1923/1971, p. 91), the manpower of the slave is not a commodity he owns—the slave himself is the commodity. Reification takes place only when the free worker ascends to the free marketplace. When he can sell his manpower to the employer, it becomes a commodity. This process is reification. On the one hand we have the 'free' individual, on the other hand, his manpower that gains the form of "a commodity belonging to him, a thing that he possesses" (p. 91). This relationship means that he comes to see his *functions*—which can mean his abilities, his strength, his intelligence, and his quickness—as possessions. He becomes alienated: not only from society, but also from *himself as a Self*.

In prostitution, sexuality is made into a commodity, which is why Hilary Kinnell compares it to food: we can exchange our kisses and caresses for food on the marketplace—*and they must therefore be treated in the same way in language*. We must be able to exchange the word 'sex' for 'a box of bananas' and no one should think: "How awful!" Because of reification, sexuality has come to look as if it were wandering around the marketplace completely independently, without corporeal human companionship. But this is an illusion, of course, and will always be. One cannot sell sex without being a living human being of flesh and blood. Thus what the story of the sex worker does rhetorically, the real-life prostitute has to do in reality. She must be present but try to convince herself that she isn't.

How this is being done is evident in the testimonies from people in prostitution. Rather than speak of sexuality as a way of being closer to another person, many speak of the necessity of maintaining distance. One Australian woman says: "I can only work it from below the neck. If I have to think of a service or involve my mind even slightly, I feel dirty. I avoid fantasies. I don't want to participate in their filth" (Wood, 1995, p. 55). Instead of a human encounter, sexuality becomes something she doesn't want to take part in. The expression 'from the neck down' is significant: the body must be sectioned off from the mind. Miki Nagata and Sandra Lundbom, who work at the Prostitution Unit in Stockholm, carried out four in-depth interviews in 2007 with women who had left prostitution. They discuss the result in their senior thesis 'Living with prostitution experience'. One of the women is called Sara. She was prostituted for two years and describes this process:

> What I also felt, during the act itself, or whatever you would call it ... I felt like I moved myself entirely into my head ... And I see that I used the same thing [in prostitution] yeah, well, it's from the incest. From there I learned to go into another reality. And that reality was in my head. So I felt like I didn't have a body, either ... But I had no feelings at all. I was completely closed. So someone could do whatever they wanted with my body without me feeling it (in Nagata and Lundbom, 2007, p. 26).

The separation is painfully obvious, more explicit than Descartes ever could have described it. He imagined it by closing his eyes for a moment, while women in prostitution must *make it happen*, try at any expense to separate body and consciousness, make the body mute, unfeeling. The same thing is said over and over, irrespective of whether the person being interviewed feels positively or negatively about prostitution. In one of the first anthologies of stories of prostitution, the French volume *Une Vie de Putain*, 'E' tells her story:

> The proof that I make this distinction is that on my bed there's always a sheet or blanket that keeps the client separate from what's mine. Never, never will he lie on my bed. He'll lie on a special sheet, on a blanket, but not on the bed that's my own bed. My sheets are my property, identity, that's where I bury my head, that's where I feel me, in my own smells. This might seem odd of course, since there's contact between the clients and my skin; you'd think my skin was closer to me than the sheet, but I can wash my skin afterwards. My body can be cleaned, and besides, this body isn't the same body—the one the client gets isn't the real one, it's not mine (in Jaget, 1980, p. 145).

It "isn't the same body," "isn't the real one," she says. The real one is the organic, feeling body—the "other" is the prostituted body. 'E' speaks positively about prostitution but says exactly the same thing as women who have left it: that sex in prostitution is "something else" and that the body isn't hers. 'E' goes on to explain how she told her boyfriend that she was a prostitute (p. 145):

> And then I made him see that my body was my body, sure, but that what he and I had between us was much more than that, it was the 'head', the soul more than anything, and that the body isn't important … There's one thing I keep for myself, and that's everything from the shoulders up. I won't let anyone touch me there.

This returns in story after story about prostitution, but it wasn't until the late 1970s that prostitution researchers understood it. While listening to women in prostitution, they heard many different life stories—but the stories had one thing above all in common: the technique of 'turning off', attempting to separate prostitution from the Self. Researchers such as Hanna Olsson in Sweden and Cecilie Høigård and Liv Finstad in Norway came to characterize the split Self/body as the core of prostitution. Swedish prostitution investigator Hanna Olsson wrote that prostitution, for the person doing the 'selling', is about raising a boundary between the private and public Self. Thus the woman attempts to defend the most important thing: her ability to feel. Olsson describes two defense mechanisms: avoiding physical contact for as long as possible, and avoiding active participation—being passive during the act. In a reflective essay, she describes how her knowledge took shape:

> I understood that the most important question was not what was agreed to in the contract with the man, but what *wasn't* agreed to. That the woman by all means possible attempted to protect herself from the man's use of her by not being mentally present, not allowing kissing or other intimate touching (Olsson, 1987).

Norwegian criminologists Cecilie Høigård and Liv Finstad, who spent a number of years in the mid-1980s in Oslo's prostitution milieu, came to the same conclusions: there was hardly "any other theme that gave so much insight into what prostitution involved for prostituted women" than the techniques of shutting off:

> And they are nearly universal. In the international literature prostitutes tell of such mechanisms—relatively unnoticed by 'professional researchers' before Olsson's investigation. In our own material there are only two of the women [of 26] who don't tell of a variety of methods of protecting the self (Høigård and Finstad, 1992, p. 64).

Høigård and Finstad developed Olsson's observations by describing six main defense mechanisms used by prostitutes: turning off (by thinking about something else or taking drugs/alcohol), establishing physical boundaries (certain body parts may not be touched, for example), limiting time, hiding one's real self (through false names, using different clothing and not talking about one's private life), tricking the client, and avoiding buyers one might begin to care about (pp. 74–75).

Høigård and Finstad stated that although there are major differences amongst women, the defense strategies were universal. Later international research in this field has noted the same thing. Women in prostitution all over the world, without communicating with each other, instinctively use these defense mechanisms. The same tactic—separating the Self from the body—returns time and again.

This is what is so tragic about turning sex into a job. For the person doing the selling, it becomes impossible to have a whole, indivisible sexual relationship. It's all the same no matter whether the surroundings are a filthy car or a bed at a luxury hotel, no matter whether it happens in South Africa or Norway. In order to survive in prostitution, one must reify one's own sexuality, see it as a function separate from the Self, and maintain the distinction between 'the sold' and the Self. 'Moving up into the head' is a perfect description of this tactic. It is performing the split between body and soul. The woman transforms herself into a commodity at the same time as she tries to transfer her Self elsewhere. Every day, she has to go through the process of transforming her body into a product that will feel as little as possible, and afterwards, she has to attempt to reawaken her body, remind it how to feel. Ida from Norway says:

> It's not easy money. I can't point to anything in particular. Not any single thing, or a single customer. Not the violence. It's more the regular, daily tricks. It's so massive. Small, unnoticeable scratches. Each scratch helps *to separate my body from my head.* The feelings I had, I've left behind on the street. They're lying down there (in Høigård and Finstad, 1992, p. 112; my emphasis).

Reification is, at its core, a defense mechanism. The individual reifies her/himself so that s/he can say: I don't sell my Self, I sell something else. *What is sold must always be something else.* It is also the same mechanism proponents of prostitution use to explain that the prostitute's Self is impaired in some way, or that the body is separate from the soul. It is reification on a collective level: to protect, restrict, keep the shame out. Andreas Malm (2003), who has written about pornography as reification, explains: "When a relationship between people is transformed into a relation between things, the authenticity, mutuality and, above all, the stark intimacy between the self and the world all disappear." For us, living in a world where everything is for sale, our sexuality may be a way of experiencing the intimate link between the Self and the world. Prostitution, in contrast, erects a razor-sharp boundary between the two.

Often, there are parts of the body the buyer isn't allowed to touch. As Sara describes it:

> My face was off-limits. No one was allowed to touch it. Or my arms. Yeah, I'm not really sure where this came from, but no one could touch my arms. My arms were mine, and I always wore long-sleeved shirts" (in Nagata and Lundbom, 2007, p. 25).

"My arms were mine"—what does that mean? That, for Sara, her Self was still alive, vulnerable, nearby, right under the skin, in her arms and face—for which reason she refused to include them in prostitution. We all have a longing for unmediated intimacy. When we don't have the option of letting it blossom completely, we have to find some body part where this longing may reside. For Sara, it was her arms. For others, it is the mouth. Or the feet. Even when we have to give almost all of our Selves, we attempt to retain private spaces where we feel complete, can fully experience the slightest touch, where we love ourselves. This bears witness to the unyielding nature of the human being.

After spending a period of time in prostitution, many people develop a split personality. One is the real Self, the other is the prostituted Self. The person is split into the being and the bought. The two Selves have different life stories. The 'stage names' taken by many women in prostitution have only partly to do with the fear of being recognized. They have as much to do with the necessity of making a distinction: he believes that he is meeting a woman with a certain name, but that woman is not me. He will ask for me by a name and call me this name, but that name cannot touch me, for it signals another. For the prostituted woman, the name becomes a protective barrier and a way to project away from herself all the unpleasantness: it happened to 'Antoinette', 'Valentine', 'Esmeralda', not to me. The names are often fluffy, sugar-sweet, and unrealistic in order to appeal to a male fantasy world, far removed from the real person. Ulla, one of the women active in the protests in Lyon in 1975, tells us:

> Strange how one can make a gesture or do a task or a chore without really participating. This is what has kept me from suffering too much. Suffice it to say that I managed to avoid suffering ...
>
> From that moment, my natural tendency to split off, even to completely divide into two, was extended. Because of this regrettable tendency I have to create private moments of being deeply alone, in which I attempt to put myself back together (Ulla, 1980, p. 149).

In many countries in the Middle East, prostituted women from Eastern Europe are routinely called 'Natashas'. These 'Natashas' are women who went to the Middle East in search of a better life after the collapse of the Soviet Union or who were forced there by human traffickers. They make up a separate class of prostituted women, a universal sex fantasy of the blond, available woman. As Marika, a Russian woman transported to Israel by human traffickers, tells us:

> We were their sexual fantasy. These fools would walk into the parlor and with a stupid grin on their face call out: Natasha! Like we were some kind of Russian doll. And we were expected to smile and rush over to them ... At first, I thought it strange to be called by another name. But very soon I came to accept it as my escape. When I was alone in my thoughts and dreams, I was Marika—free from this prison. But when I went with a man, I became this other woman, this prostitute called Natasha who was cold and dead inside me. Natasha was my nightmare. Marika was my salvation. I never told any of these men my real name (in Malarek, 2003, p. xvi).

As early as the 1800s, Parent-Duchâtelet described most prostitutes as taking a "nom-de-guerre" (1981, pp. 101–102). Prostituted women of the 'lower' classes used descriptive names such as Beefsteak, Blondie, Numbskull, Hot Legs, or Miss Perfect, while those of the 'upper' classes called themselves Arthémise, Palmire or Modeste. There are no surnames, indicating detachment from any sort of family ties. The acts in prostitution also have other names than in the outside world: 'French' (oral sex), 'Greek' (anal), 'uro' (to pee on someone), 'scato' (to shit on someone). Prostitution doesn't want to sound like prostitution, but like a menu at a restaurant.

All of prostitution is permeated by this duplicity; no one who comes into contact with prostitution goes unscathed. It also affects social workers, researchers and police officers. Dutch scholars Hugo Letiche and Lucie van Mens, who studied Dutch brothels, write that everyone involved in the culture of prostitution ends up 'double':

> Each relationship to prostitution is double. The prostitutes do not want to be identified as 'whores'. The clients try to restrict prostitution to a 'kick' and manly need isolated from the rest of their existence. The proprietors are involved in a (semi-) criminal activity, but want business respectability and social acceptance. The professionals have chosen a non-conformist career, but want to retain their 'expert' status. No one wants to reveal him or herself. The researchers do not tell what they have seen/felt. The clients keep their secrets ... The relationship between the self and prostitution remains unsettling (Letiche and van Mens, 2002, pp. 179–180).

These authors borrow a metaphor from Antonin Artaud: prostitution is a theater of cruelty that expels the Self (p. 179). No one can speak of the Self and of prostitution at the same time. There has to be a dividing line that protects the boundary and keeps things separate. Countries with legalized prostitution often even have special rules for where and how prostitution can take place. In Italy and Spain, the rule is at least 200 meters from schools and churches. In Germany, there are special areas where street prostitutes are allowed, and they can be fined for prostituting themselves elsewhere. This means that prostitution can be going on all the time, that it impacts society "as incest impacts a family," as the Chilean psychiatrist Jorge Barudy has said (in Marcovich, 2007, p. 333)—but that it is also kept at a distance, limited only to certain areas.

It appears to me, too, that the story of the sex worker is another way for society to keep prostitution at a distance. By making prostitution a discourse, a topic of debate, a semantic issue, people think they can keep 'real' prostitution away. This is reminiscent of how people in prostitution behave. It is as if society uses exactly the same defense mechanisms. As if the debate about prostitution were itself the defense mechanism against prostitution. On the one side, we should be completely preoccupied with the issue of prostitution, talk about it, debate it, interpret it, redefine it, idealize it, and speculate about it—but on the other we must never let it come near us. Something big, dark, and terrible, a black hole right inside us, is made clinical, remote and manageable.

Prostitutes who defend 'sex work' often appear on TV, at conferences, and on the internet. They say that 'sex work' is just like any other job. At the same time, they make a clear distinction between these appearances and the 'sex work' itself. It's not possible to book an appointment on these websites, nor can one approach these women after the conference and ask about prices. Prostitution happens somewhere else. One side is preoccupied with politics and campaigns while the other is selling oneself, and ne'er the twain shall meet. When we look at the big picture, we see the clear suggestion that, actually, prostitution might *not* be like any other job. It is important to understand the difference: sexuality becomes a commodity, but this does not mean that prostitution becomes work. It builds layer upon layer of shame and duplicity around itself. Feelings of shame pervade the world of prostitution, even the money isn't regular money—it's no coincidence that money made from prostitution is sometimes called 'monopoly money'. It comes and goes with incredible speed, as if the money itself were encumbered with all the shame and angst that surrounds prostitution.

Prostitution is often accompanied by boundaries. These boundaries save the Self, provide it with breathing room from the threat posed by prostitution. We might consider this a healthy sign: the boundary exists because there is something considered worth protecting. But when I discussed this with friends who have experience with prostitution, one said that she didn't have any boundaries, because at that time, she was so far gone that she didn't care what happened to her.

At the same time, this dividing line is incredibly damaging for a person because it breaks down her essential wholeness. Today's researchers no longer call this attempt to dissociate a 'defense mechanism' but instead Post-Traumatic Stress Disorder (PTSD). The largest international study to date on prostitution classified prostituted women's symptoms as belonging to the same category as the symptoms of war veterans and refugees who had experienced torture (Farley *et al.*, 2003, p. 56). Trauma researchers write that one of the symptoms of trauma is that a person becomes numb. The inability to feel one's own body is a symptom found in people who have experienced extremely traumatic situations and whose integrity has been violated. These researchers describe what Post-Traumatic Stress Disorder means for individuals in prostitution, saying they dissociate and that

> dissociation is an elaborate escape and avoidance strategy in which overwhelming human cruelty results in fragmentation of the mind into different parts of the self that observe, experience, react, as well as those that do not know about the harm ... A primary function of dissociation is to handle the overwhelming fear, pain and to deal with the encounter with systemized cruelty that is experienced during prostitution (and earlier abuse) by splitting that off from the rest of the self (Ross *et al.*, 2003, pp. 205–206).

A person who experiences pain, fear, and cruelty dissociates so that she does not have to absorb what happens. Dissociation can happen on a wide scale ranging from normal daydreaming to DID—dissociative identity disorder, where a person develops different parts of the Self, where thoughts and feelings literally exist in separate halves of the brain. According to these researchers, most people in prostitution whom they interviewed did *not* suffer from dissociative identity disorder. Many said they were depressed, while the authors claim that this shows that they still have an integrated Self. On the other hand, the majority of them showed so-called somatic dissociative syndrome: they had lost the ability to feel certain parts of the body (Ross *et al.*, 2003, pp. 206–207). This is what happens when sex becomes work. Because this 'work' isn't something that is produced and walked away from. Instead, the 'work' is one's own Self and body. The consequences are that the body shuts down, becomes numb, and disowns its own functions.

The Struggle for the Woman

Mechanization, writes Lukács, forces itself "right into the worker's 'soul'. Even his psychological attributes are separated from his total personality and placed in opposition to it so as to facilitate their integration into specialised rational systems" (1923/1971, p. 91). This is also what happens when sexuality becomes work: it is mechanized and separated from the person.

But this—a mechanical worker—is precisely what the buyer does *not* want! He doesn't want a woman who acts as if she is separated from her personality. He wants a woman who acts as if she *isn't* working; a horny, turned-on, sensual woman who loves going to bed just with him. The buyer's ideal is a woman who gives absolutely all of her Self, one who carries out the act with the precision of a machine and the enthusiasm of a wild animal. On an internet forum where buyers of sex from all over the world review prostituted women, the most common criticism is that the woman acts *as if it were a routine chore*. "Looking at the clock" is a common criticism, and we often see "passive" and "bored" along with critical comments about women who don't allow kissing, anal sex or oral sex.

And here we arrive at the core of prostitution: the buyer's paradox. He both wants and doesn't want prostitution to be work. He wants to be able to buy sex, but he doesn't want the woman to behave as if she is being paid to perform the act. The buyer wants prostitution to exist, but he doesn't want it to resemble prostitution. The more it resembles a routine chore—the more the woman acts like a cashier at a grocery store—the more displeased he becomes. No matter how much he wants her, he knows that she is doing it for the money. He therefore constantly demands something more, something genuine, something real. He wants to possess her whole body, her whole person, her whole Self. The buyer finds himself in a constant state of self-deception, which continually leads him to desire possession of what cannot be bought.

This is the central dilemma of prostitution, and one of the reasons why prostitution can never become a 'job like any other': in order for it to exist, it has to conceal its nature as work. And who is responsible for hiding this essence? The woman, naturally, the selling half of the commercial equation. She works with sex but has to pretend that she is not working.

Among men who buy sex, we often find the opinion that one cannot trust prostitutes, that they are 'liars'—exactly as Lombroso and Parent-Duchâtelet wrote. But this lie is actually one of the men's demands. There are some buyers, we have to admit, who don't care about theatricality and who even enjoy the fact that the woman is forced into prostitution. But few men want someone who says: you are ugly and stinky; can't you speed it up so that I can take my money and leave? Without the lie, there would be no prostitution.

A few years ago in Barcelona, I got to know a woman by the name of Maria who was involved in escort prostitution. Among other things, we spoke about whether sex could be regarded as work. In her opinion, that could never be the case—precisely because of this dilemma. "Sex work," she said,

> ... would be if you masturbated someone while he lay there watching a porn flick: you could do the same thing every time, he wouldn't touch you, you wouldn't involve yourself. But as soon as he reaches out a hand and touches you, you are emotionally involved—he might have cold hands, his touch might bother you, but you have to say that it's fantastic either way. That's when it stops being work.

Maria compared this to the job of a chef: the chef makes the food, but s/he isn't forced to eat it. The restaurant patron does the eating and the chef does the cooking. The chef can be a vegetarian but still prepare meat; s/he does it because it is their job. Prostitution, according to Maria, is as if the chef were forced to sit down and eat with all the patrons and say that it was delicious, that it was the best meat s/he had ever eaten, even if they were a vegetarian.

Marx wrote that commodification always conceals the social relation between two parties. Here it becomes literal: the relationship is disguised as a commodity. That's why the man wants her to be available as any other commodity would be: in display windows, at sex clubs and in online advertisements. At the same time, however, he demands that the commodity be transformed back into a relationship after he has paid: she now has to be human, real, interested in him.

Prostitution is, therefore, an eternal tug-of-war. The woman wants to keep her own private sphere intact. The man who buys sex wants all forms of touch to be for sale. But then the touch loses its charm, becomes routine, and he turns elsewhere, like a tourist who hates mass tourism. The tourist wants to escape commerce, but when he touches the authentic, it becomes commercialized. The more evident commercialization becomes, the more the tourist feels like a tourist, which disgusts him and encourages him to seek a place that is less 'exploited'. The tourist destination therefore has to wear a façade of authenticity, to fake pre-commercial conditions while at the same time charging for the show. Prostitution functions in the same way. The woman constantly has to work harder and harder in order to conceal the lie from the buyer.

The paradox is that the more prostitution is industrialized and made into work, *the less it resembles work.* In its undeveloped form, prostitution functions like a treadmill: a series of quick fucks with clothes on and minimal body contact. In its developed form, prostitution starts looking more and more like normal sexual relations between people. When prostitution becomes an industry, the women have to stop acting as if they worked in an industry. Why? Because the industry demands more and more intimacy.

The twenty-first century has already seen the rise of a new form of prostitution, called the 'GFE'—the girlfriend experience. In the 'GFE', the meeting is supposed to seem as much like a relationship as possible—there should be kissing, romantic dinners and conversation in addition to sex. Here, the boundary for what is saleable is close to dissolution. The woman's entire Self is supposed to be available. In the 'GFE', the buyer should be able to shower with her, kiss her, spend the night with her, and in exchange will pay her for the whole time. On websites all over the world, women are reviewed according to how good they are at the 'GFE'; men give each other tips about friendly and obliging women and warn against the grumpy and stressed-out ones. The general understanding is that in a 'GFE', everything typically included in a normal relationship should be for sale. One buyer, signed 'Punter X', says it all:

> GFE = a 'normal' interaction, as you might have with someone you were seeing in 'real' life. So it is a mutually enjoyable interaction between two people. No exploitation on either side. Naturally it would involve kissing, and other aspects of 'normal' intimacy that might naturally arise between those two people.[26]

The buyer wants to have exactly what tends to happen between two people who lust after one another—but he wants it on demand. Not only the sex should be for sale, but the whole woman. Sweet nothings and cuddling, maybe, but also whatever type of sex *he* wants to have. The moment the woman doesn't want what the man desires, it becomes clear that this is a paid service and not a romantic relationship. On an English-language website for buyers, featuring reviews from all over the world, one man with the username 'Errol Flynn' writes about his experience with the Columbian agency Girlfriend4aWeek, where tourists can rent a 'girlfriend' during their visit:

> [I]t was a slow and romantic experience and that part I loved, nor was she reticent to have sex. But, I agree, for top dollar I should get the blow job I might not get from a non-pro, that's what I'm paying for, and maybe she would have if I'd insisted … but that would have

---

26 <http://www.adultforum.co.nz/showthread.php?1968-Definition-of-GFE&highlight=GFE>

blown the romantic part of the experience which is what I am paying top dollar for.[27]

It is supposed to be 'romantic'—at the same time as she is supposed to obey his demands. In a chat among men on an online escort forum, they agree on what a 'GFE' must provide: oral sex without a condom, deep tongue kissing, letting the buyer perform fellatio on her and so-called 'MSOG'—Multiple Shots on Goal—meaning that he should be allowed to ejaculate multiple times on different parts of her body.

On an internet forum about Thailand, one man poetically exclaims that 'GFE' is better than "any other emotional relationship" because he not only gets exactly what he wants, but can also dump the girl without agony if she, for example, doesn't want to have sex every time he wants it:

> If a man having a GFE doesn't like how things are going—she's getting bitchy all the time, she wants to go shopping all the time, she only wants to sit in front of the TV, she doesn't want to have sex except on her terms—all he has to do, with rare exceptions, and without exception if he's been careful about protecting his privacy, is to pay up to the moment and tell the girl to get lost. And literally never see or hear from her again. There are very few married men who can so easily do this ...[28]

On the surface, it seems like a normal relationship, but if she happens to forget who is paying, who makes the decisions, all he has to do is send her away.

In order to work with sex, a woman has to be able to stop regarding it as sex. She has to construct defense mechanisms against being psychologically and sexually affected. But it is exactly this view of sex as 'work' that the man, the buyer, wants to break down—he wants sex, not work. Four of the defense mechanisms Høigård and Finstad listed as fundamental for prostituted women

---

27 <http://www.internationalsexguide.info/forum/showthread.php?2983-Girlfriend4aWeek.com>

28 <http://www.thailandstories.com/article/non-fiction/essays/why-the-gfe-is-the-best-of-all-possible-worlds.html>

are particularly negatively perceived by buyers: limiting the time, turning off, constructing physical boundaries and avoiding buyers the woman could come to care about. 'GFE' prostitution lasts for days, though; the woman has to be physically and psychologically present and her whole body must be accessible.

One of the oldest and most well-known defense strategies is not allowing kissing. Anyone who has seen a Hollywood film knows that prostitutes don't kiss their clients. Kissing is the first thing one does in most sexual encounters, but it is the big no-no of prostitution. It is no coincidence that it is specifically kissing that is prohibited in prostitution, write Høigård and Finstad (1992, p. 67):

> It is not strange that it is the mouth that is allotted this sacred position. The mouth is the organ we use in the first all-absorbing relationship we have with life, the relationship with the mother. The mouth is the means of acquiring life-sustaining nourishment. The mouth is the instrument of speech. The mouth is the most important channel of communication with other people. It is the mouth, not the eyes, that is the mirror of the soul.

But this irritates many buyers. Millions of men have posed the same question: Why can't I kiss you? The absence of the kiss is the red flag signaling that she doesn't want him. The absence of the kiss reveals the lie he so desperately wants to forget. And so the men have now found a way to introduce it. Today, kissing is a 'normal' aspect of escort prostitution. In escort prostitution, it isn't sufficient for the woman to offer the man complete possession of her body, she has to be everything else to him as well—masseuse, porn star, prostitute, therapist and a very nice girl, all in one. What the buyer most appreciates, as we have seen, is her *emotional engagement*. He wants her to kiss with passion and to make out with reciprocal desire. He wants to have constant proof of her emotional participation, proof that she is letting herself go just as much as he is. At the same time, handbooks for 'sex workers' warn: "Don't relax after the job is done—this could be when he attacks you. Relax when he is gone!" (Malarek, 2009, p. 211).

Complaints about women who openly show their indifference are quite common. The woman should give the impression that she is enjoying it just as much as he is, and many men actually believe that she does: they brag on forums about prostitutes "coming several times." The reason is not that the man cares about her orgasm, as some romantics might believe. It's more than that. It is in part a question of pride: if he believes that she has enjoyed it, he is satisfied with his manliness and goes away even more pleased with himself. But more importantly, when she fakes pleasure, she helps him to forget that the whole thing actually is prostitution. One Frenchman writes angrily and disappointedly about a Brazilian woman: "Unfortunately, no sensuality at all. Betyna does nothing; she is mechanical, not an expert courtesan! She gets wet but still uses a clump of lube for penetration. She rides me a little bit, but it is out-and-in without eroticism."[29] He finishes: "180 Euro for a blow job with a condom and no kissing, it's highway robbery!" Another man warns, "To avoid: Sonya, Russian!" This Sonya seems to see prostitution too much as wage slavery, because she "uses a condom for the blow-job. No DFK [Deep French Kissing], no social time, crabby and stressed. In brief, too short, no GFE, too commercial and banal."[30] That a buyer calls prostitution "too commercial" might seem strange and paradoxical, but this is a very typical criticism of escort prostitution. He pays for a service, but she is not allowed to reveal in any way that she does it for the money. A man from New Zealand writes: "For me seeing an escort is more than just sex, it's some *intimate human contact in its most purest* [sic] *form*, so in a way the escorts I see are also a form of therapy" (my emphasis).[31]

For the woman, the requirement of offering "human contact in its purest form" is an extreme form of reification. It is paradoxical:

---

29 <http://www.escortfr.net/1681622/viewtopic.php?t=48050> accessed 20 March 2009.

30 <http://www.escortfr.net/1681622/viewtopic.php?t=52313> accessed 20 March 2009.

31 <http://www.adultforum.co.nz/showthread.php?770-Is-French-Kissing-a-must-have&highlight=GFE> posted 8 September 2008.

the more 'human' prostitution appears, the more devastating it is for the seller, because she is required to sell her humanity, her Self. When prostitution is comprised of ten-minute fucks with clothes on, it might seem mechanical, but it allows the woman to maintain her humanity outside of it all. When prostitution resembles a normal date, the woman has to involve her whole Self. In street prostitution, violence is more prevalent, but in escort prostitution, reification is more pervasive. All aspects of social and sexual life are for sale. In a glossy Swedish teen magazine, an anonymous escort's story was published with the title: 'Jag säljer sex—och gillar det också!' ['I sell sex—and actually love it!'] (*Vecko-Revyn*, 2007). The writer says: "There are lots of others like me, whose looks work in their favor and who have an attractive, sexy body and a good personality and who love sex. For me, it's a smart business concept."

She clearly describes how her Self is not synonymous with her body; she 'has' an attractive, sexy body. This view is not abnormal in today's society. We all objectify our bodies. But here, even her personality becomes a commodity. To have a 'good personality' becomes some kind of raw material that the anonymous escort puts up for sale. Here we see a sharp distinction between her being and the commodity being bought, the Self and the body, so extremely advanced that *even one's personality is part of the commodity*. Instead of a meeting between two people who *are*, there is a meeting of what two people *have*. As Lukács writes, reification is characterized by the fact that

> it stamps its imprint upon the whole consciousness of man; his qualities and abilities are no longer an organic part of his personality, they are things which he can 'own' or 'dispose of' like the various objects of the external world (1923/1971, p. 100).

What characterizes a reification process is that previously existing parts of an organic whole become separate functions: sexuality is divided into different 'services' so that parts of the woman's body become available in and of themselves. Every body part becomes a potential commodity that can be marketed and sold as if it existed on its own. Lukács says (1923/1971, p. 93):

Just as the capitalist system continuously produces and reproduces itself economically on higher and higher levels, the structure of reification progressively sinks more deeply, more fatefully and more definitely into the consciousness of man.

In Australia, another new type of prostitution has arisen: *nursing* is now being sold. Women who have recently given birth can offer the 'service' of breast milk to be included in the act of prostitution. Men can pay a sum of money and be allowed to drink a nursing mother's breast milk. From those organizations that say they represent people in prostitution, there are no protests. On the contrary, it is encouraged by the Prostitutes Collective of Victoria (PCV) as a good way to earn extra cash: "A number of men find drinking breast milk either arousing or soothing" and women "may even be able to charge extra" for this service (in Sullivan, 2007, p. 125). Louise Eek also describes the expansion of 'services' in her book *Att Köpa eller Köpas* [To Buy or Be Bought]:

> In the 70s, a frequently requested service in Swedish porn clubs was 'oral massage' ... In the 80s, posing with piss and shit was in, in the 90s anal poses and S&M were requested. In the early 2000s, services have become more brutal than ever (2005, p. 83).

The Buyer's Dilemma

The buyer of sex is tricked—hence the term 'cod': the literal translation of the Swedish jargon for 'john', signifying the empty eyes and gaping mouth of the idiot. The woman knows that what she gives him is just an illusion. It is his false consciousness that is the basis of all of prostitution because he shuts his eyes to what he knows to be true: that she does not desire him or even like him. He prefers the illusion that he can buy 'intimate human contact in its purest form'—that he can buy not only her approval, but also her Self. The buyers on internet forums may be cynical and callous in many ways, but in one respect they show the most complete naiveté: when they speak of the woman's pleasure. Many write that the prostitute "had an orgasm" or "enjoyed it." Deep inside, they must know this is not true, and it makes them angry; so they simultaneously despise the prostitute because she has tricked them.

The buyer dumps responsibility for his dilemma on the woman: if she doesn't trick him well enough, he complains about her. *She* has to solve the problem, he demands, to bridge the gap. She must pretend and lie and compliment and moan and smile and fake pleasure. Her duty is to convince him that this isn't prostitution. The best prostitute, therefore, is the one who doesn't act like a prostitute but who never forgets that she is one.

Compared to the buyer, the prostituted woman finds herself in a much more lucid situation. She sees through the whole game and scorns him for letting himself be tricked. She knows that she has something 'behind the curtain' that is 'real', something he will never gain access to. She sees much more of his real Self than he will ever see of hers, because he is there on his time off while she is 'at work'.

But she, too, lives in a false consciousness, believing that it is possible to sell herself and protect herself at the same time, give him what he wants and stay intact. The duplicity he demands, she will have to embody: telling the world that she is just doing her job, a service like any other that doesn't affect her—and at the same time assuring him that she is horny, crazy about him, that she loves it more than anything. And it is she who pays the highest price for the duplicity that is actually his. It is he who has created the impossible paradox of buying appreciation and intimacy, but he transfers this split onto her. She is the one who has to make the man's lie real for him. The result is that he becomes whole at her expense, whereas she becomes split. Her defense mechanisms are meant to protect her Self, but instead gnaw away at its unity. Høigård and Finstad write: "*All* the other women we interviewed described how, in the long run, it was impossible to preserve yourself and your emotional life when you prostitute yourself" (1992, p. 107, original emphasis). This split, so seductive and simple in language, often proves to be impossible to maintain in reality. Colin A. Ross, Melissa Farley and Harvey L. Schwartz, American researchers who looked at trauma in prostitution (2003), quoted a woman in strip club prostitution who said:

> At work, what my hands find when they touch my body is 'product'.
> Away from work, my body has continuity, integrity … Last night,
> lying in bed after work, I touched my belly, my breasts. They felt like
> Capri's [her peep show name] and refused to switch back. When [her
> partner] kissed me I inadvertently shrunk from his touch. Shocked,
> we both jerked away and stared at each other. Somehow the glass had
> dissolved and he had become one of them (pp. 207–208).

Funari dances at a strip club and routinely imitates sexual feelings; she touches her body as if it were a 'product', she simulates being turned on but knows that it is only a performance. At the same time, she wants to maintain the organic integrity of her body when she comes home and makes love with her partner. In the end, it doesn't work to keep the two Selves separate. The product—the commodity—takes over; the product eats its way into her body even in her free time. Ulla, one of the leaders of the Lyon protests in 1975, illustrated the dilemma in this way: "I truly wish to sell my body, my flesh, but not my self. And in both pleasure and pain, it is the self that trembles. It is the self that lives. And there ain't no question that I am jeopardizing it" (Ulla, 1980, p. 122). She puts it so clearly: She wants to sell her flesh, not her Self—but the Self trembles in the flesh! The separation is an illusion. When the Swedish woman Sara speaks about her experience of prostitution, she says:

> [I]t felt like every time I let a man penetrate me, a part of me
> disappeared. And it occurred to me not too long ago, 'what on earth
> have I done? How many men haven't been inside my body? How many
> haven't touched my body?' … And then I think, it's clear that you are
> present psychologically and are affected by it. That's why I think it has
> to do with *me* and my integrity. My body … And so I let in man after
> the man … No matter how much I turn off, my *soul* is still being used
> up (in Nagata and Lundbom, 2007, p. 27).

Note that she first described her body, described the men as being inside her "body," but then went on to use the words "me" and "my soul." In other words, she was unable to maintain the distinction: her body turned out to be more than that, it turned out to be her very Self. Anne Mignard wrote in *Les Temps Modernes* (1976):

> The feminist slogan, 'My body belongs to me', seems absurd to me because it is always interpreted literally. What do the words mean? One doesn't *own* one's body, one *is* one's body. 'My body is me'. Not an object, an instrument, separated from the self, something that can be sold, rented, abandoned, or kept to oneself—but being itself. One does not belong to oneself, one is oneself. This is why the prostitutes' claims that they own their own bodies seem to me to reflect this very same alienation.

And the story of the sex worker is marked by precisely the same false consciousness. It is already clear that its ideological core is the idea that one can sell one's body, sell 'sex' without selling one's Self. But what is this idea, if not precisely a model of the dissociation that takes place in prostitution? What the story of the sex worker does is *idealize reification,* and *idealize the split that occurs in prostitution.* What happens physically in prostitution, a turning off, happens *discursively* in the rhetoric of the sex worker. Trauma becomes an ideal. The story of the sex worker says: the Split Self is not only possible, it is ideal.

The women interviewed by writers such as Petra Östergren describe precisely the same experience of dissociation as observed by trauma researchers, but she holds them up as a *positive model.* "Just like many other sex workers, Johanna points out that she does not really sell her self, but instead her sexual services," Östergren writes, and quotes Johanna with admiration when she says: "It's not for weaklings" (2006a, p. 189). In another place, she writes: "Karin doesn't put any of her own feelings into her work; when she leaves work, she says, it's history. This is how it has to be done, she believes, otherwise a woman who sells sex would go crazy" (pp. 183–184).

Seeing sex as emotionless and the body as a tool is depicted here as positive; this is "how it has to be done" and a woman who can't separate the body from the Self isn't the right person for the job. The strength she speaks of lies in the *ability to turn off.* When the woman repeats her mantra: I am not here, it will be over soon, what should I have for dinner?, only ten more minutes, focus on the money—the story of the sex worker is there to support her. It says: No, you are not here. You are a businesswoman, an entrepreneur: what is being prostituted is only a 'thing'. Deal with it, you are strong, a heroine! The story of the sex worker acts as a cheerleader standing on the sidelines, cheering for the split Self. It convinces society that this split is normal, and that it can be pursued with no harm to the Self. It even touts prostitution as a skill that only the strong are able to perform. As a political ideology, it is incredibly cruel.

The myth of 'the happy hooker' was different—it was based on what the buyer wanted to hear, that women in prostitution were horny pleasure-seekers who sold themselves to get more sex. It was a naïve, idealistic story. The myth of the sex worker is closer to the prostitute's own defense mechanisms. It is cynical and as dark as the blackest night because it is derived from the reality of prostitution. It claims that it is better for a woman to be paid for sex than, as Östergren writes, to "give men sex for free" as if sex were always something women "gave" men, as if we never had sex for our own sake (2008). In this ideology we find a mixture of man-hatred and misogyny, because this story claims that women would never really want to be with men unless we were paid—as if we couldn't love men and desire them without a constant eye on their wallets. There is resignation, cynicism, and an absence of hope for a better world. The best thing that could happen, according to this story, would be if prostitutes were murdered a little less frequently and had somewhat nicer places to work in. Men and women can apparently never meet and have sex with each other merely out of mutual desire. Sex will always be something a woman 'gives' a man for his sake, in which case she might just as well be paid handsomely for it.

For men, this is a very sad vision, and buyers should, therefore, dislike the idea of the prostitute as a worker. Even so, buyers accept the story of the sex worker because they know that its ultimate goal is to encourage the existence of the kind of prostitution they want. At the same time, they hold on tightly to the myth of 'the happy hooker'. This leaves us with two disparate myths—the buyer's idea of the 'happy hooker' and the seller's idea of rational sex work. They are as inherently contradictory as prostitution itself.

The Postmodern Story: A False Dialectic

On the surface, the story of the sex worker looks like a story that encompasses the complexity of life, insists that "there are both good and bad experiences of prostitution," and claims to present a nuanced picture that takes into account all aspects of this matter. It signals development and sensitivity to changes. An important aspect of this story of the sex worker is to take the ax to the alleged bias of radical feminism. There is hardly a text written about 'sex workers' that doesn't vilify radical feminists; it doesn't even seem possible to tell the story of sex work without an introductory tirade about radical feminists who think that all prostitutes are victims and who prevent anyone else from speaking.

These tirades never include a definition of what radical feminism is, though; it is always portrayed by way of sweeping generalizations as an extreme approach: dogmatic, man-hating and sex-hostile. In contrast, the story of the sex worker offers the alternative of its own 'sex-radical' feminism that claims to be open, nuanced and sensitive to contradictions. But if we look at the facts of prostitution, the analysis by radical feminists isn't the least bit exaggerated. Everything this analysis says about violence in prostitution isn't only valid—it also barely scratches the surface. There's much more that has not even been written about. In short, radical feminism is absolutely correct in the way it describes the reality of prostitution.

The problem with radical feminism is, in my view, not its descriptions of reality, but rather that the radical feminist analysis of prostitution tends to become static at times. It seems to me that when radical feminist works present the overwhelming evidence of men's violence against women without also giving a positive model of relationships between men and women, it can instead produce hopelessness. Social positions appear frozen, unchangeable. Since the radical feminist analysis offers few models for a positive heterosexuality, the heterosexual woman is left bewildered.

But this situation is not limited to radical feminism. In fact, the same process applies to many social movements as a consequence of the marginalization of radical forces. Those who don't buy into the prevailing neoliberal order risk being locked into a static analysis and becoming paralyzed. They stop seeing the potential for change, stop searching for ways out, stop hoping. This locked-in position sows the seeds of hopelessness and the idea that change is, after all, only cosmetic. This has taken place not only in social movements but also in art, literature, religion and relationships. A social movement must be able to identify the contradictions in society *as they are right now* and, importantly, detect the seeds of change.

Where dialectics exit, however, postmodernism and relativism enter. I experienced this in feminist groups in the late 1990s, when women, exhausted from trying to constantly and actively confront all the problems in society, turned instead to exploring the idea of 'queer', which was easier to absorb. Within queer identity, anything was all right as long as it was cool and society as a whole disapproved of it. Although radical feminists had developed a comprehensive analysis of men's oppression of women, fully absorbing these insights and integrating them into one's life is an immense challenge. In the long run, not all women had the energy for it. Especially if one leads a heterosexual life, loving men and at the same time fully understanding the concept of men's all-encompassing oppression of women can be a hard burden to bear. Human beings have a natural tendency towards dialectics, which also explains why some feminists were drawn to the story of the sex worker. It is a story that *seems* to highlight nuances and complexity, and *claims* to listen to different voices. It is a story that *claims* to be able to deal with the contradictions of life.

This, however, is nothing but the advertisement on the packaging. In reality, the myth of the sex worker *is* static and paralyzing. It fails to see where prostitution is coming from or where it is going.

The only contradiction it eagerly praises is that prostitution simultaneously challenges *and* confirms patriarchy: prostitution can be both a bad *and* a good experience, prostitution can be both oppressive *and* liberating. Where is the development in this? What is the direction? If prostitution can be both liberating and oppressive at the same time, we want to know what it is most of the time. And above all: we want to know where it is heading, and us along with it. But none of these questions are answered—the contradictions remain. Rather than the simplistic phrase 'everything is *either* black or white', the story of the sex worker posits the notion that 'everything is *both* black and white all of the time'. This is not seeing contradiction in a dialectical way; on the contrary, it is confirming a vacuum as the status quo. Moral and anti-moral, liberation and censorship, virgin and whore, good and bad—queer theory is unable to get beyond these dichotomies. The furthest queer theory ventures is to combine them in endless new variations. Although this is a way of playing with dichotomies, it turns the whole matter into a never-ending game. The fact that queer theory always returns to these dichotomous concepts says something about its being most comfortable in their presence.

The story of the sex worker, exactly like the entire postmodern story, is an example of false dialectics. It appears to offer openness, movement and nuances, but nothing moves and no doors are opened. *'The movement' is in fact static relativism.* When Marxists speak of dialectics, they are talking about how society develops through contradictions. A seemingly homogenous situation always contains its own opposite, the seeds of its own demise, which is why it is so important to identify these seeds. But when postmodernists speak of seeing contradictions, there is never any movement between them—they don't go anywhere, they simply exist. Life is a single static contradiction and consequently we will never be able to really understand anything—let alone effect change.

Instead of productive, dynamic contradictions, the postmodern story prefers exceptions. The old saying *the exception that proves the rule* shows that things can be true at the same time as there will always be exceptions. The evidence of exceptions does not preclude the possibility of generalizations. Postmodernists, on the other hand, claim that *the exception nullifies the rule*, in which case *one* exception suffices to preclude a generalization. This is how Petra Östergren can say that there are prostitutes who enjoy what they do, without having to address the 89% of all prostitutes, according to the largest international study ever carried out, who wish to leave prostitution (Farley *et al.*, 2003, pp. 33–34). In the minds of the postmodernists, the exception not only nullifies the rule: the exception *is* the rule.

The Way Out

A man in Catalonia told me the following story: he was soon to be married and a few weeks before the wedding he stopped his car on the street to buy a quick fuck. He negotiated with a woman and she got into his car, and then in the light he recognized her. She was his future wife's sister. The shock was mutual. The future brother-in-law: john. The future sister-in-law: whore. They stared at each other for a moment without saying a word. Then she jumped out of the car and slammed the door. Neither of them ever mentioned the incident to the rest of their family.

Prostitution, so normal for both of these people, became in that moment completely impossible. Because prostitution, after all, is *not* just a job like any other. No one goes into prostitution with one's whole Self. When two people meet as buyer and seller, it is their respective others who meet. Not the future husband or the wife's sister, but the flip side, the 'other Self'. The Catalonian man's story strikes like a lightning bolt: the masks fall off and the tragedy unfolds—the real people behind the masks look directly at each other. When the Self is revealed in the midst of prostitution, the cruelty of the performance is made obvious: prostitution becomes impossible. As Hugo Letiche and Lucie van Mens write:

> If you force people to react without their normal distance, if you threaten to destroy alienation, if you frustrate the reifications, your

audience will not know how to react. 'Holism' is unknown, threatening and subterranean (2002, p. 180).

Such a lightning bolt can affect society as a whole. In a moment of turbulence and social unrest, a whole society can go through a collective process of unmasking. The 1960s and 1970s were such a time. What characterized the sociological studies of the 1970s was a desire to work together with the people one was researching, to acknowledge them as subjects and resist making them into objects, to abolish the divide between the researcher and 'the Other'. According to Paulo Freire's *Pedagogy of the Oppressed* (1970), the academic researcher must live with the people s/he is studying, because the only path to knowledge is experience.

Hanna Olsson, reflecting on her research experience with prostituted women, points out that "the balance ... is particularly difficult. Namely, both to identify with the person I was meeting and take in what she told me, at the same time as I maintained my own perspective for the analytical and interpretive work" (1987, p. 11). She also says:

> It is not the distance that helps me to see in this struggle—but the closeness. Closeness breaks all social laws that reinforce inequality; while the distance facilitates a hierarchical approach to human worth. And it is when one abolishes this boundary that it becomes possible to gain new knowledge about people and social phenomena (p. 1).

Olsson writes in her research journal about how she was changed by stepping into the reality of prostitution. It was a bodily, physically disruptive experience, because she entered it in a historically new way: as one person meeting another. Not as a doctor or criminologist who is going to study an object, but as a person who has to get to know another person, a subject, to understand her—not just with the intellect, but with the body. Identification with 'the whore' began to enter her dreams. She writes: "And I had to accept it. Have it in my body." She was seized by a physical fear that pervaded her body. When she got to know the women she was interviewing more closely, she too began to develop a split Self. As she remembers:

Not until now have I begun to seriously understand that violence and assault come up in different ways in more or less every interview. My alliance [with the prostituted women] is increasing, and I am having an ever-harder time being able to draw a line between the job and myself. Sometimes I feel that I am more allied with them than with the investigation ... I find no bridge between what I am living and 'real life'. Can't describe to others how I actually feel. I am now beginning to understand how a woman's life is affected by prostitution ... I have developed two selves. A prostitution-self and my own self. And these two selves must be held apart. It is the only way to survive (pp. 7–8).

What Olsson is describing is revolutionary. She comes so close that she herself experiences the split that characterizes prostitution. Her body begins to live in prostitution. She is shaken by it. And by "having it in [her] body" she gains the in-depth understanding of what prostitution is about.

The Dutch are now in the process of realizing for the second time what they already acknowledged and acted on 100 years ago: that legal prostitution leads to trafficking. Holland today is a hub for trafficking gangs and a center for animal pornography (Koh Bela, 2007). Illegal prostitution thrives in and around legal prostitution. The Dutch authorities are slowly making adjustments. The number of display windows in the Red Light District has decreased. Germany, too, has been forced to admit that legalizing prostitution did not reach any of the goals it set. The Swedish approach has been well received internationally, and both Norway and Iceland have established similar laws in which the buyers are fined. France and Ireland are well on the way, too. Change is not only a fantasy, a utopian dream. It is possible in our time.

* * * * *

But today's prostitution is not limited to sexuality. It has expanded into other parts of the woman's body. For thirty years now, we have seen a trade in pregnancy. A reproductive type of prostitution has arisen in which women are inseminated and made pregnant in exchange for money. They are paid to bear the children of others and they give away these children shortly after the birth. This form of prostitution is called 'surrogacy'.

PART II

SURROGATE MOTHERHOOD

CHAPTER FOUR

The Reality of Surrogacy

At a clinic in Anand in northern India, women give birth to Western children. White women's eggs are inseminated with white men's sperm, and the embryo is implanted in the wombs of Indian women. The children will show no traces of the women who bore them. They will neither bear her name nor get to know her. After giving birth to the children, the Indian women surrender them. They sign a contract and receive between 2,500 and 6,500 USD the moment they give up their responsibility for the child they just gave birth to. For the women, most of whom are poor and from nearby villages (Haworth, 2007), the payment can be up to the equivalent of ten years' salary (Vora, 2009). The buyers are typically American, European, Australian, Japanese or wealthy Indians; they are childless heterosexual couples, homosexual men and single men. In a 2008 interview with the BBC, Indian surrogate mother Rubina says: "It's a miracle. I myself was wondering how I managed to deliver such a beautiful American, totally white baby. I couldn't believe it—I am very happy." One of her two children at home had a heart murmur and needed surgery; bearing a child for an American couple was the only way she could afford the operation (Thakur, 2008).

Surrogate motherhood sounds a bit like science fiction, but it is a growing and legal industry in the USA, Ukraine, India and a number of other countries. In India, thousands of children have been born via surrogacy, and in 2006 analysts estimated the value of the Indian surrogate industry at 449 million USD, due to its high potential for future growth (Chopra, 2006).[32] Two Swedish men told of their experience looking to India to have children. "I have no problem with women doing this for crass economic reasons. Just the opposite—in a way I think it is rather healthy to see motherhood in this light," said one of them in an interview with Swedish Radio (*Sveriges Radio P1*, 29 May 2008).

Surrogacy means that a woman is inseminated or has an embryo implanted in her uterus. When she gives birth after nine months, she surrenders the child to the biological parents. It can be done for free or for payment, but in either case the woman signs a contract pledging that she will birth the child for others. Neither commercial nor 'altruistic' surrogacy is currently legal in Sweden, but demands for legalization are becoming ever more frequent; in 2012 the Swedish Parliament voted to investigate the possibility of surrogacy in Sweden.

Background

The trade in pregnancy originated in the USA back in the 1970s. Advertisements began to show up in American newspapers in which men whose wives were infertile sought women who were willing to birth a child for them in exchange for payment. The women were inseminated, and the men 'adopted' their own children. It all took place on a small scale and in relative obscurity.

It was only a matter of time, though, before someone would see in surrogacy the potential for profit on a large scale. Lawyer Noel Keane established an agency with the business plan of connecting fertile women with childless couples. He knew that many couples were prepared to pay large sums of money to have a child who was genetically related to the father, and Keane guaranteed them one. He saw to it that he gained a positive reputation through spectacular appearances on talk shows where he presented his agency as a

---

32 By 2012, the surrogacy industry in India had grown to 2.5 billion USD; see <http://www.medicaltourism.com/en/news/india-s-surrogate-mothers-bear-other-people-s-babies-to-escape-poverty.html>.

charitable movement to help childless people. The young women were offered money and the potential to be recognized as Good Samaritans. Keane himself made a fortune, and the practice spread. By the end of the 1970s, there were a number of such agencies in the USA. For a while, they remained semi-legal (Chesler, 1989).

It didn't take long, however, before the first public custody battle arose. In 1986, a woman who had given birth at Noel Keane's clinic refused to give up the child. Mary Beth Whitehead, a lower middle-class mother of two, had agreed to bear a child for the upper middle-class Sterns. Whitehead had been inseminated with Bill Stern's sperm on the promise of 10,000 dollars when she gave up the child. But after Whitehead had given birth, she was struck by stronger feelings for the child than she had anticipated. When she saw her daughter, she couldn't give her up. Whitehead writes in her autobiography:

> At that point, I thought, What a mistake I've made. I did not want to make the mistake real. I wanted to pretend that it hadn't happened, that this was just my baby and we would share a normal life together. On one level, I felt guilty because of the obligation I believed I had to the Sterns and I was worried about their feelings, but now I also felt a strong obligation to the baby, as any mother would to her child … My God, I thought, how is she going to feel when she finds out that she was sold for $10 000? She's going to feel like the slaves did (1989, p. 19).

Whitehead ran off to Florida with the infant. The police followed and took the baby girl away, upon which Whitehead threatened to commit suicide. A long and trying litigation followed. Mother versus father, egg versus sperm, lower class versus upper class, blood versus contract. The trial attracted the attention of the whole USA and was even turned into a television series. Feminists took up the battle for Whitehead's right to keep the child at the same time as a smear campaign was launched by the media. The surrogacy contract was nullified in court, but in the end the Sterns were given custody since the judge decided they, being more economically stable, were more fit to be parents (Jaquith, 1988, p. 31).

127

The case came to be called 'Baby M' and led many states in the USA to outlaw commercial surrogacy. But then something happened that superseded the verdicts in custody battles and enabled the industry to move to the developing world. In the early 1990s, embryo transplantation became possible—implanting one woman's fertilized egg into another woman's uterus. Thus the surrogate could bear a child who had absolutely no genetic connection to her. This is known as 'gestational surrogacy', which distinguishes it from the traditional form in which the surrogate's own egg is used.

This was exactly when countries such as India started to become interesting for the surrogacy industry. With traditional surrogacy, the industry had been limited to the Western world. An Indian mother would have meant a child with Indian features. But suddenly, through the miracle of modern technology, it became possible for an Indian woman to give birth to a white child. Thus, Americans could pay two-thirds less than for surrogacy in the USA and still come home with their 'own' child, even though it had spent nine months in an Indian woman's body. Embryo transplantation also impacted on American courts' judgments in child custody cases. In one case from 1993, almost identical to 'Baby M'—the mother had second thoughts after the birth and wanted to keep the child—the judgment was that *she was not the child's mother*. She "was not exercising procreative choice, but was providing a service" (Scott, 2009). Because the egg wasn't hers, the pregnancy wasn't motherhood but a 'service'; therefore, she had no rights to the child she gave birth to. This has now become standard practice in the USA, and even when the egg belongs to a third woman—a so-called egg donor—custody is granted to those who paid for the child.

The surrogate industry is on the rise all over the world. It is legal in the USA, India, Ukraine, Hungary, South Korea, South Africa, Israel, the Netherlands, and is being discussed in France. Great Britain and Australia have legalized non-commercial surrogacy (see Klein, 2011). Reports from China claim that women are being offered sums equivalent to 12,000 dollars per child as a result of illegal trade in pregnancy (*China Hush*, 9 September 2009). It is difficult to know how many children have come into the world via surrogacy because few countries keep such data. The official statistics from the USA show that in 2000, there were 1,210 attempts at gestational surrogacy—the number has likely risen since (Spar, 2006, p. 82). Swedish couples, too, have put in their orders for children via surrogate motherhood from both the USA and the developing world.

The Buyers and the Bearers

Until recently, the people wanting children through surrogacy have mainly been heterosexual couples living in the Western world. They are between 35 and 45 years old and, as a rule, are highly educated (van den Akker, 2007a, pp. 53–62). On average, they have spent seven years attempting to have children with the assistance of hormones and in vitro fertilization (IVF) but eventually find that the woman cannot bear a child for any number of reasons (MacCallum *et al.*, 2003). A rapidly growing group of those seeking a so-called surrogate are homosexual couples (mostly gay men) or single men who want a biological child. (Many countries don't allow single men or homosexual couples to adopt.) What all of these people have in common is that they want to have a child who is genetically related to the father (or fathers, in the case of two men, who often 'commission' two babies)—but they don't want to share custody with the woman who gives birth to the child(ren). On the website oneinsix.com, one man writes: "I saw you web site about mother surrogate. I want to know exactly the price (all included) to get a baby ! I want to be father what i have to do? And how much for surrogate mother ? thanks." One woman who had already given birth but who didn't want to deal with another pregnancy says: "Will be 40 in August anyway – which doesn't help and yet we still long for another child or two. We would like to use our own embryo and a surrogate just for the gestation of the child/children." Others have specific wishes about appearance: "This is S from UK. Im considering to become a single father and i would love it if i can find someone who can carry my child but it'll mean it may include her own egg. I'll love an Asian child maybe a Kenyan child – whats the chance there?"

Swedish couples advertise for surrogates, too. One woman writes on familjeliv.se: "I wonder if anyone has any experience with a surrogate mother from the Ukraine or the USA? How does it work? And how do you deal with the Swedish authorities when you come home and what does it cost, approximately?"[33] In advertisements such as: "Married couple seeking surrogate. Generous compensation for your help!"[34] there is no doubt that what is being asked for is commercial surrogacy, even though all forms of surrogacy are forbidden in Sweden. Another woman writes: "We talked about surrogacy today. My spouse is skeptical about it and is afraid we'll be cheated. We wonder how much money those of you who do this want for your services? How can we guarantee that the surrogate mother doesn't change her mind when the child is born?"[35] One man writes: "I am a single man who really wants to have children. Live in Malmö and am 43 years old."[36]

The woman who gives birth, in the majority of cases, and regardless of whether she is from Ukraine, India or the USA, is poorer than those who pay for the child. In India, she often comes from a village near the surrogacy clinic. In the USA, she is typically a married woman from the working class (Chesler, 1989, p. 44).

33 <http://www.familjeliv.se/Forum-3-144/m24188434.html>
34 <http://www.villhabarn.se/content/?s=a31719e5012a78776dd55637d789
    2e68>
35 <http://www.villhabarn.se/content/?s=a31719e5012a78776dd55637d789
    2e68>
36 <http://www.villhabarn.se/content/?s=a31719e5012a78776dd55637d789
    2e68>

CHAPTER FIVE

The Story of the Happy Breeder

As could be expected, organizations and lobbyists have begun to demand that surrogacy be legalized in Sweden. These proponents include associations for childless couples, queer theorists and politicians from both the right and left wing. Surrogacy is still relatively unfamiliar territory, but The Swedish Federation for Lesbian, Gay, Bisexual and Transgender Rights (RFSL) has taken a stand in favour of commercial and altruistic surrogacy. All political parties, except the Left Party and the Christian Democrats, voted in 2012 to open an investigation on the matter. Some, like RFSL and Birgitta Ohlsson of the Liberal Party of Sweden, are only in favor of 'altruistic' surrogacy, in which no money changes hands. Others, such as philosopher Kutte Jönsson from The Swedish Association for Surrogacy and conservative politicians like Christer G. Wennerholm, advocate commercial surrogacy as well. We have started seeing a whole arsenal of texts take shape—from family stories to debates, political proposals and philosophical dissertations: all attempt to establish an ethics for the acceptance of a pregnancy contract. Two parallel stories have developed from this discourse: 'the happy family' and 'a norm-breaking practice' of 'revolutionary acts'.

Happy Families

In lifestyle sections of the daily press, and in magazine articles about surrogacy, the longing of 'childless' people to have children always takes center stage. The articles have headlines like: 'A happy family thanks to a surrogate' and focus on surrogacy as a solution to a problem. They describe how celebrities, such as Sarah Jessica Parker, Angela Basset, Michael Jackson, Elton John, Ricky Martin and Nicole Kidman, have had children via a surrogate.

It is difficult to find a more idyllic family portrait than the one that is painted in the newspaper *Svenska Dagbladet* of a Swedish homosexual couple who achieved their family happiness "thanks to a surrogate mother." They loved each other and had everything they could wish for; all they were lacking was a child.

> They look like the quintessential happy family, walking toward me with Linnea, eight months old, in her carriage. They look like a relaxed and harmonious family unit. Even if their everyday life is lined with the same routines as other new mothers and fathers, their parenthood has a very special luster (in Haverdahl, 28 September 2008).

The men fought for many years to have a child and first considered pairing up with a lesbian couple, but they felt that "the child would become a typical child of divorce, shuffled around between the pairs of parents," something "we didn't want," as Patrik remembers it. Then a woman came to their aid, a single mother of three from America who "loved giving birth" and who didn't even want payment, just "money to cover her expenses." She was willing to give birth without demanding custody or even having contact with the child.

When they finally met the woman, it was like a love story. "The minute we met, we clicked"—she was the perfect surrogate mother. "Everything matched up; our values, views on childrearing, everything." After four days, they were convinced. Marie was the right woman. The only fly in the ointment was a gnawing fear over whether she would really be prepared to give the child up when the time came.

The woman was inseminated with sperm from one of the men, and after the second try, they received the good news: she was pregnant! One of the men tells us: "I waited a few months for Mother's Day. Then I gave my mom the pattern for a baptismal gown." The pregnancy advanced, and both of the men were able to be present at the birth. They traveled to the USA, cut the umbilical cord, and then, five days later, they said a tearful farewell to Marie. She wanted to have a few more days to say good-bye to the child. Patrik was still nervous that Marie would change her mind and want to keep the child, but that didn't happen. In the morning when they were going to travel, it was pitch black. Marie, Patrik and Jens stood quietly in the hallway and held each other. Everyone cried. When the taxi came, they parted without a word. Marie's tear-drenched face in the window was the last they saw of her. Not until they were settled in on the ship with Linnea between them did they dare relax and begin to accept the full reality of what had happened. They had become parents.

The article ends with an interview in question-and-answer format with an American surrogate (it isn't clear if this is also Marie) who says things like it is a "fantastic experience to bear a child for someone else" and that she "didn't regret it for a second." She was making absolutely no demands of her own, and in response to the question of whether she would want to meet her child, she answers: "Absolutely, if the parents think it is appropriate."

An article in *Expressen* begins with the words: "André, 20 days old, has come home" (Kazmierska, 6 April 2009). A Swedish couple had hired a woman in Ukraine to bear a child for them, but the child could not get a Swedish passport since it was legally from Ukraine. The article expresses no doubt about whether the Swedish couple are the child's real parents, or that Sweden is the child's home country. The central issue is a "family" that should "be united." The parents were "confused about why *their* newborn baby didn't get a Swedish passport" (my emphasis), until the previous Conservative Party leader, politician Bo Lundgren, intervened. When the child was allowed to enter the country, it was "an enormous relief." The article ends, as they usually do, happily: "For

John, Sara and André, a happy ending. The family is back home in Sweden ..." The mother who gave birth to the child does not have a voice in the story, it is only briefly mentioned that she is from Ukraine, had two children previously and had to give birth to André via Caesarean section because the placenta was misaligned in the uterus.

The surrogate is generally presented as happy, and the buyers as well-established, stable, upper middle-class couples who will give the child the best possible upbringing. There is never any question: it is the couple that pays for the baby who comprise the 'true' family. The woman who gives birth is never presented as the child's mother or even a person with a background and a will of her own—she is just a kind soul, a fairy godmother, who helps the people who pay for the child get what they want. In Marie's case, in spite of her tear-drenched face and desire to spend a couple more days with her infant, she is ready to make this sacrifice for the men's sake. Only in passing does the reader find out that the couple paid money for the child, and such articles never say how much. Nor do they deal with the real crux of the story, that a woman signs away custody for money, or question whether this could be considered trafficking in babies.

This 'happy family' story tells us about a family that has been created via a surrogate. Her function is to create this family—but she is prohibited from being a part of it. What characterizes surrogacy is *the requirement of an absent mother*. It engages a woman whose only function is a physical one.

In the newspaper *Aftonbladet*, father through surrogacy Daniel Szpigler writes a thank-you note to himself—in his daughter's name!

> My dear dads, I am so glad you decided to have my brother and me via a surrogate. I know it wasn't an easy decision for you. You didn't want to share me with a lesbian couple or a heterosexual woman. You wanted to be full-time dads. Raise me full time. Love me full time (Szpigler, 27 July 2009).

While the daughter in question is not even two years old and is completely oblivious to having written for *Aftonbladet*, Szpigler clarifies on her behalf that "it is completely okay for me" not to have a mom. Szpigler not only takes the liberty of writing a declaration of love to himself in his daughter's name, he even arms her with political opinions. That a mother otherwise tends to be automatically seen as a parent "should be changed, I think." And what about the fact that they paid money for her? "It's not strange, I don't think. People pay to adopt a child, do in vitro fertilization or egg donation. What's the difference?" He signs the article: "A daughter of two dads through Daniel Szpigler, the driving force of surrogat.nu." The article is illustrated with a child's drawing.

Similarly, Olof Lavesson, member of Parliament for the Swedish Conservative Party, praises Ricky Martin's decision to engage a surrogate mother, writing about himself on his blog in 2008: "In my personal opinion, I don't want to plan for a 'shared' child. Cristofer is the person I have lived with for ten years. If I am going to see my own child grow up, I want to do it with him". Lavesson bases his opinion on the typical idea of the nuclear family. Since he lives with Cristofer, they should have children together. The classic mom-dad-child constellation is at play here. But because they are of the same sex, a woman is necessary to bear the child—though Lavesson doesn't want to have to 'share' the child with her.

Words such as 'whole' and 'complete' are constantly repeated in this story of happy families. We are meant to see that surrogacy creates families that would otherwise be incomplete. All of the children's drawings, talk of wonderful walks with baby carriages and families that "are reunited" in "the homeland" portray an image that something that was broken has now been fixed; something unfinished has been completed. But this 'wholeness' presupposes an absent mother. If she meets the child or takes part in the child's upbringing, it is understood to be a division or split. It is the dream of the nuclear family—but one in which the mother is suddenly a threatening figure.

A 'Revolutionary Act'

Parallel to the newspapers' sweet stories, another legitimizing story of surrogacy is being constructed by queer theorists, cultural analysts, liberal politicians, and organizations like the Swedish gay and lesbian rights organization RFSL.

The very same activity that paved the way for the perfect family in the magazines changes face completely. In this version, surrogacy has become a 'norm-breaking' and subversive practice that challenges outdated conservative models. Philosopher Torbjörn Tännsjö writes that surrogacy "dissolves the 'natural' idea of motherhood, of fatherhood and of what a family is" (1991, p. 147). Fellow philosopher Kutte Jönsson writes that surrogacy can "challenge the norm of biological parenthood" and function as "a battering ram against conservative family traditions, where the heterosexual nuclear family represents the norm" (2003, pp. 117, 13). The title of Jönsson's dissertation, 'Det förbjudna mödraskapet' ['Forbidden motherhood'], makes the reader think of a censored and therefore legitimized (because all revolutionary things should be, after all) kind of motherhood. Similarly, Ulrika Westerlund and Sören Juvas from RFSL claim that the prohibition of surrogacy is proof that "we have a biological, heteronormative, couples-oriented view of parenthood and family" (Juvas and Westerlund, 2008). Alesia Goncharik writes in the same vein that the prohibition "is simply an expression of the conservative view of gender roles and traditional motherhood we still find today" (21 May 2009).

In spite of the fact that people who want to have children through a surrogate mother stress that they *don't* want to adopt because they want to have a child who is genetically their own, the arguments presented in favor of surrogacy in the cultural arena are often anti-biological. The rhetoric is borrowed from social movements, where the concept of 'social parenthood' is emphasized and set in opposition to biological parenthood. Daniel Szpigler writes: "It is not the biological connection that is important, but just the desire to become a parent" (2009). In an essay from 2006, Sarah Vaughan-Brakman and Sally J. Scholz criticize the "biological paradigm" that stipulates that there is "a natural connection or a natural bond between mother and child." Kutte Jönsson also questions "the myth of the sacrosanct relationship between biological mother and child" and believes that it is important to "challenge the norms of biological parenthood" (2003, p. 117).

Nevertheless, they don't consider *all* of the biological connections to be unimportant. What they are criticizing is the *birth mother's* biological connection—*that* is called a 'norm' and a 'sacrosanct myth'. The *father's* biological connection, however, is not questioned at all. Despite the fact that he lays claim to the child for the same biological reasons as the mother, *he* is not accused of defending biology or the nuclear family. In other words, this criticism of the biological connections is directed only at one sex. What is never addressed is the fact that if *all* biological claims were rejected, it would be incredibly difficult to decide whose the child is. And while the argument speaks of the importance of social parenthood, it is silent about the fact that surrogate motherhood isn't about giving a child more parents; it is about keeping one of the parents away from the child.

American researcher Heléna Ragoné is a pioneer in the construction of the story of surrogacy. She claims that it can encourage people to come together, to question inequality and to help women be liberated from traditional roles. According to her, both traditional and gestational surrogacy "allow women to transcend the limitations of their family roles and to achieve a certain degree of independence and personal fulfillment" (1998, p. 128). According to Ragoné, surrogacy also counteracts racism. Since it is common in the USA for African-American and Hispanic women to bear children for white people, Ragoné claims that surrogacy breaks down racial barriers. "Class and race differences also tend to be set aside when infertility and childlessness are at issue" (p. 125). Thus even class divisions are supposedly broken down: her view is that those who pay for the children show no prejudice against a surrogate from a lower class than themselves, because they are willing to accept a lower class woman giving birth to their child.

Reading Ragoné, we see surrogacy presented as a path to social utopia, where it isn't important whose child it is. In the past, society considered it natural for a pregnant woman to be the mother of the child and to care for it. But thanks to technological progress, "the organic unity of fetus and mother can no longer be assumed" (p. 119). This is progressive, according to Ragoné, since it liberates women.

The story of the surrogate resembles the story of the sex worker in many ways. It is a story that connects a practice—in this case, pregnancy as work—to a multitude of contemporary social concepts. Defense of the practice has little to do with accounting for what actually happens in surrogacy—how it happens and what consequences it may have—but rather suggests openness, progress, and happiness. Four members of parliament from the Liberal Party of Sweden and the center-left Green Party write in an Op-Ed article 'Surrogatmödraskap nu!' ['Surrogate motherhood now!']:

> However, there is no clarity in determining what is ethical and what is not. Why is it unethical to let a woman who is willing to do so partake of the happiness of pregnancy and birth? Why should a child who is so clearly desired, since the parents go to such extremes to have one, end up being worse off than a child who wasn't planned? (Ohlsson *et al.*, 2009).

We are meant to agree that children in surrogacy situations are "clearly desired" and therefore their parents will love them and give them a good upbringing. What makes this so certain? Why is going to "such extremes to have one" a guarantee that such a child will have a good childhood? Applying this logic, children for whom parents pay more will have better childhoods than children whose parents pay less, because how desired the child is can be measured in monetary terms. Surrogacy is also presented as if it were necessarily *a desire on the part of the surrogate mother*, who wants so dearly to share the children she bears (as opposed to the buyers of these children, we presume, who are not interested at all in sharing the children with the surrogate mothers). But the surrogate mother is not the driving force here; it is the buyer who creates the demand for surrogacy. Secondly, "partaking" is not a correct description of what happens in surrogacy. The surrogate mother cannot share in the happiness associated with these children, because she doesn't have access to them.

The 'Feminist' Arguments

Just like in prostitution, 'feminist' arguments are used to justify surrogacy. Kutte Jönsson, for example, writes:

> Surrogacy, both the altruistic and commercial varieties, can be defended on feminist grounds. Similar to all liberation movements, the women's movement focuses on freedom. By tradition, duties and activities associated with women are unpaid or poorly paid. For this reason, it has been seen as a step forward when women begin to be paid for doing things that were previously unpaid … Seeing motherhood as a 'typical job' can be a way for many women to challenge the (traditional) women's role, and simultaneously transgress its boundaries. This would align with one of the overarching goals of feminism: emancipation! (2003, p. 223).

Therefore, according to Jönsson, it is "wrong to prohibit women from being surrogate mothers" (p. 220). It is wrong to object to women "lending their bodies to others who wish to have children" because "every capable, competent and consenting adult has the right of self-determination over how s/he utilizes his or her own body" (pp. 109 and 220–221). He compares this situation to the "Wages for Housework" movements from the 1970s, which demanded that women be paid for housework and childrearing, but with his own twist: instead of being paid for taking care of their own children, women should be paid for giving them away. It is hardly a "traditional women's role" to rent out one's womb. Nor has the women's movement always seen it as progress for women to receive payment for traditional women's work inside the home. It has just as often been considered a trap for women.

Both Kutte Jönsson and Torbjörn Tännsjö believe that commercial surrogacy should be legalized regardless of the fact that women's health is at risk. Jönsson writes that even if surrogacy implies both physical and psychological risks for women, prohibiting it is wrong because "one restricts their opportunity to use their bodies in exchange for payment" (Jönsson, 2003, p. 220). Tännsjö, who is only in favor of altruistic surrogacy, observes that "some of the criticism is well-founded" but that "the risks both for the women and children are worth taking" (1991, p. 143). This is remarkable: by speaking of "rights" and "opportunities," these writers arrive at a view of surrogacy as a feminist right ("emancipation!" is Jönsson's battle cry). Yet at the same time, they find it irrelevant whether women come to harm as a result.

One would be able to dismiss such words as the diatribes of feverish philosophers if it weren't for the fact that these arguments are heard from so many directions. Conservatives Christer G. Wennerholm, Jenny Edberg and Fredrik Sawestähl write in an Op-Ed that "we basically do not see anything wrong with a surrogate receiving reasonable and fair compensation for the part she plays"—even if they would prefer that she played it for free (2008).

American philosopher Christine T. Sistare follows the same train of thought. She argues for surrogacy as creating freedom for women, showing respect for motherhood and allowing women to exercise their free will. Her essay 'Reproductive freedom and women's freedom: Surrogacy and autonomy' ends with a tribute to the revolutionary potential of surrogacy:

> Finally, the acceptance and practice of surrogacy would reveal a meaningful respect for maternity. It would do so in the capitalist mode of paying well for what is deemed rare and precious. It would also encourage recognition that women—many women—really do enjoy the experiences of pregnancy and giving birth ... Surrogacy permits women who find their basic reproductive capacity to be a source of joy to display that valuation through their free choice to exercise the capacity for the benefit of others and for themselves (1994, p. 401).

In this 'feminist' argument, words like 'consensual', 'decisive', and 'individual' have become somewhat of a mantra: time and again we are reminded that we are dealing with capable, competent adults. Jönsson writes that surrogacy works only if women are completely informed, capable of making sound decisions, and receive fair payment. But hold on a second. What does this actually mean? Can a person ever be *completely* informed of something she has never done before? Who decides if somebody is capable of making sound decisions? What is truly fair payment for giving up a baby, and is everything just a question of the right price? These assurances are easy to write, but few of the writers spend any time figuring out how these rights would be guaranteed in reality, and even worse, no one seems to be particularly concerned about them.

When we study these assurances in detail, we find that what seems to automatically make people competent adults is always the same: the ownership of one's own body. They "utilize their bodies," "lend their bodies," or as philosopher H.M. Malm so clearly puts it: "[T]he action of entering a contract about one's body *confirms* a person's status as an individual because *a person is someone who owns his or her body*" (1992, p. 297).

This type of 'feminism' relies on the same assumption as the type of feminism that supports prostitution, the assumption that the woman is neither connected to her own body nor, by extension, to *the child she grows in her body and gives birth to*. The child is not a part of the woman and anything that happens in her body does not happen to *her*, but just to her *body*. And even more—the freedom of the Self stands in contrast to the freedom of the body.

Prostitution

Surrogacy can be seen as an extended form of prostitution. Someone, most often a man, pays for the use of the woman's body. In both cases, his needs take center stage, while the woman is only the means to achieving his end. Andrea Dworkin points out that the difference is that in surrogacy, it is the woman's uterus that is sold rather than her vagina, which keeps her from being stigmatized: she is a Madonna and not a whore (in Corea 1985, p. 275). These arguments have strong similarities to those put forward in the prostitution debate.

Sistare wants surrogacy to be seen as work. She believes that there is nothing inherently wrong with selling one's body:

> [W]e certainly allow people to treat their bodies as property in a variety of ways, e.g., the selling of blood, of antibodies, and (most apropos) of sperm. A fortiori, in our society, we permit people to sell their labor and even think well of them for it. In fact, the surrogate is more a laborer than a seller of body parts, since she really only sells her services while renting out her body ... (1994, p. 397).

Malm claims, in contrast, that it is not about selling one's body. He thinks the difference is that in surrogacy, it is not a *buyer* who uses the woman's body; it is the women *themselves* who use their bodies to satisfy the buyer.

> There is no need to view the payments to the woman as payments for the use (i.e. rental) of her body—the customer does not acquire a space over which he (or she) then has control. He may not paint it blue, keep a coin in it, or do whatever else he wishes provided that he does not cause permanent damage. Instead, the woman is being paid for *her* to use her body in a way that benefits him—she is being compensated for her services. But this does not treat her body as an object of commerce, or her as less than a person, any more than does my paying a surgeon to perform an operation, or a cabby to drive a car, or a model to pose for a statue (1992, p. 297).

There is something breezy and shallow about philosophers like Malm, but his writing is anything but superficial. In reality, his argument works on two levels and has a double effect: on the one hand, he denies the objectification of women; on the other, he compares a woman's body with an object. He experiments on both a literal level and a deeper, figurative level. On the literal plane, he uses concepts such as freedom, independence, individuals, free will and work. On this level, he claims that surrogacy is not exploitative, that it is not human trafficking, that it does not compromise women's integrity. On the figurative plane, he does the opposite:

he compares the woman with dead things. When he wants a metaphor, he uses a taxi driver who drives a car, a surgeon who performs an operation … in other words, he creates a metaphor that *de facto* compares the woman's relationship to her body with a taxi driver's relationship to his car, even as he, on the superficial level, distances himself from these comparisons: "To illustrate it, suppose that you own a lawnmower. (I do not mean to suggest that women's bodies are on a par with machines.)" (1992, p. 297).

Malm continues his comparison by claiming that if you pay someone to mow the lawn, you don't make a claim on the lawnmower but on the service of having the lawn mown. That is, lawn mowing is a service and not the purchase of a lawnmower. On a figurative level, he draws an analogy between a woman and her body and a gardener and his lawnmower. It is this analogy that drives his argument forward; it is this association we are urged to make: women relate to their children in the same way as men relate to their lawnmowers. Being a surrogate is like mowing a lawn. Still, Malm assures us that he *doesn't* mean that women's bodies are comparable to machines.

Thus the surrogacy story works on two levels simultaneously. It accustoms us to the idea that women are objects in the marketplace at the same time as the arguments for surrogacy deny this. We are supposed to become accustomed to being objects, but we are not supposed to understand what that means, because, *naturally*, we are not objects.

While philosophers such as Tännsjö and Jönsson only attempt to convince us of the benefits of surrogacy by using proven concepts, British philosopher Stephen Wilkinson goes further and questions the very concepts of harm, exploitation and consent. His *Bodies for Sale: Ethics and exploitation in the new human body trade* (2003) is a defense of surrogacy, trade in human organs and patents on DNA. He also aims to question and reinterpret concepts like commodification, objectification, consent, exploitation, welfare and force. The title is interesting: Bodies *for Sale* and *the new human* body *trade* make it sound like the whole issue is about bodies, not people. Compare the impression it would have made if the title instead were *People for Sale: Ethics and exploitation in the new traffic in human beings.* Bodies, somehow, always denote someone else.

Exploitation is a vague concept, Wilkinson writes. So he invents an alternative term: "mutually advantageous exploitation" (2003, p. 70). He thinks it is wrong to always talk about exploitation as harmful to the exploited. On the contrary, in his view, it is to the *advantage* of the exploited. He goes on to claim that "exploitation should be allowed because the exploitees are better off with it than without it" (p. 71). This manner of thinking is echoed by Kutte Jönsson, who believes that there "are advantages to being exploited, especially when they are living in total misery" and that "it is not obvious that commodification as such is degrading, except (possibly) on a symbolic level" (2003, pp. 148, 170). Both Wilkinson and Jönsson claim that exploitation and commodification are not degrading, because we also have to question the word degrading. It isn't necessarily degrading to be degraded, etc., etc. ...

A dilemma arises when philosophers who defend surrogacy and prostitution get to the subject of slavery. In liberal democracies, slavery represents the ultimate form of exploitation; if you don't distance yourself from slavery, you disqualify yourself as a theorist. But what are philosophers supposed to do, having already pulled the rug out from under their own feet? Having gradually rejected each and every concept that forms the framework of the argument against slavery: exploitation, human trafficking, harm, oppression, autonomy and commodification, how can they prove that they are against slavery? Wilkinson solves this by simply trumpeting: "Clearly, ownership of this kind is wrong" (2007, p. 32). He has no ground left to stand on from which to condemn slavery and must therefore appeal to common sense—in spite of the fact that he has just completely sent common sense back to the Stone Age.

Child Trafficking

These philosophers want us to regard pregnancy as just like any other job. We are not to see childbirth or the womb as something 'sacred'; we should liberate ourselves from biological prejudice and see women as the owners of their bodies. Pregnancy is a 'service' just like factory work or lawn mowing. To this end, they argue in exactly the same way as prostitution proponents. But if pregnancy is a job—what, then, is the product? In contrast to prostitution, the *product* cannot be brushed aside as an abstract concept such as 'sex'. The product of surrogacy is absolutely tangible—it is a newborn baby. If pregnancy is the same as working in a factory, then the child is comparable to a car or a mobile phone. The woman bears and births a child and hands the product over. At the same moment she gives up the child, she receives payment. The first thing we wonder is: Why should this *not* be considered human trafficking?

Concurrently with surrogacy becoming a lucrative industry, dissertations arrive on the scene from faculties of philosophy and law all over the Western world, in which all similarities to child trafficking are contested. And here the philosophers perform a strange maneuver: on the one hand, we are to see the surrogate mother as a worker, while on the other hand, we are prevented from seeing the child as the consequent commodity.

According to philosopher Kutte Jönsson, surrogacy is not child trafficking "because the child didn't exist when the transaction was sealed. It is therefore not a question of child trafficking" (2003, p. 221). In spite of this, he consistently calls the child a "product" in his dissertation.

Martha M. Ertman, professor of law, claims that the child is not what is being sold; what is being sold is parenthood. She speaks of the "parenthood market" and asserts that even though "most people believe parenthood should not be bought and sold … a parenthood market, in some circumstances, can be a good thing" (2008, p. 299). According to Ertman, since there is already a marketplace in which "people routinely exchange funds to obtain parental rights"—adoption—there is no use arguing against the practice. When we read Ertman's term 'parenthood market', we could very well imagine that it is the children who buy and sell parents—extremely enterprising children indeed, who sign contracts before they are even conceived!

According to Wilkinson, surrogacy is not child trafficking because one cannot trade something one does not legally own. Because parents don't have the right of ownership to their children, Wilkinson claims that it is by definition impossible to engage in child trafficking. What is sold is "a limited bundle of parental rights, not the baby itself" (2003, p. 147). Certainly, money changes hands when the child is given up, but Wilkinson suggests that "we can think of surrogacy contracts instead as service contracts with success clauses" (p. 146). He states that although surrogacy does resemble child trafficking, we cannot definitively say that it *is*:

> But at least we can conclude that it is *very far from obvious* that the surrogate's handing over the baby for money is baby selling. This in itself is enough to render the baby selling argument weak, since (in order to justify legal prohibition) its proponents must demonstrate that commercial surrogacy *really* is baby selling (p. 148).

Wilkinson stands as a staunch defender of the precautionary principle—if we can't be certain, it's best not to take action. But 40 pages later, he has suddenly made up his mind: "Commercial surrogacy *isn't* baby selling, *needn't* commodify or exploit women, and *can* be validly consensual" (my emphasis, p. 181). Suddenly, the need for proof and complete certainty disappears; that surrogacy does not *necessarily need* to be exploitative and that it *can* be voluntary suffices for Wilkinson to recommend legalization.

Another way to avoid the question of child trafficking is to tone down the role of money. In her 'anthropological critique of the psychosocial scholarship of surrogate motherhood' Elly Teman believes that surrogacy isn't about selling children, but rather "constructs families through the marketplace" (Teman, 2008, p. 1,005). Others believe that although the child is transformed into a product, the buyers don't need to *treat* the child as a product. Martha Ertman's argument for why surrogacy isn't child trafficking is that in the marketplace, the buyer can purchase exactly the item he wants, while "parents have the duty to help the child develop a healthy sense of self" (2008, p. 304). She compares surrogacy to the purchase of a car and claims that, while the car owner has the right to destroy the car, parents do not have the right to destroy the child. Law professor Marjorie Shultz agrees:

> We simply say that money is one dimension of human interaction and valuing. The critical issue is not whether something involves monetary exchange as one of its aspects, but whether it is treated as reducible solely to its monetary features (in Shultz, 1990, p. 336).

Now this is intriguing: children are being exchanged for money, but we should not see it as trafficking because children are people and *by definition* cannot be seen as products. Here, the philosophers appeal to our humanist tendencies and empathy to cover up the system they are defending—in which children *de facto* become products.

These philosophers have a giant problem on their hands when they attempt to defend surrogacy. They see it as a job like any other, but the product is naturally *not* like any other—which is why they treat us to a display of daredevil rhetorical contortions. The argument for why surrogacy isn't child trafficking reads: either there is no child to buy, or there *is* a child, but one cannot buy children by definition, or it is the parents who are bought by the children. With the same logic, nothing that is ordered in advance—a cake from the bakery, a painting by an artist, dinner at a restaurant—can be bought, because none of these things existed when they were ordered. We could also argue that it is the dinner that buys its eater. Or that human trafficking by definition cannot exist, because one cannot own human beings.

Sold with Fatal Relativism

The story of surrogacy tells us about the new, the modern. It tells us what will bring unique happiness to everyone: a baby. Everyone can now have a baby: childless couples, infertile couples, heterosexual or homosexual couples, older women, single men. And the best thing of all is that everyone can have their very own biological baby without having to go to the trouble of bearing or birthing it. We can outsource this bodily hardship, exactly as we have outsourced manufacturing, and still have our very own newborn babies the minute they are born.

When we hear the story of surrogacy, we hear about social revolutions, about dismantling norms—and at the same time, we hear about the wonders of the happy nuclear family. We hear a feminist story about women who rebel against traditional motherhood—and simultaneously a description of the hell of being childless, and about surrogacy as the only remedy. Conservative or radical, patriarchal or feminist—the story of surrogacy has something for everyone. We hear of happy intended parents and surrogates who beam when they give up the child. Surrogacy, says Elly Teman, "threatens dominant ideologies" and challenges the "ideology of motherhood" (2008, p. 1,105). She criticizes feminist research on surrogacy as being under the influence of Western cultural conceptions, such as that 'normal' women don't give up their children and 'normal' women don't give away their children for money (p. 1,105). She writes that surrogacy *threatens, challenges, breaks, revolts*, and sets these active verbs against *dominant ideologies, the Western world, prejudice* and *traditional motherhood*. Thus, Teman successfully aligns feminism, postcolonialism, queer theory, liberalism and all kinds of rebellion on the same pro-surrogacy team.

But not all people are radical breakers of norms. Especially not those who pay for surrogacy, the majority of whom are still heterosexual couples longing for a biological nuclear family. Conveniently enough, the argument has a tendency to adapt to its surroundings. When surrogacy was about to be legalized in conservative parts of the USA, it was said to strengthen the nuclear family. Scholar John A. Robertson writes that surrogacy "may shore up, rather than undermine, the traditional family" and "thus serves the purposes of the marital union" (1992, p. 50). Additionally, he claims, it helps infertile women to fulfill their natural longing for children. Heléna Ragoné believes that surrogacy is "a reaffirmation of the importance of the family" and is "consistent with American kinship ideology in the sense that biogenetic relatedness is achieved (for the father)" (Ragoné, 1994, pp. 2, 110).

There is something for everyone, which is the red flag of a story driven by profit. As in the field of advertising, all tricks are legit, as long as they sell the product. Images of rebellion are interwoven with images of tradition, images of the happy family with images of the independent woman. *Time* is an important component in this kind of story. The solution has to be new and fresh—but not untested. It has to be the future—but decidedly not science fiction. Surrogacy is therefore described *both* as a new, revolutionary practice *and* as an ancient tradition. Surrogacy has "existed since the dawn of time," writes Fredrik Larsson of the Swedish Association for Surrogacy; it is "a traditional way of having children" (Larsson, 2006). Nearly every book on the subject begins with quotations from the Bible and the story of Sara, Abraham and Hagar in which a servant woman bears a child in place of the wife. These quotations are assumed to have a placating effect: we mustn't rush off and start associating surrogacy with Huxley's *Brave New World*. Calm down folks, this goes way back to the Bible! Surrogacy speaks to us from every direction. It is a modern phenomenon at the same time as it has always been practiced, exactly as prostitution is explained as both 'the world's oldest profession' and a modern business for the liberated woman. Its opponents, on the other hand, are only positioned in the negatively charged past. People who stand against surrogacy are accused of being both conservative biologists *and* deniers of the biological drive for children!

In this way, the story is able to speak to people of all groups and political leanings at the same time, and to contradict itself again and again—it doesn't matter, as long as it serves its purpose. The consequence is that we become confused. Norm-breaking can mean just about anything. The nuclear family can be seen as a negative in one version of the story, but can just as well appear in the next as a self-evident human right. The strategy is to present oneself as challenging the status quo. But since 'the status quo' isn't tangible like economic, military or physical power, but is rather like 'norms' and 'social expectations', it could be just about anything. That norms are bad *per se* and exist only to be broken, is then understood without further explanation needed.

In the case of surrogacy, as in the case of prostitution, we see how the postmodern story is used as the theoretical superstructure for contemporary capitalism. Doing away with concepts such as 'truth' and 'reality' makes the postmodern story infinitely adaptable; it can be used to justify anything. But surrogacy poses its own special challenges for the postmodern story. How can we justify a situation in which wealthy people use poor people as breeders, inject them full of hormones, take children away from them and leave pocket money in exchange? A good dose of relativism always does the trick. Elly Teman describes how she does it (2008, p. 1,004):

> I apply a social constructionist approach toward analyzing the scholarship, arguing that the cultural assumption that 'normal' women do not voluntarily become pregnant with the premeditated intention of relinquishing the child for money, together with the assumption that 'normal' women 'naturally' bond with the children they bear, frames much of this research. I argue that this scholarship reveals how Western assumptions about motherhood and family impact upon scientific research.

Turning the Law of Supply and Demand into a Human Right

There are two initial parties in surrogacy, and they are inextricably intertwined. On the one hand, we have wealthy people from developed countries. On the other, we have women from developing countries or women of lesser means from developed countries. The former have money and a longing for children. The latter have only their bodies—making them the proletariat in a very literal sense. The word *proletariat* comes from the Latin word *proles*, meaning 'children'. The proletariat comprised the poorest class in the Roman Empire; they had no property, only themselves, their bodies and their fertility. Their purpose was to have children. 'Proletariat' is a patronizing word that I never use otherwise—like the term 'bodies', it always sounds like it's referring to somebody else. In this context, though, it is fitting, since detachment is exactly the point.

We can see surrogacy as an attempt to regulate the traditional relationship between the proletariat and the upper classes by means of a *contract*. Via a contract, the economic power differential between the wealthy and the proletariat is 'cleansed' and remade as an equal relation: "mutually advantageous exploitation," as Wilkinson puts it.

People who seek a surrogate have a very specific desire. It is not enough for them to get to know a child or to help to raise a child who is already alive. Nor is it enough to adopt an orphaned child or to have a child with a woman who also wants a child. No, it has to be their own genetic offspring, a newborn baby of whom the buyer has sole custody. This is always concealed in discussions about surrogacy—that it is not only a *desire* to raise a child, but also a *demand that the mother be absent*.

The surrogacy story follows a slippery logic. It begins by stating that this *desire* exists and when the people in question have money, it becomes a *demand*. This demand is reformulated according to suitable argumentation and thus lands in the realm of being a 'right'.

Many people either don't want to or are unable to have a child themselves, Kutte Jönsson writes in 'Det förbjudna mödraskapet' ['Forbidden motherhood'] (2003). He identifies the potential clients in a surrogate market: infertile women, single men, homosexual couples, female athletes who don't want to lose years of their careers but still desire a child who is genetically related to them—not to mention those women who have aesthetic reasons for not wanting their bodies to be compromised by a pregnancy. The last group can surely seem a bit superficial, but: "Who are we to judge?" Jönsson asks rhetorically.

The desire is then reformulated into a need. Ulrika Westerlund writes in an Op-Ed in the magazine *Ottar* about "those who *need* a surrogate in order to have children" (2008, my emphasis). She doesn't tell us why a *surrogate* is needed rather than a mother who will be present for childrearing—but the desire of one or two men to raise a child without the mother being involved has clearly become a *need*. In another Op-Ed by Westerlund, this one coauthored with Sören Juvas, we read: "Sweden must be able to ignore antiquated ideals about the right way to have children and respect people's varying needs, expectations and choices about building a family" (Juvas and Westerlund, 2008). Here, personal choice is confused with need: whoever requests something, no matter how specific the desire is, *needs* it. Kutte Jönsson writes: "Sometimes, people's interests and preferences demand that a surrogate bear the child" (2003, p. 125). Who is doing the demanding? Interests and preferences, or people themselves? By formulating it in this way, Jönsson legitimizes the need as if *it* were something that was *needed* rather than *someone* who needed *it*. Then, the need becomes a right: suddenly, we are talking about "everyone's right to have a child"— this very specific desire has thus been transformed into a human right. Robertson calls this "the right of a couple to raise a child" and "a married couple's right to procreative autonomy," which he calls a "fundamental right" (1992, pp. 52–53). If the demand goes unmet, according to his logic, we have a denial of basic human rights on our hands. Surrogacy is presented as the only solution to the problem, as an article in the newspaper *Sydsvenskan* formulates it: "[F]or homosexual men, surrogacy may be the only way to have a child" (Gunnarsson, 2009). A general longing for children has suddenly been narrowed to mean that surrogacy is an absolute necessity—end of discussion.

The longing to have children could indeed be seen as a universal human emotion. People all over the world, from all social classes and of all sexual orientations, long to have children. This longing is, in itself, a beautiful feeling. There is nothing bad about the longing to protect a little life, to see a child grow up, to be part of the cycle of life. But there is a huge difference between longing for a child and demanding a surrogate. The longing to have children is simply an emotion, but the demand for a surrogate is a requirement that the child's mother never get to know the child or be present during its childhood. As Marx pointed out, food is a human need, but "hunger that is satisfied with cooked meat eaten with fork and knife is a different kind of hunger from the one that devours raw meat with the aid of hands, nail and teeth" (in Miklitsch, 1996,

p. 23). The former is a desire, the latter is a need. Desires and needs are two completely separate things; while a need is something one will die of if it is not satisfied, a desire is something one wants for a variety of reasons and that may even stand in opposition to one's needs. Swedish intellectual Nina Björk has written that one sign of an affluent society is having difficulty distinguishing desires from needs: we learn to desire the things we don't need and to call these desires needs (2008). And our so-called needs become ever more specific: the longing for children becomes the right to use another woman's womb for our own purposes. Behind this slippery logic stands, naturally, the forceful, violent logic of profitability, which makes it all too easy for the wishes of economically strong groups to be transformed into self-evident rights.

On the Term 'Surrogate Mother'

Of everyone involved in the making of a child, the birth mother has spent the most time with it. She has carried it inside her day and night for nine months. She is the one who feels the child inside her. She is the one who makes it grow from a seed into a person. She is the one who puts her life and her health on the line by giving birth to it. She is the one who risks gestational diabetes, pre-eclampsia, a Caesarean section, and infertility. She is the one who has hormonal shifts, starts to dream differently at night, who suddenly has cravings for new foods or is disgusted by foods she used to eat. She is the one who can no longer sleep on her stomach and who feels the child kick. It is her breasts, her skin that will bear the marks of the child. The child's navel is the eternal reminder that it was once connected to her body. Psychologist and child psychotherapist Pia Risholm Mothander writes that pregnancy is "one of the most complete physical transformations ever" and that it "carries with it radical psychological changes that are at least as great" (1994, p. 32).

They say that blood is thicker than water, but in this case, money is thicker than blood. In surrogacy, linguistic tricks are played to distance the mother from the child, to claim that she doesn't have a right to the child and that she is not the child's mother. "It is simply not and has never been her child," Kutte Jönsson writes about gestational surrogates—thus revealing his own extremely genetically oriented view of parenthood (2003, p. 158). "Think of it as if someone's child comes to stay at your place for nine months," says Dr. Nayna Patel, director of one of the clinics in India, to her surrogates. A father who ordered a child via surrogacy says: "She was an oven ... *We don't see her* as *the mother* and that's the way it is" (in Berkhout, 2008, p. 105). It is "like providing day-care or nanny-services," said one American judge who ruled against a surrogate in a child custody case (in Tong, 1992, p. 293). The mother is "no more than a vehicle for bearing someone else's baby, as is common with farm animals" says lawyer Russell Scott (in Corea, 1985, p. 124). Kutte Jönsson compares a woman's womb with other possessions when he discusses whether surrogacy is exploitative: "[I]magine that you find a lost wallet—are you then exploiting the owner?" (2003, p. 158). Now, I don't know about Jönsson's world, but as for mine, I have never seen a lost womb lying around on the street. It is telling that all of these metaphors are external and speak about things being where they don't actually belong. To illustrate the place of human origin, we are supposed to think of temporary loans and the renting of objects.

The woman is called a bearer, a provider, a suitcase, an incubator, a surrogate—she is never simply called 'mother' or 'mom'. The very word 'surrogacy' is, etymologically, incorrectly used. The definition of 'mother' in the Oxford English Dictionary is "the female parent of a human being; a woman in relation to a child or children to whom she has given birth." The definition of 'surrogate' is "replacement." It is therefore the woman who pays who should be called the 'surrogate mother', because she replaces the mother who gives birth. But words mirror power: the 'real' mother is the one with economic resources, while the 'false' mother only has her own body.

But in the full phrase 'surrogate motherhood' we have the word 'mother', which weighs it down with an emotional and historical burden which requests, entreats, and encourages us to feel that she is still some type of mother. And so the displacement is hastened: the word 'surrogate mother' is shortened to 'surrogate' and is further shortened in American everyday speech to 'surro'. This moves us further away from motherhood—we don't even have to say the word. It is not a question of being a mother, but of being a surrogate: a substitute, a function, not a mother. The woman who gives birth can also be called the 'bearer', as in the French *mères porteuses*, or by American agencies that offer their clients "both bearers and egg donors": neither the woman who gives birth to another woman's inseminated egg nor the biological mother is referred to as 'mother' here. Kutte Jönsson discusses the term 'surrogate mother' and argues for the complete elimination of the word 'mother' from the term:

> In principle, surrogacy doesn't implicate a surrogate mother, and according to the dictionary definition, 'surrogate' literally means 'substitute', 'ingredient used as a last resort', 'replacement'. The substitute needed in surrogacy is, however, not the *mother/the female parent*, but the *uterus* (2003, p. 15, original emphasis).

Jönsson does admit that, as of yet, no uterus has ever appeared without a woman, and so he agrees to accept the term 'surrogate mother'. But he can perfectly well imagine that it would be possible to create an independent uterus. This "might be a realistic alternative—and presumably a better one—to surrogacy." Jönsson concedes that today, unfortunately, "a woman is necessary for child-bearing," but insists again that what is actually needed is not the woman as a person, but her uterus, as if they were two completely separate entities (2003, p.15).

Another way of handling the issue of the birth mother is to ignore her completely. The Liberal Party of Sweden's Martin Andreasson, chairman of the LGBT Liberals, doesn't even mention the mother when he argues for the legalization of surrogacy: "It isn't any more difficult than any other form of in vitro fertilization—since that is what it is about. And yet surrogacy would make it possible for many longed-for, planned children to be born into loving families" (2009).

Here, it is the paying couple that longs for, plans for, and is going to be loving toward the child. The birth mother is presented only as a technical function, not as a feeling person. Andreasson doesn't take into account that she could also plan, long for and be loving toward the child—he ignores her existence altogether and pretends that surrogacy is only a type of in vitro fertilization, in spite of the fact that the entire controversy is not about technology, but about the divorce between mother and child.

And when we suggest that paid pregnancy might not stop a mother from loving her children, Stephen Wilkinson counters with:

> [I]t is not clear that a) the child is really hers (the surrogate's) or b) that the surrogate is really the child's mother (a fortiori that she is the child's only mother) or c) that gestational mothers' rights to love 'their' children (if such rights exist at all) are inalienable (2003, p. 177).

With what ease, with what arrogance and Latinizations do these philosophers do away with physical realities and equally real emotions! This rhetorical process is an analogy to what happens in the story of the sex worker; *she is not a mother* is a parallel to the statement *the body is not the Self.*

The child is also affected. In his research, John A. Robertson writes of "donors and offspring" instead of mothers and children, and believes that the central question is not "the deliberate separation of biologic and social parentage, but how the separation is effected" (1992, p. 54). Instead of talking about how *mother* and *child* are separated, he speaks about the distinction between biological and social *parenthood*. Instead of being about a woman giving birth to a child and then, a few hours later, still in the afterpains of childbirth, having to give up custody of that child, for Robertson it is about an abstraction, about cultural preconceptions, about the biological versus the social. This spares him the need to take up the burning issue of how *people* are affected.

In fact, most texts that defend surrogacy share this trait: the *physical reality* is subordinated to an abstract, theoretical idea. Torbjörn Tännsjö asks in a typical formulation: "Is it actually important that biological, genetic, social, etc. parenthood coincide?" (1991, p. 148). He has already fragmented motherhood into three parts and presents them as if they just happened to coincide; like if your birthday happened to coincide with both your anniversary and Christmas. Of course "biological" and "social" motherhood need not always coincide—and in the long run, social can be more important than biological. But this doesn't mean that biological motherhood is completely meaningless. Besides, pregnancy is not only a question of biology; being pregnant is itself a form of social parenthood.

In the same way as the woman in prostitution is abstracted away and becomes 'sex', the birth mother is abstracted away and becomes a substitute, a 'surrogate'. People tend to speak disdainfully about what has been called 'uterofeminism' in Scandinavia, a term for 'essentialist' feminism in which biology is put on a pedestal, but in the case of surrogacy the woman is reduced to only her uterus without the slightest trace of feminism. The woman is presented not as a feeling human being who experiences her pregnancy on an existential level, but as a container, an incubator. The process of abstraction follows a similar pattern as in prostitution:

mother $\rightarrow$ uterus $\rightarrow$ container

which becomes linguistically

mother $\rightarrow$ surrogate mother $\rightarrow$ surro

Exactly as sex is indivisible from a person, the fetus is indivisible from the woman during pregnancy. Philosophers can't do much about this union in practice. What they can do, however, is deconstruct it in theory. The fetus is something else, they claim, something that doesn't actually have anything to do with the woman, that only *happens to coincide* with her. The fetus comes to term inside the woman, but is a separate individual or a product. The idea of the fetus' independence from the mother is a foundational patriarchal idea that has long been used to control women. The Vatican's opposition to abortion is built on exactly this same thesis: that the embryo/fetus is a separate person as soon as there is a fertilized egg, and that the woman is only a container.

The Capitalist Creation Myth

There was a time when women were the center of the universe. Archeological finds from southwestern Europe, the Middle East and Asia Minor show that, at one point in time, women had significantly higher status than today (Moberg, 1999, p. 12; see also Foster with Derlet, 2013). Author Eva Moberg writes that these finds indicate a radically different society in which sexuality was sacred, war was highly unusual, and no signs of sex-based oppression were evident. Researchers do not believe that these societies of the past were matriarchal in the same way that today's society is patriarchal. They were, however, matrilineal and matrilocal. Families were traced through the mothers, and when a couple married, they moved in with the woman's parents. These societies often viewed sexuality and childbearing as sacred (Sjöö and Mor, 1991, p. 50).

Then, approximately 6,000 years ago, the shape of society began to transform. A paradigm shift occurred in many parts of the world, including India and China: the shift from goddess worship to belief in gods. Societies shifted from believing in female deities and sacred birth to believing in a male god and the oppression of women. Why this happened is as strongly disputed as why dinosaurs became extinct. Some believe that warring tribes invaded these societies. Others think it had to do with agriculture and the rise of private property. Still others speak of increasing animal husbandry and the slaughter of animals as factors (Moberg, 1999, p. 16).

In patriarchal societies, it is no longer the woman who is the most important giver of life, but the man. It is the man who counts as the most important parent, and the child is given his surname and inheritance. Aeschylus' *Oresteia* depicts this transformation and how the father's rights were established over the mother's. In the play, Orestes stands before a judge for having murdered his mother. He is acquitted, not because he is innocent, but because there is no such thing as a mother. The god Apollo hands down his judgment:

> … That word mother—
> we give it to the one who bears the child.
> However, she's no parent, just a nurse
> to that new life embedded in her.
> The parent is the one who plants the seed,
> the father. Like a stranger for a stranger,
> she preserves the growing life, unless
> god injures it. And I can offer proof
> for what I say—a man can have a child
> without a mother (Aeschylus, 2007, p. 141).

It is striking to see how surrogacy so aptly realizes this patriarchal wishful thinking. The gestational surrogate mother is literally made into a container for the seed and a stranger to her own child. In an interview on a Swedish website, Fredrik Larsson, chairman of the Swedish Association for Surrogacy, says that the idea of parenthood needs to be revised:

> Today in Sweden, we have a prejudice about motherhood that means that the woman who gives birth to the child is considered the child's mother. I see it as more appropriate that whoever *takes the initiative* to have the child should be regarded as the child's parents. They are the ones who will be taking responsibility (Kolehmainen, 2008, my emphasis).

Just like Apollo, Fredrik Larsson questions the mother's rights. He believes that the woman who gives birth to the child should not necessarily have the right to be the mother. This is exactly the same ideology we find in the Bible, in Aeschylus' dramas and Aristotle's philosophy. According to Larsson, the mother should not even get to take care of the child, she should only bear him/her—not to the advantage of the father in his capacity as *Father*—but in his capacity as *Buyer*.

In this way, Fredrik Larsson has formulated a new type of patriarchal creation myth—a *capitalist* one. The father is not the man who begets a child, but the man who buys one ("takes the initiative"). The buyer does not even need to do the minimum that once was the man's duty—no physical contact with the woman is necessary. All he has to do is place an order. He donates his semen, and the child is born on the other side of the globe, bearing his name and carrying his genes.

Thus what is reified in surrogacy is not only the individual woman or the individual child—but life. Existence itself is commodified. When a child is produced via surrogacy, the market is pivotal *to the child's very existence.*

Surrogacy is therefore a comprehensive reification of our existence. In surrogacy, a transaction replaces intercourse as the source of life. Commodity exchange becomes the answer to a basic existential question: why do I exist? I exist because someone paid for me. In this capitalist creation story, the parent has become a consumer: *the parent is the one who pays.*

'For a Friend's Sake' – About Altruistic Surrogacy

Many people agree that it should not be possible to buy and sell pregnancy for money—but what if someone bears a child for a friend or a relative? What if a woman bears a child for her infertile sister, a mother gives birth to her infertile daughter's child or a friend of a homosexual couple offers to carry a child for them? Altruistic surrogacy is advocated by, for example, Birgitta Ohlsson of the Liberal Party of Sweden. She believes that altruistic surrogacy is completely different from commercial surrogacy. Other commentators think that we *must* legalize altruistic surrogacy if we are to avoid commercial surrogacy. "Allow surrogates in Sweden—otherwise people will look elsewhere," write RFSL's Juvas and Westerlund in their article in *Expressen* (2008). According to their argument, if we don't accept this 'milder' variant, we will instead get the 'worse' form in which Indian women are exploited. This is reminiscent of the distinction between prostitution and trafficking in which 'voluntary, humane sex work' is set against the forced and inhumane trafficking.

If it were just a matter of allowing one form of surrogacy in order to avoid another, we would never see Britons or Americans seek out the Indian market. The fact that altruistic surrogacy is legal in Great Britain and commercial surrogacy is legal in many American states ought to suffice to keep people from looking abroad, according to this argument. On the contrary, however, Americans and Britons are dominant amongst the foreign buyers in India (Pande, 2009). Americans who look to India explain their actions as follows: since surrogacy is well known and widely available in the USA, a doctor may advise them to try surrogacy after establishing infertility. When they begin to look into it, they find that it is expensive and since it is difficult to find someone who is willing to be a surrogate mother for free, they begin to consider India.[37]

There is no proof that altruistic surrogacy will hold back the commercial market. In fact, it is even difficult to prove that 'altruistic' is an accurate term. In England, where only reimbursement of expenses is allowed, surrogates often get around this by claiming they need "long vacations abroad and a whole new wardrobe" (Barbour, 2010). If the procedure is legalized—a woman will bear a child as laid out in a contract—the risk that a black market will develop increases. As Kelly Oliver has shown in her studies of American surrogacy, few people actually bear children for others completely without compensation (1992, p. 269). When some states in the USA banned commercial surrogacy, agencies noticed that the number of willing surrogates sank dramatically (Corea, 1985, p. 229). Just as trafficking is a *consequence* of prostitution and nothing else, commercial and altruistic surrogacy are different levels on the same scale.

The next question is, of course, whether altruistic surrogacy is more humane. Is it reasonable that a woman bears a child for someone else, with everything it involves, without receiving any compensation? Are familial relationships always equal, and do they

---

37 See, for example, 'Our journey to surrogacy in India—Blaze's story' at <http://ourjourneytosurrogacyinindia.blogspot.com>.

guarantee that things will be done right? In US child custody cases involving altruistic surrogacy, some women claim that they were manipulated and forced into surrogacy by their relatives (Saul, 2009).

In my opinion, the distinction between altruistic and commercial surrogacy is a dishonest one. There is not actually any difference. What happens is the same in both: the woman is reduced to a container. Altruistic surrogacy *functionalizes* motherhood, even when it doesn't *commercialize* it. Instead of being an existential and spiritual experience for the woman, pregnancy is made into a *function* to serve others.

Functionalization always precedes commercialization, as we have seen in prostitution. In order for something to be sold as separate from the seller, it must first be *constituted as a separate function*. What happens in the rhetoric of altruistic surrogacy is that it subversively accustoms people to seeing pregnancy as something a woman can lend to others—if she is not yet selling it.

CHAPTER SIX

Inside The Surrogate Industry

Uterus Pimps—About the Agencies

Proponents of surrogacy claim that it is completely different from prostitution. Agencies declare that potential surrogates are carefully investigated, and that only women who are determined to be appropriate candidates are approved. They must, for example, have had children before, their spouses must approve of the arrangement and they must pass psychological tests. Daniel Szpigler, the central figure of surrogat.nu, explains:

> Surrogates are middle-class women, have their own children and see it as a chance to help others and simultaneously earn a few bucks. Most of them are connected to a clinic where everything is taken care of, via lawyers and a supportive medical team (Szpigler, 2009).

How this actually comes about was revealed by journalist Susan Ince when she went undercover as a potential surrogate mother in the USA. In 'Inside the surrogate industry', she describes what happens when a woman applies to become a surrogate.

Ince answered an ad in a local newspaper. The agency had a good reputation and was well established. At the first meeting, the female director told moving stories about childless couples:

> The director did most of the talking. I was touched by her stories of infertile couples—the woman who displayed the scars of multiple

163

unsuccessful surgeries creating a tire-track pattern across her abdomen; the couple, now infertile, whose only biological child was killed by a drunk driver ... (1989, p. 100).

Ince was told that she would be interviewed and would speak with a psychologist and have a physical examination by a doctor. To become a 'traditional surrogate', she would be inseminated twice a month for six months. During this time, she would not be allowed to have intercourse. If she did not become pregnant, she would be removed from the program and would not receive any compensation beyond her expenses. Even if she did become pregnant but miscarried, there would be no compensation. If she were to give birth to a stillborn child, however, she would receive full compensation. The director explained that they were really looking for married women with children, because if a woman has already given birth, the chances of a positive outcome are higher. Still, the fact that Ince was single and childless did not pose a problem.

In the 'psychological test,' Ince was asked about her religious beliefs, her age, her eye color, her hair color and whether she had relatives in the area.

> [A]nd I was surprised to find he had no more questions. 'I just needed to be sure you're still positive 100 percent. You are, aren't you?' Without a nod or a word from me, he continued, 'You seem like it to me' ... Because I was 'obviously bright,' there would be no IQ testing. I was never asked whether I had been pregnant before, whether I was under medical or psychiatric treatment, or how I would feel about giving up the baby (1989, pp. 102–103).

Once the surrogate has signed the contract, she finds herself in the hands of the agency. She may not have intercourse, smoke or drink. She has to submit to all of the physical examinations and treatments the program prescribes. She has to have an amniocentesis, and in some cases, the buyers have the right to demand that she have an abortion if the results are abnormal—but not based on the sex of the child. If the surrogate herself changes her mind and wants to have an abortion, she can be accused of breach of contract and have to pay damages of 25,000 dollars (Ince, 1989, p. 107). While Szpigler assures us that 'everything is properly handled by lawyers and a supportive medical team', it was clear to Ince that the agency's lawyers are on the side of the agency and its clients—if the surrogate wants to have her own lawyer, it will be at her own expense, as will any litigation expenses. All actions that "can be seen as dangerous for the health of the unborn child" are deemed a breach of contract and the agency has the right to sue her. The medical team is not on her side, either: if the doctor prescribes a Caesarean section, the surrogate has no right to refuse it (Ince, 1989, p.106). The meaning of all of this is that the fetus that grows inside her is not hers—it is the buyers'. She is simply taking care of it for them.

Susan Ince began to ask questions, irritating the director who "admonished me for asking too many questions" (p. 108). Ince's conclusions about her undercover investigation were that anyone would be accepted as a surrogate just as long as she was fertile and seemed compliant. Scholar Olga van den Akker challenges the "reliable psychological tests," saying that they continue to be a myth. Women are not tested to see if they are psychologically stable but rather to see if they can be counted on being tractable about giving up the child (2007b).

In terms of 'work', surrogacy is not particularly lucrative. An American surrogate earns less than $1.50 per hour, and her Indian sisters earn barely half as much. The physical process which surrogates must undergo is complicated. In gestational surrogacy, they are subjected to multiple drug treatments. They have to inject themselves with hormones 2 to 3 times a day for 3 to 4 months (Ragoné, 1998, p. 122). To maximize the chances that a child will result, the doctor often implants more than one fertilized egg at a time, usually between 4 and 6. Because surrogates are younger and more fertile than other women who undergo in vitro fertilization, it is not uncommon for the result to be twins (Ragoné, 1998, p. 123). Twins often necessitate a Caesarean section. Women have become infertile as a result of serving as surrogates (Barbour, 2010). One woman tells of her attempt to become a surrogate mother:

I've experienced things that I never wanted to experience. My body has been pumped full of medications and poked and prodded. I've had a D&E and a natural miscarriage. And now, I'm done. I can't do it anymore no matter how much I love my IPs [intended parents] because my body just isn't working. I have lost tangible things like money and jobs that I didn't take because they wouldn't have been conductive [*sic*] to pregnancy. I have lost intangible things like time and days of my daughter's life when I was traveling or too wrapped up in hormonal meds to pay attention.[38]

The Most Surrogacy-Friendly Courts in the World

The point of moving the surrogacy industry to the developing world was not only to get the cheapest prices, but also to avoid child custody cases. The agencies learned their lesson from the 'Baby M' case in the USA: it was important not to give the birth mother too much time to think. But while a surrogate mother or egg donor in Great Britain has the right to make a claim to the child during the first two years, women in India relinquish their rights in the hospital immediately after childbirth. Their decision is irrevocable. We Care India, a company offering medical tourism and surrogacy, assures Western couples that the law is on their side:

> Indian courts are the most surrogacy-friendly in this part of the world. In fact, the courts have consistently upheld the intended parents' rights when they have chosen to use a surrogate or egg donor, regardless of whether they have used their own genetic material, donor ovum, or donated sperm.[39]

In India, the parties involved have virtually no more contact than a buyer of a mobile phone has with the factory worker who made it. The birth mother and the buyers often only meet once in the introductory period, and sometimes not even then. After that, all contact takes place via the clinic. Sometimes the surrogate doesn't even know what country the child in her womb will end up in, and

---

38 <http://www.surromomsonline.com/support/showthread.php?t=158332>

39 We Care India (n.d.) <http://www.indiahospitaltour.com/surrogacy/surrogacy-facts-india.html> accessed 26 April 2013.

her own information is not always saved, making it difficult if the child ever wants to contact her when s/he grows up (Vora, 2009).

An important in-depth study of the Indian surrogate industry was conducted by Amrita Pande from the University of Massachusetts. She is herself of Indian descent and spent nine months at a clinic in Gujarat, conducting 42 detailed interviews with surrogates (Pande, 2009). Some women, Pande states, decided on their own to become surrogates and were aware of what it would entail. But she also tells of women who don't speak English, who don't understand the details of the contract—written in English— who are sometimes forced by their husbands to become surrogates and who, having neither money nor lawyers, have no access to their legal rights (Pande, 2009). Because primarily gestational surrogacy is practiced in India, the women must go through comprehensive hormonal treatments to prepare their bodies for embryo implantation.

Surrogate mother Gauri tells Amrita Pande that no one really prepared her for the experience (2009, p. 147–148):

> The only thing they told me when I came in was that this thing is not immoral, I will not have to sleep with anyone and that the seed will be transferred into me with an injection. They also said that I have to keep the child inside me, rest for the whole time, have medicines on time, and give up the child.
> We are not really told much about the medicines and injections. In the beginning I used to get ten-ten injections that hurt so much, along with the pills required to make me strong for the pregnancy. We [her husband and she] are not as educated as you are, you know. I won't really understand much else! And I trust Doctor Madam, so I don't ask.

The women live in apartment-hotels for the duration of their pregnancies. According to the contract, the buyers have the right to demand that they submit to medical check-ups—and, if they become pregnant with twins, force them to have either an abortion or a medical reduction of one of the fetuses. The pregnant women's existence is regulated in the minutest detail. In a society with almost non-existent prenatal care for poor women, surrogates are treated as if they were as fragile as glass. Women sleep nine to a room, are not allowed to go downstairs and must have permission from the clinic to leave the hotel (Hochschild, 19 September 2009).

One myth spread by proponents of surrogacy is that the Indian women come from the middle class. Swedish Conservative MPs Christer G. Wennerholm, Jenny Edberg and Fredrik Sawaståhl write in a placating tone:

> Our opponents believe that poor women from the Third World are at risk of being exploited. The experiences of Swedish couples who have had biological children with the help of Indian surrogates show the opposite: that these women come from an ever-growing Indian middle class (Wennerholm *et al.*, 2008).

What the clinics might have told the Swedish customers is one thing, but 'middle class' is hardly a suitable description of the Indian women who become surrogates. Amrita Pande reports that 34 of the 42 women she interviewed had a family income that was at or below the poverty line (2009). According to Pande, their average income is 2,500 rupees per month *per family*. That is just over 45 USD each month for a family that may consist of up to eight or ten people. The director, Dr. Khanderia, told Pande (2009, p. 166):

> I had to educate them about everything because, you see, all these women are poor illiterate villagers. I told them, 'You have to do nothing. It's not your baby. You are just providing it a home in your womb for nine months because it doesn't have a house of its own. If some child comes to stay with you for just nine months what will you do? You will take care of it even more because it is someone else's. This is the same thing. You will take care of the baby for nine months and then give it to its mother. And for that you will be paid.' I think finally how you train them, showing the positive experiences of both the parties, is what makes surrogacy work.

In an interview in *The Wall Street Journal*, some Indian women recall what led them to surrogacy. Sudha, a 25-year-old mother of two, had borrowed money to use as bribes so she could get a job as a street sweeper. When she didn't get the job, surrogacy was a way she could pay back her debts. Lakhsmi, 29 years old, has two children and an alcoholic husband, and debts totaling 4,000 USD. For her, the 'choice' was either to sell a kidney or become a surrogate. A doctor advised her to opt for surrogacy: "[W]ith a single kidney left, I might live for a shorter time. I have a daughter. I have to get her married ... I prefer to be a surrogate" she says (in Cohen, 2009). Anjali, just 20 years old, has "no idea about the money involved in the contract or the exact medical procedures. Her husband seems to be the one in control of the finances" (in Pande, 2009). Salma tells Amrita Pande (p. 141):

> Who would choose to do this? I have had a lifetime's worth of injections pumped into me. Some big ones in my hips hurt so much. In the beginning I had about 20–25 pills almost every day. I feel bloated all the time. But I know I have to do it for my children's future. This is not work, this is *majboori* (a compulsion). Where we are now, it can't possibly get any worse. (She uses a local proverb.) In our village we don't have a hut to live in or crops in our farm. This work is not ethical—it's just something we have to do to survive. When we heard of this surrogacy business, we didn't have any clothes to wear after the rains—just one pair that used to get wet—and our house had fallen down. What were we to do?

The United Nations Development Programme (UNDP) warns that human trafficking for the purpose of surrogacy will eventually develop (UNDP, 2009). Indian lawyer Anil Malhotra, an international law expert, writes that "exploitation, extortion, and ethical abuses in surrogacy trafficking are rampant, go undeterred and surrogate mothers are often misused with impunity" (Malhotra, 2008).

Nevertheless, custody battles are still waged in India. The former Indian Minister of Women and Child Development said in an interview in *The Telegraph* that "custody cases often occur between surrogates and the paying couple" (2008). Not all of them arise because birth mothers become attached to the child; the opposite also occurs: the buyers don't want the child they have paid for. When a child becomes a 'thing' that can be ordered via the internet, there is also the risk of buyer's remorse, second thoughts about the 'purchase'. This has happened, for example, when the mother has given birth to twins and the buyers only agree to take one child (in Whitehead, 1989, p. 14). In other cases, buyers have refused a child because it is developmentally delayed (Corea, 1985, p. 219). In one very publicized case from 2008, a heterosexual Japanese couple had used an Indian woman as a surrogate. During the pregnancy, however, the couple divorced, and when the child was born, they didn't want it any longer. According to Indian law, the mother must be present for the child to receive a passport, and therefore the child remained at the hospital in India. Pictures of the child's Japanese grandmother watching over the cradle in India were circulated all over the world as a symbol for the complexity of such an arrangement. According to the Indian authorities, these cases don't prove that there is anything wrong with the practice, only that it requires clearer regulation.

"If I do feel sad after the birth, I won't show it"

Because a surrogate acts as a container for the embryo, she is not expected to become attached to the child. Her feelings after the separation are seen as a passing affliction. "If I do feel sad after the birth, I won't show it" says surrogate mother Vohra, one of the many women waiting to give birth in Nayna Patel's clinic in Anand (Haworth, 2007). Ulrika Westerlund, who advocates surrogacy, explains that "surrogates did not have any problems with giving up the child, and the child developed in the same way as other children" (2008).

In both the Indian and the American surrogacy industries, women are coached to be detached from the children they carry. American agencies follow women during their entire pregnancies "to ensure that they understand whose child they are carrying and giving up," writes scholar Olga van den Akker (2007a, p. 56). In the USA, it is normal for surrogate mothers to attend support groups arranged by the agencies, where they learn the art of being pregnant without relating to the developing child. While support groups can be positive places where a woman can meet others in the same situation, they also function as training camps where women learn which feelings are 'right' and which are 'wrong'. A woman who expresses herself in an unacceptable way may be reported to the agency (Tong, 1992, p. 277). There are similar arrangements in India, where surrogates receive a short training course in the art of distancing themselves. According to anthropologist Kalindi Vora (2009, p. 9):

> This is meant to help them both to understand that surrogacy does not involve their bodies sexually, and also to encourage them to emotionally distance themselves from the fetus and the child they will deliver. Through counseling and conversation, medical personnel encourage surrogates to see themselves as gestation-providers whose only link to the fetus is the renting of a womb imagined as an empty and otherwise unproductive space.

Surrogates all over the world—regardless of whether they speak of surrogacy in positive or negative terms—tell of the techniques of turning off their emotions. First and foremost, this has to do with *creating a mental distance* and can be done in various ways, using techniques such as ignoring, turning off, or transferring feelings to someone else. In Heléna Ragoné's study, skin color is a major factor used by surrogates to distance themselves from the child. Black and Mexican women therefore prefer to carry white and Japanese children. Ragoné writes (1998, p. 127):

> My preliminary findings suggest that the majority of gestational surrogates do not object to and may actually find it desirable to be matched with a couple from a different racial background. One of the reasons for this preference, as mentioned earlier, is that racial/ethnic difference provides more 'distance' between them, a degree of separation the gestational surrogate is able to place between herself and the child.

Ragoné interviews Linda, a Mexican-American woman, who says that the fetus in her body "is totally Japanese. It is a little hard for me. In some way, she will always be my Japanese girl, but she is theirs" (1998, p. 125). A different skin color, a different ethnicity, makes the separation easier to manage. Ragoné sees this as one of the positive sides of surrogacy—that races mix. Except that they don't at all, because the buyers' intent is that the black or Mexican woman will not 'rub off' onto the child, and skin color is used by the birth mother as a way to create distance rather than attachment.

Women can also try to transfer their feelings to their own children. Geeta from India, who is pregnant with a 'Caucasian' couple's child—she doesn't know what country they come from—explains it this way to Arlie Hochschild (19 September 2009): "'I keep myself from getting too attached', she says. 'Whenever I start to think about the baby inside me, I turn my attention to my own daughter. Here she is'. She bounces the child on her lap. 'That way, I manage'."

The most widely used strategy is to repeat: "It is not my child." As one 30-year-old surrogate describes it:

When you go into a surrogacy you have to have a certain mindset. These children aren't yours. They were never yours. You have no rights to them. I know my role in all of this. I'm simply a babysitter for my great friend, T. This is her baby. I'm simply watching over and taking care of him until he's born.[40]

This attitude is very typical amongst surrogates. Law professor Lori B. Andrews explains (1995, p. 2,352):

In my interviews with surrogate mothers, I found that they did not refer to the fetus as 'my baby', as do biological mothers in the context of adoption, but as the intended parents' baby ... When they talked to their pregnant bellies, they said 'This is what your parents are doing today'—referring to the infertile couple.

Repeating that the child belongs to someone else is the surrogate world's most popular mantra. Like the prostitute who says "my body is not myself," the surrogate says "the child is not mine." But in order to mentally construct the child as an individual of its own, an individual who furthermore *belongs to someone else*, the woman

---

40 The Life of a Surrogate Mother (29 January 2009) 'Bad surrogacy story revisited' <http://surrolife.blogspot.com/2010/01/bad-surrogacy-story-revisited.html>.

makes *a part of herself* into something that belongs to someone else. This is reification: a part of the Self is made into 'something else' that belongs to 'someone else'. Now, the fact that some children don't grow up with the women who gave birth to them and call another woman 'Mom' is in itself nothing new. But in the surrogacy situation, the child is *intended* for someone else even while existing in the woman's body. In this way, surrogacy is an extended form of reification. Few workers would say that their hands or feet are not their own, as prostitutes or surrogates insist that parts of their bodies *are not themselves.*

In order to sell a part of herself, the surrogate, like the prostitute, must distance herself from it. Anyone familiar with prostitution who listens carefully to what the surrogate is saying will notice the many similarities between their coping strategies. But where prostitution research has put words to these emotions, surrogacy research has hardly noticed them. No one has expressed any *concern* about surrogate mothers dissociating. On the contrary— researchers state that this distancing is exactly what proves that surrogacy works. The best surrogate is the one who feels the least.

The Ultimate Reification

Surrogacy is the trade in women's bodies, but it is, in some ways, a 'softer' trade than prostitution. The occurrence of violence, murder, drug abuse, homelessness and sexual exploitation is lower. Mortality is considerably lower, even though some surrogates have died during childbirth (*Daily Mail*, 29 January 2005). At the same time, the reification is much more extensive. Philosopher and Marxist Kelly Oliver writes that most people would perceive a job carried out around the clock as slavery:

> Most people do not perform their services 24 hours a day unless they are slaves. And most people only sell their labor, labor performed by the body, perhaps but distinguishable from it. Surrogates, on the other hand, perform their services 24 hours a day and sell the body itself (1992, p. 268).

Surrogacy is ongoing for at least nine months, day in and day out. During this time, the woman must abide by a host of restrictions. She is not allowed to exert herself, smoke, drink or take drugs. She must, if the buyers wish, submit to medical tests. Her body goes through numerous changes, she deals with morning sickness, her stomach grows, she can suffer various complaints such as back pain—not to mention the labor and birth itself. She can't escape from any of this; she can't take a break from it for even one minute. She is in it, and it is in her. 'The work' is her very existence, 24/7. For although she lives in symbiosis with the child, she doesn't have the least bit of power over it because the child belongs to someone else. Indian surrogates, it seems, are sometimes not even worthy of knowing what country the child will live in. Surrogacy is thus not something one *does*, it is something one *is*: a being who can be bought.

Karl Marx wrote that a person who works in a capitalist system is estranged in four ways: from nature, from his/her own role in the production process, from the social aspects of work and from other people (Marx, 2003, pp. 64–66). A person who produces goods in a capitalist system does not see his/her work as an integrated part of life in a society. Work—those activities through which a person creates civilization and culture—could be a source of pleasure for a person, where s/he can feel like a creative being. But in capitalism, where a person *sells* his/her labors to another, the work instead becomes something 'other' and s/he is reduced to a machine. We all know how the world's most exciting activity suddenly becomes boring and monotonous when it is labeled 'work'. As Marx writes: "The worker puts his life into the object; but now his life no longer belongs to him but to the object" (2003, p. 59). Work often becomes a necessary evil and a person takes refuge in leisure time—which is when s/he can feel like a whole person. By extension, if we judge people according to what they do (work) instead of what they are (being), we split the human Self into disconnected fragments.

Kelly Oliver believes that surrogacy is something so deeply alienating that even Marx' definitions are too narrow (1992, p. 275). The surrogate is not only estranged from nature, the fruits of her labor and other people around her, but also from her own body and the child growing inside her. The alienation is direct, not indirect. This is why it is so treacherous when philosophers like Kutte Jönsson try to acknowledge the critique of surrogacy but are unable to see the difference between a factory and a female body:

> There are those who, for example, fear that the surrogate industry, which follows the principles of mass production, will lead to surrogates being alienated from their *products* in the same way as the labor force is alienated from production in capitalism (Jönsson, 2003, p. 208, my emphasis).

Jönsson wants to show empathy for the situation of the mothers and children at the same time as he alienates them from each other on a deeper level. His worst possible scenario is that the surrogate becomes like any other worker and is alienated *in the same way as* the worker. But such criticism begs Jönsson to counter: If we are already alienated and sell ourselves in all kinds of ways, why would this be any different? It is like comparing a prostitute to a secretary who sells the use of her hands—these aren't apples and apples. But the point is that there is a dramatic difference in surrogacy, and Kutte Jönsson completely ignores it. He compares the child, *a living being and a part of the living woman*, to a product a worker makes outside of his/her body. That he is not able to differentiate between internal and external, or between person and thing, becomes shamefully obvious when he writes "product" instead of child.

Prostitution and surrogacy cause an immediate short circuit in Marxist theories about alienation and reification. The work doesn't *feel like* selling oneself—the person *literally* sells herself. This is why comparisons with other jobs seem so strange. To compare one's job with prostitution says a whole lot about the job, but to compare prostitution with work doesn't tell us anything about prostitution. Correspondingly, 'I slave away at my job' can be a description of working, but anyone who calls slavery a job has not understood much about slavery. Kelly Oliver writes about the surrogate who, contrary to other workers, is not an appendage of the machine. She *is* the machine (1992, p. 275).

Marx wrote that when work in the capitalist system becomes mechanized, the worker takes refuge in leisure time and 'animal pleasures'—eating, drinking, sleeping, having sex. It is a paradox, then, that we should feel human when we act like animals, but feel 'mechanical' when we engage in that genuinely human act of creating and producing a new life. But even leisure time becomes impossible for the surrogate, as Oliver notes, and she is therefore doubly estranged (1992, p. 276).

Whereas people in prostitution can escape by living destructively, all mechanisms of creating a physical distance are impossible for the surrogate. She can't cut the time short or stop being pregnant for an afternoon. She cannot create an alter ego, even if she uses a false name (Ragoné, 1994, p. 103). She cannot escape by taking drugs, smoking and drinking—she has to take care of herself. She must live for the child, think of the child in every daily action. Simultaneously, she must create distance between herself and her body, between herself and the child she bears— because a person must always make a distinction between what is her being and what is being bought. She must care about the child, but not get attached to it. And this may be the hardest part: to sell yourself and yet have to be kind to yourself. In prostitution, drugs and alcohol are a form of self-medication to more easily cope with selling yourself. But the surrogate cannot numb her body. She cannot turn off her daughter's kicks—but she must not relate to her. She cannot distance herself from her son or daughter in the same way as a prostitute can distance herself from a john.

What are you to do in a situation in which you have to distance yourself from a part of yourself (and your Self) at the same time as you have to take care of it, and care about it?

The Virgin Mary in the Marketplace

In surrogacy, pregnancy and childbirth are made into work and submitted to the rules of the marketplace. It is partially this adaptation to the marketplace that makes proponents enthusiastic: motherhood is no longer sacred—it is a commodity just like everything else!

But the surrogate doesn't see herself as a worker; quite the contrary. Of all the studies I have read and time I have spent on British and American surrogate forums on the internet, I have not heard a single surrogate mother talk about it as work. Instead, they speak of emotional motivation. They emphasize their generosity, talk of wanting to help, of heeding a call. Even though few women are willing to become surrogates without compensation, the women say that they don't do it for the money (Oliver, 1989, p. 269). In an English study of 34 surrogates, only 3 of the women said they did it for the money, while the others said that they mostly "wanted to help a childless couple" (Jadva *et al.*, 2003). Lori B. Andrews, who interviewed surrogates in the USA, writes that almost all of them found that the greatest payment was "the creation of a family, giving the gift of life, seeing the beautiful baby or seeing the couple's happiness" (1995, p. 2,353). The women she interviewed spoke of "the tremendous psychic benefits they received from the feeling that they were helping someone meet a joyous life goal" (p. 2,354).

The women Heléna Ragoné interviewed spoke of a "mission", "a sacred obligation" and "the ultimate act of love" (Ragoné, 1994, pp. 40–41). According to scholars Ciccarelli and Beckman, it is something women do for "altruistic reasons" and because they have "empathy for childless couples and want to help others experience the great joy of parenthood" (2005, p. 30). An often-cited American study by Betsy Aigen, *Motivations of Surrogate Mothers*, includes 90-minute interviews with each of 200 potential surrogates. Aigen claims that "being a surrogate is a life experience that allows some women real success in altering their emotional state in a direction they desire and fulfilling ideal images of themselves." Money is not their most important motivation, she writes; "it is, for these women, a particularly female experience" (1996).

This perspective is universally admired by scholars. That women don't do it for the money makes surrogacy a little more humane, makes it feel a little less market-driven. The industry takes on a human face; it can even be presented as an idealistic charity movement comprised of good-hearted souls. The scholars' enthusiasm over the women's goodness may be explained by the fact that a number of them are funded by the industry. Betsy Aigen, who owns the agency Childbirth Consultation Services, was a founder of the American Association for Surrogate Agencies and herself has two children who were borne by surrogates.[41] The interviews presented in her study are actually employment interviews with potential surrogates. Lori B. Andrews, as board member of the American Bar Association (ABA), has taken a clear position in favor of surrogacy and pushes campaigns for buyers' rights to keep the child even when the surrogate has changed her mind (Scott, 2009, p. 136, footnote 166). Other scholars have only spoken with the women once, sometimes only by telephone and for a maximum of two hours (Ragoné, 1994, p. 7).

We should, perhaps, be careful about believing that these researchers are interested in uncovering deeper truths about surrogacy. Rather, they confirm the overall story used by surrogate mothers to explain the experience. And it isn't about work; it is the story of the *Virgin Mary*.

In this story we find four central points: 1) the surrogate gives birth without having had sex; 2) she does it only to give joy to a childless couple; 3) she requires nothing for herself except to see the other couple's happiness; 4) she is happily married and lives in a nuclear family. Far from Kutte Jönsson's dreams of surrogacy driving "a wedge through conservative family norms," the surrogate world is permeated with a strong belief in the 'Holy Family'. I have never felt so close to a conservative nuclear family norm than during the time I've spent on online American and British surrogate forums. The surrogate's duty is clear: to have a selfless nature, be a loyal wife and give birth to many children. Women are

---

41 <http://www.donorconcierge.com/motivations-of-surrogate-mothers-parenthood-altruism-and-self-actualization-author-dr-betsy-p-aigen-a-three-year-study>

valued according to how many children they have borne—both for themselves and for others.

On most internet forums, surrogates introduce themselves with profiles of their accomplishments. There is a photo of the woman herself and her children, as well as information about her family relationships and how many children she has given birth to. Examples include: "Michele, wife of Ethan, mom to Kailee and Stephen, GS X 1, TS X 4," which means that Michele has two children who live with her (Kailee and Stephen), has borne and given away four children through traditional surrogacy ('TS')—insemination—and one via gestational surrogacy ('GS')—embryo transplantation. And: "[D]evoted wife and mother in Texas, pregnant with twins for P&F." Another reads: "Ann, happily married mother of 4, GS X 1 twins 2009, GS X 2 for E&W" which means that Ann has four of her own children, gave birth to twins via embryo transplantation and is currently in her second gestational surrogacy for a couple with the initials E and W. (A rule on surrogate forums is that the buyers' names are never revealed.) The woman is always 'happily married' and a 'loving wife'. Many are housewives or write about how they wish they could be, if their husbands could afford it. A striking number of their husbands are serving in the military in Iraq or Afghanistan. In almost all of the profiles, the women say they have a happy nuclear family and stress how much they love to give other families the same family happiness. Sometimes the women sell other reproductive functions. Some say they donate eggs. Others sell their breast milk, sometimes to a couple that have just received a 'surrogate' baby.

The surrogate world has its own jargon. It has similarities with the world of prostitution in its use of obliquely technical abbreviations for everything physical, like 'TS'—traditional surrogacy—for those women who are inseminated and give birth to their own genetic children, 'ED' for egg donors and 'BFP' (Big Fat Positive) for a positive pregnancy test. That women *de facto* sell their own flesh and blood for money is made manageable via the abbreviation 'TS': it is technical, short and doesn't remind us of what actually happens—in the same way as the 'service' of being pissed on is comfortably called 'uro' in prostitution. But the surrogate claims emphatically that she is not a prostitute. Quite the contrary: she is not sexual at all. When a woman who was said to have worked as a stripper enlisted as a surrogate, many on the forum Surromomsonline reacted thus: "She is a stripper and heavy drinker!" or "WOW!!!!!!!!!!!! That is scary about where she is known from!!!!"[42] And an Indian surrogate justifies her decision in contrast to prostitution: "At least I am not like some other women who have [sexual] relations for money, just because they are so desperate" (in Pande, 2009)—in other words, because surrogates don't have sex, they are better than prostitutes.

Here it is not the entrepreneur but the good mother who is the ideal. If the 'happy hooker' can be said to be an enterprising and clever woman, the 'happy breeder' would describe herself as a generous and self-sacrificing Madonna figure. Kutte Jönsson may call the child a product and praise a society where nothing is too holy to have a price tag—but the surrogate would absolutely never do this. She makes all of surrogacy into a sacred calling. An overwhelming number of American surrogates are deeply religious and have a Christian background. Many are Catholics and, even though the Vatican does not approve of surrogacy, these women speak of surrogacy as a religious duty. One woman believes that surrogacy is to "honor God's gift to me by giving back the gift" (in Hanafin, 1987). Laschell, surrogate for the third time, claims that surrogacy is a way to rectify one's sins (ChristiaNet, 27 February 2009):

> I feel God has given me this gift not to be selfish but to give back to my brothers and sisters that are unable to conceive on their own. Dont [sic] you think that's why God gives us 'special gifts'? I do. He wants us to share and love each other so I do. I am a sinner, but I am grateful that I have Christ in my life to forgive my sins and take my sins from me.

---

42 <http://surromomsonline.com/support/showthread.php?t=59122&highlight=stripper>

Even when pregnancy is made into work, *it is too painful to see it as a job*. It must have a protective, concealing façade. And what works better than the cult of the Virgin Mary? In this way, surrogacy gains a saintly dimension. The cult of the Virgin Mary lets the woman forget that it is work. The cult of the Virgin Mary soothes the loss of the child by making the surrogate even more motherly in her own mind. Even if the superstructure of the surrogacy myth is all about stating that the women 'are not mothers' to the children they bear, these women cultivate the idea that they become *even more motherly* by giving up their children. The cult of the Virgin Mary allows the surrogate to feel pious, clean and exalted, because she becomes a model of the most archetypal mother Western culture has. The cult of the Virgin Mary is the defense mechanism of the surrogate industry, defending surrogates against the view that women sell their bodies and their children. It is encouraged by agencies that urge women to "give the gift of life" and advertise: "It's not about the money, it's about the experience."

The story of the Virgin Mary is a story of exaltation. It is about a woman of the people who, through divine intervention, becomes pregnant with the son of God. Through this, she is canonized. She is married, but her spouse is faithful, asexual and supportive. He will not risk getting in the way of the virgin birth. Mary becomes a saint because she has not had sex, because she isn't an unmarried mother, because the child's father is God. And because she doesn't require anything for herself, giving the child up for a higher purpose.

If we look at surrogacy, we see that it strangely contains the very same ideological elements. The surrogate is a married woman from a lower class who gives birth to a child without having sex. Her husband doesn't get in the way; he defers to the other man. The woman gives up the child who must go away, if not to Heaven then to a notably higher social class. Suffering is also a central element of surrogacy: the woman risks her life and her health and becomes a martyr for a sacred cause. One woman recalls (Ragoné, 1994, p. 62):

I had a rough delivery, a C-section, and my lung collapsed because I had the flu, but it was worth every minute of it. If I were to die from childbirth, that's the best way to die. You died for a cause, a good one.

But where does this need to be like the Virgin Mary come from? And why must the Virgin Mary suffer? Why do these women sacrifice themselves, put up with everything that pregnancy entails: pain, childbirth and hormones for nine months—just for a smile on the faces of a mystery couple? The official explanation in the surrogate world is that it is simply female nature. The idea that this insane risk-taking is some sort of typically female action hovers over the surrogate industry like a thin, fluttering film. But if we wash away this film of traditional gender myths, we see that under this longing to be the Virgin Mary often lies deep pain.

Pain and sacrifice are not just something these women have to put up with because they are being paid. Pain and sacrifice are *the whole point* (van den Akker, 2007a). As one surrogate says: "Not everyone can do it. It's like the steelworkers who walk on beams ten floors up; not everyone can do it, not everyone can be a surrogate" (Ragoné, 1998, p. 128). She is proud of having gone through pains that few others would be able to endure. Another woman says that she loved her son so much that she gave birth to him and gave him away (Ragoné, 1994, p. 41). Love, to her, means sacrificing what you love.

Why this pain? One of many reasons can be that childhood sexual assault survivors and women who have lost a child are overrepresented amongst surrogates (Ciccarelli and Beckman, 2005). If a person has experienced a great deal of pain in life, s/he may begin to seek out pain. Feminist psychotherapist Phyllis Chesler, who has treated surrogates, writes that surrogacy is, for many, a way to cleanse themselves of guilt and shame (1988, p. 45). Christian motives such as guilt, cleanliness, forgiveness, asexuality, motherhood, innocence and sacrifice of children in order to demonstrate one's faith all come together in surrogacy. Chesler writes that a woman may have been a victim of incest, had an abortion, or given a child up for adoption. She feels guilty. To be a good woman, she sacrifices her body. She has found the perfect way to atone for her sins. It is similar to prostitution, but without the sexual shame: she suffers, subordinates herself, sacrifices her body. The archetypes of the virgin and the whore are similar in that they represent women who *give*, who offer themselves as a gift to the world and whose resources are endless. And is this not the classic female way to try to set things right? To suffer for a better world? To sacrifice our bodies in order to satisfy others? To identify pain with goodness? To believe that something good will come of our pain, that our wounds shall free us from a guilt that will otherwise never stop weighing us down?

Unfortunately, women are rarely compensated for this type of masochistic sacrifice. Having given up a child can lead to even greater feelings of guilt—am I a bad mother, will they take care of the child, what will s/he think of me? Many surrogates describe a mixture of grief, longing, guilt, and emptiness. The solution is often to go through the whole procedure again. As many as 30% want to become surrogates again, according to Heléna Ragoné. American doctors have begun to speak of an addiction (Ragoné, 1994, p. 82). Because surrogacy was the answer to the first problem, it is also the answer to its own problem. It becomes a never-ending circle of losses, where the woman recreates the feeling of wholeness with the child she lost just to lose it again and start over from the beginning.

Many people who are critical of prostitution and surrogacy point to economic coercion. They use arguments like: 'As long as poverty exists, women will be forced to become prostitutes and surrogates; it is not a free choice because they have few other possibilities'. This is correct in many cases, but sometimes the money is simply unimportant. The goal can be to harm oneself, to punish oneself. Prostitution and surrogacy accomplish this: two industries feed off women's self-destructiveness. They are industries that have everything to win by celebrating our destructive tendencies as positive and admirable; they are industries that do not hesitate to play on women's self-sacrificing tendencies. One Indian surrogate agency encourages women to become surrogates so they can see the smiles on the Western couple's faces:

> Share Your Motherhood
> Unlike the western countries, we understand the awareness in Indian people and the myths they believe in. This decision of yours is indeed the most rewarding act of kindness in history of human mankind ... At the end of nine months, you feel, its 'YOU', who can gave happiness & smiles to the other couple.[43]

Women who Change their Minds: "I am not a surrogate; I am a mother"

The woman who gave surrogacy a face in the USA was Elizabeth Kane, mother of three. In 1980, she became the USA's first legal surrogate by being inseminated and then giving birth to a child for a childless couple who contacted her via an agency. During the pregnancy, she went public and talked about her decision. She said that she wasn't doing it for the money, but to help a childless couple. Even though her husband, her friends and her mother were against it, she stood by her decision.

In Elizabeth Kane, the agencies had found the perfect poster woman and they displayed her on talk shows and in reports. One month after the birth, she spoke out in *People Magazine* about what she saw as "a pure gift of love," saying that her happiness only came from "knowing that he is home, and that his Christmas gifts will be under another tree" (in Moore Hall, 1980). She said that she had no anguish over giving up the child:

> The joy I had received from seeing him in their arms would last a lifetime. Before I left Louisville I went to court and signed papers dissolving any legal rights I had to the baby, and once again I felt good. I knew that this was the most important day for his new parents, and I went home with no regrets at all.

---

43 <http://www.surrogacyindia.com/s_Surrogatebenefits.html> accessed 6 February 2013.

Kane told of experiencing negative reactions from those closest to her, but even so, she never doubted her decision: "I always knew I was doing the right thing, as a woman and a Christian." Kane became the emblem of the good surrogate and those who came after her both spoke and acted remarkably like Kane.

Six years later, Elizabeth Kane had changed her mind. Together with 17 other American surrogates, she founded the National Coalition Against Surrogacy (Allis, 1995). In 1988, her biography *Birth Mother* was published, further confirming her position against surrogacy. In the book, Kane describes how she had gotten "high" on personifying the image of the good, generous woman (p. 277): "I understand now that it was important to me to project an apple-pie image to the public. I wanted to make surrogacy work so much that I refused to let myself feel or think negatively about my decision to have Justin."

Kane introduces her biography by telling how she, as a young, unmarried mother, had given up her newborn daughter for adoption. With this experience behind her, she was certain that she could 'manage' surrogacy—she had already given up one child. At first, everything felt fantastic: "For months following the birth I was euphoric. I would get high just remembering the look on Adam's and Margo's faces as they held their son in the delivery room" (p. 276).

But after all of the attention around her had died down and the buyers had settled in with the child, she went into a deep depression.

> Time lost all meaning after June 1981. I cannot honestly say how long my depression lasted. It could have been six months or twelve. Perhaps eighteen. I became obsessed with Justin's absence. I knew where he was, but I could not reach out to him. He belonged to another woman and my heart was slowly turning into stone ... The depression soon grew into fantasies of my death (p. 277).

It took six years for Elizabeth Kane to process the events and to be able to say to herself that "I missed my son, that I had never gotten over the loss of him and that surrogate motherhood was a terrible mistake" (p. 285). She sums up surrogacy succinctly:

> I now believe that surrogate motherhood is nothing more than the transference of pain from one woman to another. One woman is in anguish because she cannot become a mother, and another woman may suffer for the rest of her life because she cannot know the child she bore for someone else (p. 275).

Kane's story is typical in many ways. During the pregnancy, the surrogate is the center of attention. The buyers are concerned about her health, buy presents for her and take her along to restaurants and on excursions. She is special. She is valuable. She is bearing their child. Because the child is inside her, the buyers want to get along well with her. Many surrogates say that they enjoy the attention. Because the buyers come from a higher social class, the woman gets a temporary peek into another walk of life. "They were pretty well off and they spoiled me rotten," one woman tells Ragoné. Others say they learned to sail, could swim in the buyers' pool every other weekend and were invited on a two-week, all-expense-paid trip to Hawaii (Ragoné, 1994, pp. 68–69).

But as soon as the umbilical cord is cut and the child is given up, the birth mother is out of the picture. She returns to her normal life as a housewife or at a poorly paid job. No one calls her every day to hear what she ate or how she slept. She is no longer special; she returns to being just another person. Her power over others has dissolved. It is then that the feeling of having been exploited can come rushing in. 'Mervl' describes her feelings after the birth:

> I was upset at the hospital because my FIPs [the intended parents] wouldn't let me hold my surro son, and then it hurt me quite a bit when they handed me my final comp check just seconds (literally) after I signed the adoption papers. And when we were leaving, it was my attorney that convinced my FIPs to let me hold my surro son one last time. But with everyone staring at me, I didn't dare cuddle him much or give him a kiss as I had desired to do. Upon leaving, they got him into the car quickly, so I just rushed (as quickly as I could being just a few days post-c/s) into our car and hid my face as I cried.

THAT and then later realizing they weren't going to hold up their end of the bargain with sending photos/updates often—that is what hurt and made things hard.[44]

Many surrogate mothers continue to ask for pictures of the child, about milestones and his/her health, just "whatever, it doesn't take much time to send a message," vents one woman.[45] On the surrogate forum, a majority of the women have installed a clock that ticks and shows their surrogate child's age to the second. Even women who have carried a child for a friend or relative can have these same feelings. Sherrie, who gave birth to a child for her infertile sister, writes:

> I can't describe the depth of sadness I felt when I came home without the child I loved, carried within me, and gave birth to. It was as if I had a child die ... I knew I would never try to keep the baby for myself. I could never hurt my sister like that. I just couldn't help but love this child like my own, because it was my own ... As I watched their car driving away that day on the gravel road, I felt like the dust left behind to scatter in the corn fields.[46]

The buyers' and industry's greatest fear is that the woman will keep the child. In most countries with legalized surrogacy, except India, there is a waiting period during which time the birth mother is allowed to change her mind. A report from the British Department of Health estimates that 4 to 5% of surrogates change their minds and refuse to give up the child (in Edelmann, 2004). Mary Beth Whitehead, mother of 'Baby M', writes about her process (1989, pp. 11–12):

> The clinic's staff told me how wonderful I was. They said: 'This couple will thank you for the rest of their lives and will always think of you' ... Looking back, I now believe that the praise was a form of brainwashing. Over and over, the staff told me that it was the 'couple's

---

44 <http://www.surromomsonline.com/support/showthread.php?t=160016& page=2> post from 8 February 2010, accessed 5 December 2012.

45 <http://www.surromomsonline.com/support/showthread.php?t=160016& page=2> post from 8 February 2010, accessed 5 December 2012.

46 <http://www.fertilitystories.com/sherrie.htm> accessed 5 December 2012.

baby' … They never said that it was Betsy who would actually be the surrogate mother, since she was the one who wished to substitute for me … It wasn't until I delivered my daughter that I fully comprehended the fact that it wasn't Betsy Stern's baby. It was the joy, and the pain, of giving birth that finally made me realize I wasn't giving Betsy Stern *her* baby, I was giving her *my* baby.

When Whitehead realized that this was "*my* baby," it was a healing discovery. She had been told that she was like a broodmare, that the child she bore didn't have anything to do with her, that she would only give birth to it and hand it over. Her consciousness was reified; she saw herself as a tool, and was proud of her ability to deliver as good a product as possible. But at the birth, something happened that caused her to see she was not simply a breeder. Body and soul united, the sight of her daughter brought her back to life. And when she says, "I am not a surrogate; I am a mother," she revolts against her mechanical role. She refuses to be an oven, an incubator, a factory. She says: I have given birth and I am a mother. For the surrogate industry, this is a failure and, naturally, a huge shock for the buyers who have waited and longed for a child. The woman who keeps the child is transformed into an evil, demonic person—especially in the eyes of other surrogates, whose ideological foundations she thereby threatens.

In 2009, the Christian three-time surrogate mother Laschell Baker—the staunch defender of surrogacy quoted earlier who had claimed that God had given her "this gift not to be selfish but to give back to my brothers and sisters that are unable to conceive on their own"—decided to keep the twins she had given birth to. She refused to hand them over to the intended parents and made up her mind to raise them herself. She was consequently subjected to hate campaigns on multiple surrogate forums. She was called "shameful," a "witch," "just evil," "worse than a whore," and, paradoxically enough, a "baby-selling hoe."[47] One woman who had been a surrogate five times wrote:

---

47 <http://www.surromomsonline.com/support/showthread.php?t=153025>

This whole thing is DISGUSTING and makes me SICK!!! As a surrogate it is NOT your descision [*sic*] of where these babies go ... GIVE those helpless little babies back to their PARENTS!!!! IF they are NOT fit parents the law will decide that, that is NOT your decision ..."[48]

Time and again, the others remind her of her role as a carrier: "You need to step back and realize your role as a GESTATIONAL SURROGATE."[49] What they were saying was that she was a tool and should not have any pretensions of being anything more. Religious insults such as "You shouldn't have tried to play God", "And you call yourself a Christian?" followed.[50] A group of surrogates even began a collection to benefit the buyers. One of them explained that Baker was not "a true surrogate" and that this was not "a true surrogacy."[51]

Why are they so threatened by this woman? They have no intention of keeping their 'surrogate' children; what does it matter if others come to different decisions? Furthermore, Laschell Baker's excuse was that the buyers were using cocaine; shouldn't it be seen as a responsible and motherly action not to want to see your child treated poorly? But none of this was as important as the fact that Baker was approaching the most tender of topics: healing the wound between being a tool and being human, between Self and body, child and mother on a completely different level: by unification instead of by punishment. And suddenly, the others begin to feel their wounds much more deeply. Baker's actions reveal immediately how much their own wounds hurt, how deep they are. She is hated because she opens them again and again, causing them to bleed. Because she crossed over from the self-sacrificing, obedient surrogate to the real mother, she is called an

---

48 <http://www.surromomsonline.com/support/showthread.php?t=153025&page=3> post from 13 September 2009, accessed 5 December 2012.

49 <http://www.surromomsonline.com/support/showthread.php?t=153025&page=2> post from 13 September 2009, accessed 5 December 2012.

50 <http://www.surromomsonline.com/support/showthread.php?t=153025&page=18>

51 'Bad surrogacy revisited' <http://surrolife.blogspot.com/>.

evil witch. Despite the fact that the surrogate world—thousands of surrogates, agencies, doctors, buyers, lawyers, and judges—applaud the decision to give up a child, one woman's refusal is enough to completely upend their emotions.

It is just like prostitution all over again, coming back to haunt us. It is the same division of the Self and the body, person and function, mother and child, soul and sexuality. And the same fear that the two will be reunited. The division is made sacred while the unity is demonized. What everyone in surrogacy longs for—whole families, happiness, sacredness, Virgin Mary status, forgiveness and atonement—is the diametric opposite of the functionalization and commodification that is actually taking place. What Daniel Szpigler (2009) calls "the creation of a whole" is, in actuality, a compulsory divorce. We all know it, exactly as we know when we are lying, but we convince ourselves that if everyone agrees with the lie, it becomes truth. Constantly singing the praises of surrogacy or prostitution, as some surrogates and prostitutes do, is to be constantly caught up with covering the wound. That is why all the negative stories have to be eliminated. That is why organizations such as *Les Putes* cannot accept talk of a single raped or drug-addicted prostitute. Everything that is negative must be quickly covered up. The cover-up comes from a belief in the magical healing powers of words, a belief that is actually the manifestation of the longing to escape the pain. If we cover it up with a blanket of positive words, maybe it will be transformed? But reification remains, no matter what we decide to call it.

Isn't this same dualism actually the normal state in capitalist society, since it is a prerequisite for reification? When we sell ourselves or produce ourselves as 'objects', 'tools' or 'personal trademarks'—must we not then, somewhere, split? We create two (or more) Selves: the one we sell and the one we hold back. The more we sell, the greater the need to create another private Self. Even if there is no objective difference between body and soul, we have to create this difference in order to survive psychologically. We create it as the being and the bought, the Self versus the product, the private life versus the trademark, my psyche versus my body, my real smile versus the false waitress' grin. It is this division that is prized in capitalist societies, exactly this split that forms the foundation of the story of the sex worker: a Self that 'owns' a body has come to characterize all of femaleness today.[52] A woman's Self is declared equal to a man's while her body becomes an object.

The division has deeper roots in patriarchal society: between reproduction and sexuality, the virgin and the whore, image and text, practice and theory. It is women being forced to bear male psychological complexes, complexes that have become industries. When one makes large industries out of psychological complexes, the psychological complex stands out in all its absurdity. Never before has the desire to separate 'the whore' from 'the Virgin Mary' made such a clear imprint on the physical geography of the Earth. Thailand delivers women for having sex with. India delivers women for bearing children. The Earth is structured, literally, in man's own image, according to man's desires. And because the need to separate is so strong: the whore may not become pregnant, the surrogate may not have sex; women all over the world are denied their complete humanity. We are limited, imprisoned, turned off, made numb.

The Girls Who Went Away by Ann Fessler contains interviews with women who gave up their children for adoption before abortion was legal. Their stories have a great deal in common with the testimony of surrogates. Many women describe how they became numb inside when their children were taken from them. Diana became "unconscious inside." Judith describes how she "cut herself off" and "wouldn't look in the mirror at myself other than from the waist up" during the pregnancy." She describes how she still struggles with trying not to feel like a robot (Fessler, 2006, p. 271). What returns time and again is the sense of loss, the loss of the whole Self. The inability to feel how one's Self hangs together. Prostitution and surrogacy fragment the person, and the story of those industries and the people who fall victim to them has the same effect on society. We forget how things fit together; we teach

---

52 See, for example, Susan Bordo (1993).

ourselves to separate, not to think about two things at the same time.

Something different happens when we claim humanity as a whole. When we say: enough is enough, I don't want to play games, I don't want to hide, I am not a whore, I am not a Virgin Mary either, I am a person, and I have the right to feel. I am not either/or, I am both–and. I have a right to the children I give birth to. I don't need to go and meet up with men I don't like. My body is alive and I am going to listen to its signals. It is not my possession, it is not an object for me to use—it is my opportunity to *be* in the world. Our legs are not first and foremost 'things'; they give us the opportunity to walk. Our eyes are first for seeing and only second for being looked at, as Sartre wrote (1943, p. 344). This is un-reifying a violent, physical process. It is healing the wound that resulted from dualism. Judith describes experiencing the beginning of this process when she is reunited with her daughter after 35 years (Fessler, 2006, p. 272): "With that wall breaking down, I started to feel just what I had done and what had happened to me, in a way and at a level that I had never felt before. I was no longer numb."

Bibliography

'A global alliance against forced labour: Global report under the follow-up to the ILO Declaration on Fundamental Principles and Rights at Work' (2005) International Labour Organization, Geneva.

Abrahamsson, Maria (27 November 2006) 'Men låt fler kvinnor komma till tals' *Svenska Dagbladet*, Stockholm.

Abrahamsson, Maria (1 March 2009) 'Damen i baren minns jag tydligt' *Svenska Dagbladet*, Stockholm.

Aeschylus (2007) *The Oresteia*, trans. Ian Johnston, Richer Resources, Arlington, VA.

Aftonbladet (25 May 1997) 'Nunnan: Jag födde barn åt en svensk direktör' Stockholm.

Agustín, Laura (2002) 'Challenging "Place": Leaving home for sex' *Development* 45 (1) pp. 110–117.

Agustín, Laura (2006) 'The disappearing of a migration category: Migrants who sell sex' *Journal of Ethnic and Migration Studies* 32 (1) pp. 29–47.

Aigen, Betsy P. (1996) *Motivations of Surrogate Mothers: Parenthood, altruism and self-actualization*. The American Surrogacy Center Inc., Marietta, GA.

Allis, Trevor (1995) 'The moral implications of motherhood by hire' *Indian Journal of Medical Ethics* 5 (January–March).

Altink, Sietske and Sylvia Bokelmann (2006) 'Rechten van prostitutees' *Stichting Den Rode Draad*, Amsterdam <http://www.prostitutie.nl/fileadmin/nl/6._Studie/6.3_Documenten/6.3f_Sociale_positie/pdf/rechten_van_prostituees.pdf> accessed 26 April 2013.

Andersson, Patrik (3 January 2003) 'Sexarbetare har en viktig funktion att fylla' *Kristianstadsbladet*, Kristianstad.

Andreasson, Martin (3 July 2009) 'Tillåt surrogatföräldraskap i Sverige' *SVT Debatt* <http://martinandreasson.wordpress.com/2009/07/03/tillat-surrogatforaldraskap-i-sverige/> accessed 26 April 2013.

Andrews, Lori B. (1995) 'Beyond doctrinal boundaries: A legal framework for surrogate motherhood' *Virginia Law Review* 81 (8), pp. 2,343–2,375 <http://www.lfip.org/laws822/docs/2.htm>.

'Angående anmälan om oredlighet i forskning' (10 June 2009) DNR H5 2152/09, Gothenburg University.

'Aqui trabajamos con otra realidad, trabajamos con la historia de vida de las mujeres' (19 February 2009) Entrevista a Constanza Jacques, psicóloga de Ámbit Dóna <http://grupos.emagister.com/documento/entrevista_a_ambit_dona_/1017-111657> accessed 26 April 2013.

Arbetarmakt Newsletter (2002) No. 115 (04/02) – 020322, Sweden.

Arena Baubo (2007) *Fackmöte för Prostituerade* <http://www.arenabaubo.se/html/fackmote.html> accessed 26 April 2013.

Australian Sex Party <http://www.sexparty.org.au> accessed 26 April 2013.

Barbour, Matthew (27 February 2010) 'I gave birth to my friend's baby—and it nearly cost me my life' *Daily Mail*, London <http://www.dailymail.co.uk/femail/article-1253601/I-gave-birth-friends-baby--nearly-cost-life.html> accessed 26 April 2013.

Barry, Kathleen (1979 *Female Sexual Slavery*. Avon Books, New York.

Benér, Theresa (25 February 2008) 'Samtidsskildring med närvaro' *Svenska Dagbladet*, Stockholm <http://www.svd.se/kultur/scen/samtidsskildring-med-narvaro_907499.svd> accessed 26 April 2013.

Berkhout, Suze (2008) 'Buns in the oven: Objectification, surrogacy, and women's autonomy' *Social Theory and Practice* 34 (1) pp. 95–117.

Bindel, Julie (7 July 2003) 'Sex workers are different' *The Guardian*, London <http://www.guardian.co.uk/politics/2003/jul/07/tradeunions.gender> accessed 26 April 2013.

Björk, Nina (16 June 2008) 'Tvånget att begära' *Dagens Nyheter*, Stockholm <http://www.dn.se/kultur-noje/debatt-essa/tvanget-att-begara> accessed 26 April 2013.

Boom! Free Guide (2008) [Amsterdam tourist magazine] 15 (1).

Bordo, Susan (1993) *Unbearable Weight: Feminism, Western culture and the body*. University of California Press, Berkeley.

Borg, Arne, Folke Elwien, Michael Frühling, Lars Grönwall, Rita Liljeström, Sven-Axel Månsson, Anders Nelin, Hanna Olsson and

Tage Sjöberg (1981) *Prostitution. Beskrivning. Analys. Förslag till åtgärder.* Liber Publishing, Stockholm.

'Brev till bokhora.se – och deras svar' (Letter 2008) <http://www. nätverketpris.se/bokhora.html> accessed 26 April 2013.

Brownmiller, Susan (1975) *Against Our Will.* Fawcett Books, New York.

Carpenter, Belinda J. (2000) *Re-thinking Prostitution: Feminism, sex and the self.* Peter Lang Publishing, New York.

Chavez Perez, Inti (31 May 2006) 'Våga kallas hora' <http:// tidningenmacho.blogspot.com/2006/05/vga-kallas-hora.html> accessed 26 April 2013.

Chesler, Phyllis (1988) *Sacred Bond: The legacy of Baby M.* Vintage Books, New York.

China Hush (9 September 2009) 'Surrogate pregnancy in China, be aware of escort girls' <http://www.chinahush.com/2009/09/09/surrogate-pregnancy-in-china-be-aware-of-escort-girls/> accessed 26 April 2013.

Chopra, Anuj (3 April 2006) 'Childless couples look to India for surrogate mothers' *Christian Science Monitor,* Boston.

ChristiaNet (27 February 2009) 'A Christian surrogate mother' <http:// christianblogs.christianet.com/1147469391.htm> accessed 26 April 2013.

Ciccarelli, Janice C. and Linda J. Beckman (2005) 'Navigating rough waters: An overview of psychological aspects of surrogacy' *Journal of Social Issues* 61 (1) pp. 21–43.

Cohen, Margot (29 October 2009) 'A search for a surrogate leads to India' *Wall Street Journal,* New York <http://online.wsj.com/article/SB100 01424052748704252004574459003279407832.html> accessed 26 April 2013.

Corea, Gena (1985) *The Mother Machine: Reproductive technologies from artificial insemination to artificial wombs.* HarperCollins, New York.

Cornell, Peter (2009) *Mannen på Gatan: Prostitution och modernism.* Gidlunds Publishing, Örlinge, Sweden.

'D' (1980) 'What right have they got?' in Claude Jaget (ed.) *Prostitutes: Our life.* Falling Wall Press, Bristol, England.

Dahl, Ulrika (2006) 'Femme-inism' *Arena* 4, pp. 12–16.

Dahl, Ulrika (2007) 'Straight light district' *Re:public service* 7, pp. 16–18.

Daily Mail (29 January 2005) 'Surrogate mum dies after giving birth', London <http://www.dailymail.co.uk/news/article-335871/Surrogate-mum-dies-giving-birth.html> accessed 26 April 2013.

Demirbag-Sten, Dilsa (13 November 2006) 'Hör horan' *Expressen*, Stockholm <http://www.expressen.se/kultur/bocker/hor-horan/> accessed 26 April 2013.

Descartes, René (1971) *Descartes: Philosophical writings*, trans. and ed. Elizabeth Anscombe and Peter T. Geach. The Bobbs-Merrill Company, Indianapolis.

Dodillet, Susanne (2009) *Är sex arbete?* Vertigo Publishing, Stockholm.

Dodillet, Susanne (16 March 2009) 'Omyndigförklara inte sexsäljarna' *Göteborgs-Posten*, Göteborg <http://www.gp.se/nyheter/debatt/1.120320-replik-omyndigforklara-inte-sexsaljarna> accessed 26 April 2013.

'E' (1980) 'It kind of kills you but it's over fast' in Claude Jaget (ed.) *Prostitutes: Our life*. Falling Wall Press, Bristol, England.

Eagleton, Terry (1996) *The Illusions of Postmodernism*. Blackwell Publishers, Oxford.

Edelmann, Robert J. (2004) 'Surrogacy: The psychological issues' *Journal of Reproductive and Infant Psychology* 22 (2) pp. 123–136.

Eduards, Maud (2007) *Kroppspolitik: Om Moder Svea och andra kvinnor*. Atlas Book Publishing, Stockholm.

Eek, Louise (2005) *Att Köpa eller Köpas: Frihet och makt i sexindustrin*. Atlas Book Publishing, Stockholm.

Ekberg, Gunilla (1 December 2009) 'Keynote address' at European Union conference against Prostitution and Trafficking in Human Beings, organized by the Swedish Coalition of Unions (LO), Trade Unions against Trafficking, UNIFEM and the Swedish Institute, Stockholm, Sweden.

Ekman, Kajsa Ekis (2006) 'Det spanska exemplet: Hur man kan få en aktiviströrelse att vilja behålla kvinnor i prostitution' *Pockettidningen R* 2/3.

Ekman, Kajsa Ekis (2007) 'Den koloniala hormyten' *Bang* 1.

Elliott, Cath (9 January 2009) 'The great IUSW con' <http://toomuchtosayformyself.com/2009/01/09/the-great-iusw-con/> accessed 26 April 2013.

Ellis, Havelock (1927) *Studies in the Psychology of Sex* (Vol. 3 of 6) <http://archive.org/stream/studiesinthepsyc13612gut/13612.txt>.

Ertman, Martha M. (2008) 'What's wrong with a parenthood market?' in Nancy Ehrenreich (ed.) *The Reproductive Rights Reader: The construction of motherhood*. New York University, New York, pp. 299–307.

European Commission (May 2006) Executive Agency for Health and Consumers (EAHC) Grants for Projects, Project No. 2006/344/EC (OJ L 126).

Fagerström, Linda (3 September 2009) 'Subversivt på sängkanten' *Helsingborgs Dagblad*, Helsingborg, Sweden <http://hd.se/kultur/2009/09/03/subversivt-paa-saengkanten/> accessed 26 April 2013.

Fanon, Frantz (2008) *Black Skin White Masks*. Grove Press, New York.

Farley, Melissa, Ann Cotton, Jacqueline Lynne, Sybille Zumbeck, Frida Spiwack, Maria E. Reyes, Dinorah Alvarez and Ufuk Segin (2003) 'Prostitution and trafficking in nine countries: An update on violence and posttraumatic stress disorder' in Melissa Farley (ed.) *Prostitution, Trafficking, and Traumatic Stress*. Haworth Press, New York <http://www.tandf.co.uk/journals/haworth-journals.asp>.

Farley, Melissa (ed.) (2003) *Prostitution, Trafficking, and Traumatic Stress*. Haworth Press, New York <http://www.tandf.co.uk/journals/haworth-journals.asp>.

Fessler, Ann (2006) *The Girls Who Went Away: The hidden history of women who surrendered children for adoption in the decades before Roe v. Wade*. Penguin Books, London.

Foster, Judy with Marlene Derlet (2013) *Invisible Women of Prehistory: Three million years of peace, six thousand years of war*. Spinifex Press, North Melbourne.

Foster, Sarah (7 August 2006) 'We don't sell sex for a living' *The Northern Echo* <http://www.thenorthernecho.co.uk/features/echowoman/866713.we_dont_sell_sex_for_a_living/> accessed 26 April 2013.

Fox, Douglas (19 November 2008) 'Don't criminalise our clients' *The Guardian*, London <http://www.guardian.co.uk/commentisfree/2008/nov/19/prostitution-ukcrime> accessed 26 April 2013.

Freire, Paulo (1970) *Pedagogy of the Oppressed*. Seabury Press, New York (republished in 2000 by Continuum, New York and London).

Gallin, Dan (2003) 'Informal employment: Note on the international sex workers' movement' Global Labor Institute <http://www.globallabour.info/en/2007/09/note_on_the_international_sex.html> accessed 26 April 2013.

Goncharik, Alesia (21 May 2009) 'JA till surrogatmammor!' *ETC*, Örebro, Sweden <http://orebro.etc.se/blogg/ja-till-surrogatmammor> accessed 26 April 2013.

Gunnarsson, Ida (27 April 2009) 'Fyra roster om surrogatmödrar' *Sydsvenskan*, Malmö, Sweden <http://www.sydsvenskan.se/inpa-livet/fyra-roster-om-surrogatmodrar/> accessed 26 April 2013.

Hanafin, Hilary (1987) *Surrogate Parenting: Reassessing human bonding.* Center for Surrogate Parenting Inc., Oklahoma.

Haverdahl, Anna-Lena (28 September 2008) 'Familjelycka tack vare surrogatmor' *Svenska Dagbladet*, Stockholm <http://www.svd.se/nyheter/inrikes/familjelycka-tack-vare-surrogatmor_1794799.svd> accessed 13, July 2013.

Haworth, Abigail (29 July 2007) 'Surrogate mothers: Womb for rent' *Marie Claire* <http://www.marieclaire.com/world-reports/news/surrogate-mothers-india> accessed 26 April 2013.

Hermodsson, Elisabeth (1999) 'Det tillåtna modermordet' in Birgitta Onsell (ed.) *Någonting annat har funnits*. Carlsson Bokförlag, Stockholm, Sweden.

Hochschild, Arlie (19 September 2009) 'Childbirth at the global crossroads' *The American Prospect* <http://prospect.org/article/childbirth-global-crossroads-0>.

Høigård, Cecilie and Liv Finstad (1992) *Backstreets: Prostitution, money and love.* Polity Press, Cambridge; Pennsylvania State University Press, University Park, PA.

'Human Trafficking for Sexual Exploitation' [European Conference] (2009) Swedish National Committee for UNIFEM, Stockholm.

IBISWorld (2006/2009) 'Sexual services in Australia: Q9528', IBISWorld Pty Ltd, Melbourne and Sydney, Australia, pp. 1–37.

IBISWorld (26 July 2007) 'Boomers put boom back into sex industry' [Press Release] IBISWorld Pty Ltd, Melbourne and Sydney, Australia.

Ince, Susan (1989) 'Inside the surrogate industry' in Arditti, Rita, Renate Duelli Klein and Shelley Minden (eds) *Test-Tube Women: What future for motherhood?* Pandora Press, Unwin Hyman, London, Winchester, MA and Sydney.

Jadva, Vasanti, Clare Murray, Emma Lycett, Fiona MacCallum and Susan Golombok (2003) 'Surrogacy: The experiences of surrogate mothers' *Human Reproduction* 18 (10) pp. 2,196–2,204.

Jaget, Claude (ed.) *Prostitutes: Our life.* Falling Wall Press, Bristol, England.

Jaquith, Cindy (1988) *Surrogate Motherhood, Women's Rights, and the Working Class.* Pathfinder Press, New York.

Bibliography

Jeffreys, Sheila (1990/2011) *Anticlimax: A feminist perspective on the sexual revolution.* The Women's Press, London; Spinifex Press, North Melbourne, Australia.

Jeffreys, Sheila (1997) *The Idea of Prostitution.* Spinifex Press, North Melbourne, Australia.

Jeffreys, Sheila (1 December 2006) 'Prostitution and trafficking in Australia' Presentation to Finnish Parliament.

Jennes, Valerie (1993) *Making it Work: The prostitutes' movement in perspective.* Aldine de Gruyter, Berlin.

Jönsson, Kutte (2003) *Det förbjudna mödraskapet.* Bokbox Publishing, Malmö.

Jonsson, Lars (5 October 2009) 'Sexarbete undersöks' *RFSL Aktuellt* <http://www.rfsl.se/?p=4257&aid=11605> accessed 26 April 2013.

Josefsson, Erika (25 November 2006) 'När sexsäljare själva får tala' *Corren*, Linköping, Sweden <http://www.corren.se/kultur/artikel.aspx?articleid=4261886> accessed 26 April 2013.

Juvas, Sören and Ulrika Westerlund (17 July 2008) 'Tillåt surrogatmödrar i Sverige – annars åker folk utomlands' *Expressen* Stockholm <http://www.expressen.se/debatt/tillat-surrogatmodrar-i-sverige---annars-aker-folk-utomlands/> accessed 26 April 2013.

Kane, Elizabeth (1988) *Birth Mother: The story of America's first legal surrogate mother.* Houghton Mifflin Harcourt, Boston.

Kazmierska, Natalia (6 April 2009) 'Bebisen som väckt debatten om att få hyra en livmoder' *Expressen*, Stockholm <http://www.expressen.se/nyheter/dokument/bebisen-som-vackt-debatten-om-att-fa-hyra-en-livmoder/> accessed 26 April 2013.

Kemp, Tage (1936) *Prostitution: An investigation of its causes, especially with regard to hereditary factors.* Levin & Munksgaard, Copenhagen.

Kempadoo, Kamala (1998) 'Globalizing sex workers' rights' in Kamala Kempadoo and Jo Doezma (eds) *Global Sex Workers: Rights, resistance and redefinition.* Routledge, London.

Kinnell, Hilary (16 December 2002) 'Why feminists should rethink on sex workers' rights', UK Network of Sex Work Projects <http://www.nswp.org/sites/nswp.org/files/KINNELL-FEMINISTS.pdf> accessed 26 April 2013.

Klein, Renate (June 2011) 'Surrogacy in Australia: New legal developments' *Bioethics Research Notes* (23) 2, pp. 23–26.

Klepke, Martin (7 December 2007) 'Den lyckliga horan, myt eller sanning?' *Arbetet*, Stockholm <http://arbetet.se/2007/12/07/den-lyckliga-horan-myt-eller-sanning/> accessed 26 April 2013.

Koh Bela, Amely-James (2007) *Mon combat contre la prostitution*. Jean-Claude Gawsewitch Éditeur, Paris.

Kolehmainen, Anne (26 September 2008) 'Vi vill skaffa barn med surrogatmamma' <http://alltombarn.se>.

Kulick, Don (2005) '400 000 perversa svenskar' in Don Kulick (ed.) *Queersverige*. Natur och kultur, Stockholm.

Larsson, Fredrik (2006) 'Dags för surrogatmödraskap' *Kom Ut* 3, Stockholm.

Larsson, Lennart (27 January 2009) 'Kommunalråd stoppar kondomer till sexköpare' *Skånskan*, Malmö <http://www.skanskan.se/article/20090127/NYHETER/293974749/-/kommunalrad-stoppar-kondomer-till-sexkopare> accessed 26 April 2013.

Larsson, Mariah (1 March 2008) 'Porrstjärna i en ny roll' *Sydsvenskan*, Malmö.

Larsson, Stig (1983) *Könshandeln: Om prostituterades villkor*. Skeab Publishing, Stockholm.

Leidholdt, Dorchen A. (2004) 'Demand and the debate' [Speech], Coalition Against Trafficking in Women <http://action.web.ca/home/catw/readingroom.shtml?x=53793&AA_EX_Session=d58e5f2983971d01efc791fb44871fcb>.

Letiche, Hugo and Lucie van Mens (2002) 'Prostitution as a male object of epistemological pain' *Gender, Work and Organization* 9 (2) pp. 167–185.

The Life of a Surrogate Mother (29 January 2009) 'Bad surrogacy story revisited'<http://surrolife.blogspot.com/2010/01/bad-surrogacy-story-revisited.html>.

Lim, Lin Leam (1998) *The Sex Sector: The economic and social bases of prostitution in Southeast Asia*. International Labour Office, Geneva.

Lombroso, Cesare and Guglielmo Ferrero (2004) *Criminal Women, the Prostitute and Normal Women*, trans. and intr. by Nicole Hahn Rafter and Mary Gibson. Duke University Press, Durham, NC.

Lönn, Maria (7 May 2008) 'Motstånd med höga klackar' <http://rfsu.se/motstand_med_hoga_klackar.asp>.

Lopes, Ana (4 June 2004) 'Ana Lopes' [web page] <http://manifestor.org/mi/en/2004/06/100.shtml> accessed 26 April 2013.

Lopes, Ana (n.d.) 'IUSW history' <http://www.iusw.org/node/9>.

Bibliography

Lukács, Georg (1923/1971) *History and Class Consciousness*, trans. Rodney Livingstone, MIT Press, Cambridge, MA.

Lundberg, Lotta (12 June 2006) 'Lotta Lundberg om prostitution: Att välja att sälja sig' *Sydsvenskan*, Malmö <http://www.sydsvenskan.se/kultur--nojen/lotta-lundberg-om-prostitution/> accessed 26 April 2013.

MacCallum, Fiona, Emma Lycett, Clare Murray, Vasanti Jadva and Susan Golombok (2003) 'Surrogacy: The experiences of commissioning couples' *Human Reproduction* 18 (6) pp. 1,332–1,342.

Maîtresse Nikita and Thierry Schaffauser (28 January 2008) 'Fières d'êtres putes' <http://www.impudique.net/2008/01/fieres-detres-putes/> accessed 26 April 2013.

Malarek, Victor (2003) *The Natashas*. Arcade Publishing, New York.

Malarek, Victor (2009) *The Johns: Sex for sale and the men who buy it*. Arcade Publishing, New York.

Malhotra, Anil (14 December 2008) 'Business of babies' *The Tribune*, Chandigarh, India <http://www.tribuneindia.com/2008/20081214/spectrum/main2.htm> accessed 26 April 2013.

Mallik, Ira (2004) 'Fritt valt arbete?' in Gunilla Edemo and Ulrika Westerlund (eds) *Femkamp: Bang om nordisk feminism*. Bang Feministisk Kulturtidskrift, Stockholm.

Malm, Andreas (2003) 'När allt blir till varor' *Arbetaren* 29.

Malm, H.M. (1992) 'Commodification or compensation: A reply to Ketchum' in Helen Holmes Bequaert and Laura M. Purdy (eds) *Feminist Perspectives in Medical Ethics*. Indiana University Press, Bloomington, IN.

Månsson, Sven-Axel (1981) *Könshandelns främjare och profitörer: Om förhållandet mellan hallick och prostituerad*. Doxa, Lund, Sweden.

Månsson, Sven-Axel (12 March 2009) 'Får man göra så här?' *Socialpolitik* <http://www.socialpolitik.com/far-man-gora-sahar/> accessed 26 April 2013.

Månsson, Sven-Axel and Ulla-Carin Hedin (1998) *Vägen ut: Om kvinnors uppbrott ur prostitutionen*. Carlsson Book Publishing, Stockholm.

Månsson, Sven-Axel and Jenny Westerstrand (19 June 2009) 'Angående anmälen om oredlighet i forskning' DNR H5 2152/09, Göteborg University.

Marcovich, Malka (2007) 'Handeln med kvinnor i världen' in Christine Ockrent and Sandrine Treiner (eds) *Kvinnornas svarta bok*. Damm Publishing, Oslo.

Marklund, Annika (11 September 2009) 'Dirty Diaries är som hederlig hemmaporr' *Aftonbladet*, Stockholm <http://www.aftonbladet.se/nyheter/kolumnister/annikamarklund/article11991640.ab> accessed 26 April 2013.

Marx, Karl (1915) *Capital: A critique of political economy*, Vol. 1: *The Process of Capitalist Production*, trans. Samuel Moore and Edward Aveling, Frederick Engels (ed.), Charles H. Kerr & Company, Chicago.

Marx, Karl (2003) 'De ekonomisk-filosofiska manuskripten' in Sven-Eric Liedman and Björn Linnell (eds) *Karl Marx: Texter i urval*. Ordfront Publishing, Stockholm.

Matsson, Caroline (20 November 2006) 'Tiden har kommit ikapp Petra Östergren' *Stockholms Fria Tidning*, Stockholm.

Merchant, Carolyn (1994) *Naturens död: Kvinnan, ekologin och den vetenskapliga revolutionen*. Symposion, Höör, Sweden.

Mignard, Anne (March 1976) 'Propose élementaires sur la prostitution' *Les Temps Modernes* 356, Paris.

Miklitsch, Robert (1996) 'The Commodity-Body-Sign: Toward a general economy of "commodity fetishism"' *Cultural Critique* 33, pp. 5–40.

Millett, Kate (1970) *Sexual Politics*. University of Illinois Press, Urbana.

Ministry of Health, Welfare and Sport (1 September 2004) 'Antwoorden Kamervragen over voortbestaan stichting de Rode Draad' <http://www.nieuwsbank.nl/inp/2004/09/01/R221.htm> accessed 26 April 2013.

Moberg, Eva (1999) 'Någonting annat har funnits …' in Birgitta Onsell (ed.) *Någonting annat har funnits*. Carlsson Book Publishing, Stockholm.

Montgomery, Heather (1998) 'Children, prostitution, and identity' in Kamala Kempadoo and Jo Doezma (eds) *Global Sex Workers: Rights, resistance and redefinition*. Routledge, London.

Moore Hall, Sarah (8 December 1980) 'Surrogate mother Elizabeth Kane delivers her "Gift of Love"—Then kisses her baby goodbye' *People Magazine* <http://www.people.com/people/archive/article/0,,20078051,00.html> accessed 26 April 2013.

Moran, Rachel (2013) *Paid For: My journey through prostitution*. Spinifex Press, North Melbourne, Australia.

Nagata, Miki and Sandra Lundbom (2007) 'Att leva med prostitutionserfarenhet: Kvalitativa intervjuer med fyra kvinnor', senior thesis, Stockholm University, Stockholm <http://urn.kb.se/resolve?urn=urn:nbn:se:su:diva-7081> accessed 26 April 2013.

Bibliography

Nordic Council of Ministers (2008) 'Prostitution in the Nordic countries' Conference Report, Copenhagen <http://www.norden.org/en/publications/publikationer/2009-756> accessed 26 April 2013.

Ohlsson, Birgitta, Barbro Westerholm, Thomas Nihlén and Gunvor Ericson (2009) 'Surrogatmödraskap nu!' *Arena* 2 <http://www.eurozine.com/journals/arena/issue/2009-04-21.html>.

O'Neill, Maggie (2001) *Prostitution and Feminism: Towards a politics of feeling*. Blackwell Publishers, Oxford.

Oliver, Kelly (1992) 'Marxism and surrogacy' in Helen Bequaert Holmes and Laura M. Purdy (eds) *Feminist Perspectives in Medical Ethics*. Indiana University Press, Bloomington, IN.

Olsson, Hanna (1987) 'Det svåra sökandet efter kunskap eller Vem är jag och vem är den andra?' *Socialt Arbete* 7.

Oriel, Jennifer (2006) 'All quiet on the Western Front: The international politics of HIV/AIDS', doctoral dissertation, University of Melbourne, Melbourne.

Östergren, Petra (2006a) *Porr, Horor och Feminister*. Natur och kultur, Stockholm.

Östergren, Petra (2006b) 'De oberörbara' *Arena* 5 <http://www.eurozine.com/journals/arena/issue/2006-11-07.html>.

Östergren, Petra (8 April 2008) 'Med dagens feminister finns ingen sexuell revolution i sikte' *Expressen*, Stockholm.

'Our journey to surrogacy in India: Blaze's story' <http://ourjourneytosurrogacyinindia.blogspot.com/>.

Pande, Amrita (2009) 'Not an angel, not a whore: Surrogates as "dirty" workers in India', *Indian Journal of Gender Studies* 16 (2) pp. 141–173.

Parent-Duchâtelet, Alexandre (1981) *La prostitution a Paris au XIXe siècle*. Seuil, Paris.

Pateman, Carole (1988) *The Sexual Contract*. Stanford University Press, Palo Alto, CA.

Persson, Louise (2006) 'Statliga sexbås vid fotbolls-VM: Fantasti eller verklighet?' NMI Briefing Paper <http://www.timbro.se/pdf/nmi/nmibp1.pdf>.

Peterson, Jenny (18 February 2008) 'Karim i porrigt relationsdrama' *Helsingborgs Dagblad*, Helsingborg, Sweden.

Pheterson, Gail (ed.) (1989) *A Vindication of the Rights of Whores*. Seal Press, Seattle, WA.

Pheterson, Gail and Margo St. James (2005) '$ex workers make history: 1985 & 1986: The World Whores' Congress' <www.walnet.org/csis/

groups/icrse/brussels-2005/SWRights-History.pdf> accessed 26 April 2013.

Pierini, Leo (10 May 2007) 'En myt att folk tvingas till prostitution' *Expressen*, Stockholm <http://www.expressen.se/nyheter/en-myt-att-folk-tvingas-till-prostitution/> accessed 26 April 2013.

'Pornography and prostitution in Canada: Report of the Special Committee on Pornography and Prostitution' (1985) Minister of Supply and Services Canada <https://www.ncjrs.gov/pdffiles1/Digitization/131616NCJRS.pdf> accessed 26 April 2013.

Potterat, John D., Devon D. Brewer, Stephen Q. Muth, Richard B. Rothenberg, Donald E. Woodhouse, John B. Muth, Heather K. Stites and Stuart Brody (2004) 'Mortality in a long-term open cohort of prostitute women' *American Journal of Epidemiology* 159 pp. 778–785.

ProCon.org (31 January 2008) 'Ana Lopes PhD', Santa Monica, CA <http://prostitution.procon.org/view.source.php?sourceID=846> accessed 13 July 2013.

Ragoné, Heléna (1994) *Surrogate Motherhood: Conception in the heart.* Westview Press, Boulder, CO.

Ragoné, Heléna (1998) 'Incontestable motivations' in Sarah Franklin and Heléna Ragoné (eds) *Reproducing Reproduction: Kinship, power and technological innovation.* University of Pennsylvania Press, Philadelphia, pp. 118–131.

Rapin, Anne (2002) 'La prostitution, un rapport hommes-femmes comme les autres?' in France Diplomatie, Label France <http://www.diplomatie.gouv.fr/fr/article_imprim.php3?id_article=21420>.

Raymond, Janice G. (1989) 'Reproductive technologies, radical feminism, and socialist liberalism', *Reproductive and Genetic Engineering. Journal of International Feminist Analysis* (2) 2, pp. 133–142.

'Report by the Federal Government on the impact of the Act Regulating the Legal Situation of Prostitutes' (2007) Federal Ministry for Family Affairs, Senior Citizens, Women and Youth, BMFSFJ, Berlin, Germany.

Ribbing, Magdalena (13 July 1980) 'Utredare vill avskeda 10 experter' *Dagens Nyheter*, Stockholm.

Risholm Mothander, Pia (1994) *Mellan mor och barn.* Liber Utbildning, Stockholm.

Bibliography

Robertson, John A. (1992) 'Surrogate motherhood: Not so novel after all' in Kenneth D. Alpern (ed.) *The Ethics of Reproductive Technology.* Oxford University Press, New York/Oxford.

Ross, Colin A., Melissa Farley and Harvey L. Schwartz (2003) 'Dissociation among women in prostitution' in Melissa Farley (ed.) *Prostitution, Trafficking, and Posttraumatic Stress.* Haworth Press <http://www.tandf.co.uk/journals/haworth-journals.asp>.

Rubin, Gayle (1984) 'Thinking sex: Notes for a radical theory of the politics of sexuality' in Carol S. Vance (ed.) *Pleasure and Danger: Exploring female sexuality.* Pandora, London.

Ryan, Chris and Michael C. Hall (2001) *Sex Tourism: Marginal people and liminalities.* Routledge, London.

Säfve, Torbjörn (1987) *Siki.* Prisma Publishing, Stockholm.

Sandblad, Moa (27 February 2009) 'Dodillet vill tillåta sexköp: För kvinnornas skull' *Fria Tidningen*, Skarpnäck, Sweden <http://www.fria.nu/artikel/78108> accessed 26 April 2013.

Sartre, Jean-Paul (1943) *L'être et le néant.* Gallimard, Paris, France.

Saul, Stephanie (30 December 2009) 'New Jersey judge calls surrogate legal mother of twins' *New York Times*, New York <http://www.nytimes.com/2009/12/31/us/31surrogate.html> accessed 26 April 2013.

Scott, Elisabeth S. (2009) 'Surrogacy and the politics of commodification' *Law & Contemporary Problems* 72 (3) pp. 109–146.

Sex Worker Internet Radio Library (SWIRL) (November 2007) 'Interview with Petra Timmermans' <http://swirlwebcast.blogspot.com/2008/12/new-on-swirl-interview-with-petra.html?zx=54d8ac834c398446> accessed 26 April 2013.

Shachar, Nathan (9 September 2008) 'Elena vågade ta strid mot polisvåldet' *Dagens Nyheter*, Stockholm <http://www.dn.se/insidan/insidan-hem/elena-vagade-ta-strid-mot-polisvaldet> accessed 26 April 2013.

Shultz, Marjorie M. (1990) 'Reproductive technology and intent-based parenthood: An opportunity for gender neutrality' *Berkeley Law* pp. 298–396 <http://scholarship.law.berkeley.edu/cgi/viewcontent.cgi?article=1343&context=facpubs> accessed 5 July 2013.

Sistare, Christine T. (1994) 'Reproductive freedom and women's freedom: Surrogacy and autonomy' in A.M. Jaggar (ed.) *Living with Contradictions: Controversies in feminist social ethics.* Westview Press, Boulder, CO.

Sjöö, Monica and Barbara Mor (1991) *The Great Cosmic Mother.* HarperCollins, New York.

Spar, Debora L. (2006) *The Baby Business: How money, science and politics drive the commerce of conception.* Harvard Business School Press, Watertown, MA.

Sullivan, Mary Lucille (2007) *Making Sex Work: A failed experiment with legalised prostitution.* Spinifex Press, North Melbourne, Australia.

Svanström, Yvonne (2006) *Offentliga kvinnor: Prostitution i Sverige 1812–1918.* Ordfront Publishing, Stockholm.

Svenska Dagbladet (25 April 2009) 'Rysk liga sålde sex i Finland', Stockholm.

Sveriges Radio P1 (29 May 2008) 'Homosexuellt par anlitar indisk surrogatmamma', Sweden <http://sverigesradio.se/sida/artikel.aspx?programid=2938&artikel=2623288> accessed 26 April 2013.

Sveriges Radio P3 (27 June 2009) 'People like sex, this is Amsterdam', Sweden <http://sverigesradio.se/sida/artikel.aspx?programid=1646&artikel=2862521> accessed 26 April 2013.

Szpigler, Daniel (27 July 2009) 'Surrogatmamma måste bli lagligt' *Aftonbladet* Stockholm <http://www.aftonbladet.se/debatt/article11938880.ab> accessed 26 April 2013.

Tännsjö, Torbjörn (1991) *Göra barn: En studie i reproduktionsetik.* Sesam Publishing, Stockholm.

The Telegraph (26 June 2008) 'Proxy womb law set for birth', Calcutta.

Teman, Elly (2008) 'The social construction of surrogacy research: An anthropological critique of the psychosocial scholarship on surrogate motherhood' *Social Science and Medicine* 67 (7) pp. 1,104–1,112.

'Thousands of sex workers could be endangered by Home Secretary's proposed changes in the law' (2009) British International Union of Sex Workers (IUSW) <http://www.iusw.org/2009/03/thousands-of-sex-workers-could-be-endangered-by-home-secretarys-proposed-changes-in-the-law/> accessed 26 April 2013.

Thakur, Sunita (21 March 2008) 'Mother for only nine months' *BBC News*, London <http://news.bbc.co.uk/2/hi/south_asia/7202043.stm> accessed 26 April 2013.

'Tomorrow's children: Australia's National Plan of Action Against the Commercial Sexual Exploitation of Children' (2000) Department of Family and Community Services, Canberra, ACT.

Tong, Rosemarie (1992) 'The overdue death of a feminist chameleon: Taking a stand on surrogacy arrangements' in Kenneth D. Alpern (ed.) *The Ethics of Reproductive Technology*. Oxford University Press, New York/Oxford.

Truong, Thanh-Dam (1990) *Sex, Money and Morality: Prostitution and tourism in South-East Asia*. Zed Books Ltd, London.

Ulla (1980) *L'amour amèr*. Éditions Garnier Frères, Paris, France.

Ullén, Magnus (2009) *Bara för dig*. Vertigo Publishing, Stockholm.

UNDP Newsroom (4 August 2009) 'South East Asia's first "Women's Court" on Trafficking and HIV', Bali <http://www.unodc.org/southeastasiaandpacific/en/2009/08/UNDP-WOMEN/south-east-asias-first-womens-court-on-trafficking-and-hiv.html> accessed 26 April 2013.

van den Akker, Olga B.A. (2007a) 'Psychosocial aspects of surrogate motherhood' *Human Reproduction Update* 13 (1) pp. 53–62.

van den Akker, Olga B.A. (2007b) 'Psychological trait and state characteristics, social support and attitudes to the surrogate pregnancy and baby' *Human Reproduction* 22 (8) pp. 2,287–2,295.

Vaughan-Brakman, Sarah and Sally J. Scholz (2006) 'Adoption, ART, and a re-conception of the maternal body: Toward embodied maternity' *Hypatia* 21 (1) pp. 54–73.

Vecko-Revyn (2007) 'Jag säljer sex—och gillar det också!' No. 24, Stockholm.

Vora, Kalindi (February 2009) 'Indian transnational surrogacy and the disaggregation of mothering work' *Anthropology News*, pp. 9–12.

Wallace, Michele (1990) *Black Macho and the Myth of the Superwoman*. Verso Books, Brooklyn and London.

Wästberg, Filip and Per Pettersson (8 May 2009) 'Det är sexlagstiftningen som upprätthåller förtrycket' *Newsmill*, Stockholm <http://www.newsmill.se/artikel/2009/05/08/det-ar-sexlagstiftningen-som-uppratthaller-fortrycket> accessed 26 April 2013.

We Care India (n.d.) 'Surrogacy facts' <http://www.indiahospitaltour.com/surrogacy/surrogacy-facts-india.html> accessed 26 April 2013.

Weeks, Jeffrey (1981) *Sex, Politics and Society: The regulation of sexuality since 1800*. Longman, London.

Wennberg, Jenny (2002) 'Soutien financier de l'Union européene à des projets et organizations promouvant la legalization et la réglementation de la prostitution', Parlament européen, Brussels.

Wennerholm, Christer G., Jenny Edberg and Fredrik Sawestähl (18 August 2008) 'Dags att agera för surrogatmammor' *QX Debatt*, Stockholm

<http://www.qx.se/samhalle/debatt/7747/dags-att-agera-for-surrogatmammor> accessed 26 April 2013.

Westerlund, Ulrika (2008) 'Surrogatbabes' *Ottar* 4.

Westerstrand, Jenny (2008) 'Mellan mäns händer: Kvinnors rättsubjektivitet, internationell rätt och diskurser om prostitution och trafficking', doctoral dissertation, Uppsala University, Uppsala, Sweden.

Whitehead, Mary Beth (1989) *A Mother's Story: The truth about the Baby M case*. St. Martin's Press, New York.

Wigorts Yngvesson, Susanne (19 December 2006) 'Att sälja sin kropp är en moralisk rättighet' *Svenska Dagbladet*, Stockholm.

Wijers-Hasegawa, Yumi (16 March 2002) 'Dutch approach prostitution with pragmatism' *Japan Times*, Tokyo.

Wilkinson, Stephen (2003) *Bodies for Sale: Ethics and exploitation in the new human body trade*. Routledge, London.

Williams, Linda (1989) *Hardcore: Power, pleasure and the frenzy of the visible*. University of California, Berkeley.

Wirtén, Per (16 June 2007) 'Gränsriddare' *Expressen*, Stockholm <http://www.expressen.se/kultur/gransriddare/> accessed 26 April 2013.

Wood, Marianne (1995) *Just a Prostitute*. University of Queensland Press, St. Lucia, Queensland, Australia.

Wu, Joyce (2007) 'Left Labor in bed with the sex industry' in Rebecca Whisnant and Christine Stark (eds) *Not for Sale: Feminists resisting prostitution and pornography*. Spinifex Press, North Melbourne, Australia.

Zaitzewsky, Maria (18 January 2008) 'De vägrar se sig som offer' *Metro*, Stockholm <http://www.metro.se/nyheter/de-vagrar-se-sig-som-offer/Objhaj!07_2315-62/> accessed 26 April 2013.

Index

210

Index

Index

'safe sex' projects 55
Millett, Kate 48
Moberg, Eva 158
Mongard, Hanka 55–6, 56–7, 77
Montgomery, Heather 22–5
Moran, Rachel 5
Motivations of Surrogate Mothers (Aigen) 177, 178
Muslim women
  burkas and free choice 21, 28
  headscarves seen as revolutionary 82

Nagata, Miki 94
'Natashas' 99
National Coalition Against Surrogacy 185
National Task Force on Prostitution 50
National Union of General and Municipal Workers 62
neoliberal Right
  and abolition of victimhood 26, 27, 29
  pact with postmodern Left 83–4
  pro-prostitution stance 78–9
  prostitution as free choice 81
Network of Sex Work Projects 20, 21, 55, 92
New Zealand 3
newspapers, and the 'organized whore' 49–50
Nilson, Ulf 85
non-commercial surrogacy *see* surrogacy, 'altruistic'
Norway, purchase of sex xiv, 3, 121
  prostitution research 18
nursing 111

Ohlsson, Birgitta 131, 160
Oliver, Kelly 173, 174, 175–6
Olsson, Hanna 35, 94–5, 120–1
O'Neill, Maggie 12
oneinsix.com 129
'Only for you' (Ullén) 82
Oresteia (Aeschylus) 158–9
Oriel, Jennifer 54, 55, 56

Östergren, Petra
  claims prostitutes enjoy their work 9, 119
  financed by conservatives 78
  paid versus free sex 115
  praises dissociation 114–15
  prostituted woman as narrator 31–2
  prostitutes not victims 7, 20
  prostitution as liberating 74
  prostitution seen as work 4, 5
  'sex' as a commodity 85
  and 'sexual services' 90–1
  supported by right-wing Timbro 78–9n
  whores versus feminists 9, 10, 12–13
Our Bodies Ourselves (Boston Health Collective) 70n

Pande, Amrita 167–9
Parent-Duchâtelet, Alexandre 42
'parenthood market' 145
parenthood, revision of 159 *see also* biological parenthood; social parenthood
Patel, Dr. Nayna 154
Pateman, Carole 5
patriarchal creation myths 158–60
patriarchal societies
  father's rights over mother's 158–9
  feminism and 9–10, 12–13, 73
  impact of division on women xiv, 190–1
  and prostitution 91
  women go from goddess to oppressed 158
Patten, Fiona 70
Pedagogy of the Oppressed (Freire) 120
Petterson, Per 90
Pheterson, Gail 53, 53–4
Pierini, Leo 60, 61
pimps 54, xi, xii *see also* Fox, Douglas
  children as 23–4
  in France 65
  necessary for protection 64
  relations with prostitutes 18–19

215

Index

defined xi

defined as a sexual orientation 10–11, 73

'double' nature of the culture 100

and economic coercion 183

encourages trafficking 21

feeds off women's self-destructiveness 183

and the free market 88–9

and gender 4, 5

image of good versus evil 73

language of 4–5

legalization of *see* legalized prostitution

little change in 100 years 45–6

in the market economy 91–2

moral and sexual issue 87

moral legitimacy of 6

motives for 42

opponents of *see* feminists

as a patriarchal phenomenon 91

romanticization of 73–4

seen as revolutionary 11–12, 13–14, 46, 81, 82

socially necessary 41, 42, 43, 46

source of profit 3, 6

split Self/body at the core 95–6

terms for acts 100

unlike other work 101

viewed as an active choice 73

women's departure from 19, 51, 68, 119

prostitution (1970s)

analysis of the sexual oppression of women 48

attacked by social movements 47–8

global protest against 48

promoted by advocacy groups 49–50 *see also* COYOTE

prostitution (1980s), push for normalization 51–4 *see also* Holland

prostitution (1990s) 54–8 *see also* HIV/ AIDS

prostitution (21st century) 59 *see also* 'trade unions' for prostitutes

Prostitution: An investigation of its causes, especially with regard to hereditary factors (Kemp) 43–4

Prostitution and Feminism: Towards a politics of feeling (O'Neill) 12

prostitution as work 73, xiii *see also* 'sex work'

and *de Rode Draad* 51

demand for more intimacy 105–7

depends on concealing its nature 104

legitimized as 83–4

mechanization of sexuality 103

renamed 'sex work' 6

sellers and customers 4–5

threat of unmasking 119–20

'Prostitution Group', Sweden 18

prostitution in the arts *see* whores, cult of

'Prostitution in the Nordic countries' Conference report 72

Prostitution Inquiry (1977), Sweden 16–18, 19–20, 35

prostitution of children

in Australia 25–6

not seen as victims xiii, 22–6

in Thailand 22–6, 53

prostitution research

in Norway 18

from prostitutes' perspective 17–20, 48

in Sweden 16–18, 48

on trauma 112–14

Prostitution Unit, Stockholm 94

prostitution zones 47

queer theory 117, 118, 136

radical feminists

accurate about violence 116–17

alleged bias of 116

'oppressors' of women 117

and static analysis 116–17

Ragoné, Heléna 137–8, 148, 171–2, 177, 183

Rankka, Maria 78–9n

217

Index

Index

*If you would like to know more about Spinifex Press
write for a free catalogue or visit our website.*

SPINIFEX PRESS
PO Box 212 North Melbourne
Victoria 3051 Australia
www.spinifexpress.com.au